LITERACY
in the
Cyberage

Composing Ourselves Online

R.W. BURNISKE

SkyLight
Professional
Development

Arlington Heights, Illinois

Literacy in the Cyberage: Composing Ourselves Online

Published by SkyLight Professional Development
2626 S. Clearbrook Dr., Arlington Heights, Illinois 60005-5310
Phone 800-348-4474, 847-290-6600
Fax 847-290-6609
info@skylightedu.com
http://www.skylightedu.com

Senior Vice President, Product Development: Donna Nygren
Senior Acquisitions Editor: Jean Ward
Editor: Dara Lee Howard
Cover Designer and Illustrator: David Stockman
Book Designer: Bruce Leckie
Production Supervisor: Bob Crump
Production Assistant: Christina Georgi

LCCCN 00-131512
ISBN 1-57517-280-1

2657-McN
Item Number 1962
Z Y X W V U T S R Q P O N M L K J I H G F E D C B
06 05 04 03 02 01   15 14 13 12 11 10 9 8 7 6 5 4 3 2

I dedicate this book to the most literate
teacher I know—my wife, Jackie.

Contents

Foreword

The cyberage has arrived and with it e-mail, chat rooms, World Wide Web access, unedited information and misinformation, hackers, and an incredible range of communication possibilities both locally and internationally. We as literacy educators have no choice but to accept our responsibility to help students negotiate these new forms of communication. While some of us feel inadequate in using computers, especially regarding the technical skills needed to use the myriad of possibilities that confront us, we do know a great deal about communication. It is this expertise that is desperately needed by young cyberage enthusiasts. How can they determine the "author" of texts? How can they construct the meaning contained in these electronic messages? How can they identify the subtle emotional intents and messages contained in the visual and verbal presentations? How can they most honestly and effectively present themselves and their ideas to audiences they meet in electronic communication? How can we, their teachers, most effectively guide them in reading, responding to, and composing messages?

On my way to the library in an elementary school recently I became intrigued by the hall bulletin board. At the top was the question, "What do we mean when we say appropriate use of the internet?" Large sheets of paper contained lists of students' responses to the question. Heading their lists were: Don't use chat rooms without teacher's permission; Don't be mean; Don't send viruses; No swearing; Don't chat with strangers; No naughty sites; Don't give out personal information; Don't pretend to be someone else. These statements of caution by children sobered me. What responsibilities this generation of young people has to assume. Every form of seduction and persuasion can be accessed easily via the computer. Students are more vulnerable than ever before to unidentified and unregulated messages. And they have all the more reason to take literacy seriously. What an opportunity to explore with them key concepts like authorship, voice, and critical evaluation.

They also have access to an incredibly rich resource via electronic communication with people across the globe and information and documents unavailable locally. The new technology enables them to collaborate in new ways in researching, writing, illustrating and presenting information and ideas. They deserve teachers who can help them use this potential effectively.

Into this new reality comes R.W. Burniske's refreshing message to literacy educators. What a treat it is to read! Here is a book that puts the possibilities of computers in perspective for literacy educators. Burniske examines both the potential and problems of the cyberage technologies for literacy educators. Instead of a "technologically" focused guide, this book takes a philosophical and communications perspective. Readers are challenged to expand our concept of "literacy" as we follow his examination of the various aspects of literacy—from civil to pedagogical. Burniske has constructed a wonderful bridge for us and leads us to the new age by building on what we know and do well. He shows us how to expand our instruction so that electronic literacy becomes an essential component of our classrooms. He challenges us to realize our commitment to develop our students as critical and reflective language users. In the process both our students and we, their teachers, will compose ourselves online.

This is a book all serious literacy professionals need to read and discuss with our colleagues. My thanks to Burniske for providing such an inviting guidebook for the journey.

DONNA OGLE
President
International Reading Association,
2001–2002
Professor, Reading and Language Department
National-Louis University

Preface

Training is everything. The peach was once a bitter almond;
cauliflower is nothing but cabbage with a college education.
(Twain 1964, 46) Pudd'n head Wilson's Calendar, Chapter 5

Like most teachers, I did not enter the classroom with a well-developed,
educational philosophy. Early in my career, which began at an international
school in Cairo, I dedicated myself to the mastery of material, often leaving
a class session feeling satisfied because my "presentation" or "performance" seemed well received. Clearly, I suffered the delusion that if I left
class feeling good about things then the students must share that sentiment. It did not take long to discover the flaws in this logic, however, nor
to recognize that the best students retain the intellectual courage and curiosity of childhood, daring to think in unconventional terms while asking
difficult questions.

Unfortunately, outcome-based educational systems within the secondary schools that I served—in Egypt, Ecuador, Malaysia, and the United
States—conditioned many of my students to believe that education was a
product rather than a process. They seemed to think the best way to
achieve a quality "product" was to mimic the teacher by reciting answers
absorbed through lectures and textbooks. One of my greatest challenges,
therefore, was to inspire students to take greater responsibility for their
education, encouraging them to pursue their own questions and become
more self-conscious of their thought processes.

Fifteen years of apprenticeship in secondary schools served me well
when I began teaching in the Computer Writing and Research Lab at the
University of Texas. By then, I had acquired an extensive repertoire of
teaching strategies designed to empower individual students while forging
a community of learners. My experiments with global educational
telecomputing had reinforced the notion that learning was a distributed

enterprise in which students and teachers engaged in the social construction of knowledge. Thus, the old dispensation, the "teaching philosophy" that believed one could deliver knowledge by pouring it into the heads of student receptacles, gave way to a "learning philosophy." This not-so-subtle shift challenged students to interrogate information through activities that made them more conscious of their learning style and more critical of the conclusions they reached through personal, idiosyncratic methods and social interactions.

While this liberated me from the one-dimensional role of "sage on stage," it also introduced new responsibilities, ones suggesting that computer-assisted classes required more than just a "guide on the side" in order to function. Indeed, if we approach each class as a "community of inquiry" (Lipman 1991), then we, as educators, need to encourage each member to explore questions and ideas that promote genuine, intellectual odysseys. I include teachers in this conception because they teach best when inspired and inspiring, which means they must nurture their own curiosity, as well as that of their students, to foster a dynamic community of learners. To succeed, teachers must demonstrate respect for student inquiries while encouraging exploration of "discovered" and "created" questions (Getzels 1982). Every classroom activity and every encounter between student and teacher should contribute to an environment that supports this community of inquiry, stimulating an appreciation of its value and the value of each class member's contributions to it.

Confessions of a "Pedagogical Junkie"

In order to achieve such lofty goals, we must give careful thought to the impact of personal pedagogy and institutional curricula. Toward that end, it helps to understand what Elliot Eisner (1985) calls the *explicit*, *implicit*, and *null curricula*. For while we train our eyes upon the explicit curriculum described in course catalogs, we often fail to consider the impact of implicit curricula conveyed by indirect means (e.g., dress codes, class schedules, student assemblies, etc.) as well as the null curriculum defined by omissions from the formal course of study (e.g., woodworking, home economics, typing, etc.). We would do well to draw the implicit and null curricula into the foreground, asking how they serve—or subvert—the purposes of the explicit curriculum. Although educators may state their concern with "community" in the explicit curricula of their syllabi, it is the implicit values expressed through their pedagogy and omissions that weaken or strengthen that ideal (Eisner 1985).

Pedagogical praxis, after all, stems from the personality and convictions of an individual teacher. More often than not, this is defined by the choices we make while determining which method suits a particular objective and group of students. When teaching Shakespeare's drama, for example, I ask students to enact the text so that they can participate in questions of interpretation. For composition and rhetoric, however, the enactment is more effectively accomplished in rhetorical amphitheaters constructed in face-to-face discussions, electronic mail exchanges, Web-based discussion forums, or synchronous online sessions—all of which require that students learn by doing, continually refining their skills as readers, writers, speakers, and thinkers.

In essence, I conceive of each course as an extended inquiry. In its ideal form, students generate authentic questions and offer meaningful contributions to a collective discussion. In reality, this requires hard work, particularly with a group of indifferent scholars. Such students have turned me into a "pedagogical junkie," an educator willing to try just about anything to inspire dialectical discourse from the first class session to the last. The Computer Writing and Research Lab (CWRL) at the University of Texas has provided a supportive environment for such people because it encourages the kind of experimentation that helps teachers see their students, academic disciplines, pedagogical repertoires, and themselves in a new light. Like teachers everywhere, instructors in the CWRL develop pedagogical favorites even as they explore new ones. However, few teachers are blessed with such a liberal and creative environment, replete with a flexible curriculum, innovative colleagues, and state-of-the-art technology. In many ways, this book is an effort to share this embarrassment of riches, which has enabled me to develop a number of online learning activities. I hope my experience and insights will assist teachers who wish to preserve humanist traditions while helping students acquire a more robust form of *computer literacy.*

The learning activities that inform much of this book offer a glimpse of the promises and perils of a computer-assisted classroom. While considering their potential, we must beware the seductions of new technologies and pedagogical tricks, lest they distract us from our purpose and become an end in themselves. I encourage the reader to cast a critical eye upon the activities described in the following chapters. They include: role-playing in synchronous, online sessions and asynchronous mailing lists; online writing workshops conducted in Web-based discussion forums; electronic portfolios that enable students to capture their writing process; and an Online Learning Record that offers an alternative assessment method. Although these activities provide a glimpse of the pedagogical tools and strategies I have employed, they cannot convey a chronology or the thought process involved in deciding when to introduce them. That depends upon an admittedly idiosyncratic judgment of student needs, course objectives, learning styles, and many other factors.

Ultimately, a community of inquiry requires sensitivity to the tension between stability and chaos within a classroom. Students express boredom when classroom activities are predictable, yet they are equally resistant to excessive variations and innovations. As a result, the craft of teaching demands attention to student anxiety and *ennui*, provoking a delicate tension for the teacher. On the one hand, educators must introduce a destabilizing element when tired strategies prove ineffectual or monotonous; yet, on the other, they're wise to abandon or postpone an innovation when destabilizing forces push the community toward chaos. In other words, we must be moderate even in our moderation, finding the proper balance between innovation and tradition.

Inspirations: Teaching as a Work-in-Progress

One does not arrive at a philosophy for teaching and learning without the help of influential teachers and experiences. I am indebted to a number of talented and compassionate mentors who generously shared their gifts through the craft of teaching. As an undergraduate, I had the privilege of participating in creative writing seminars conducted as workshops at the University of North Carolina. From there, my formal studies took me to the Bread Loaf School of English, where I encountered remarkable minds committed to the study and teaching of literature. This led to a combination of workshop discussions and dialogical inquiry in my own classroom.

To complete my MA, I traveled to Lincoln College, Oxford, where I was introduced to the idea that each essay is part of a journey rather than a destination in itself, a notion that profoundly affected my approach to writing and research exercises. Finally, my study of "Computers and English Studies" at the University of Texas has helped me combine these influences and find their fullest expression in the computer-assisted courses that I have taught in the Computer Writing and Research Lab. I would be remiss if I failed to acknowledge the mentors who have influenced my thinking and the many students and colleagues who have shaped my teaching. This book reflects a lifetime of collaboration with all of them, and I am deeply grateful to everyone who has contributed to this work—and encouraged my behavior—along the way.

A number of other personal and professional experiences have shaped my teaching practices in important ways. As a football, basketball, and baseball coach, I learned that "coaching" is something all educators must learn to do, for it demands simultaneous attention to individual development and collaborative efforts. Much of this escaped me while I was a student-athlete, but enrollment in an Outward Bound course as well as independent travel through Africa, Asia, Europe, and South America helped me understand the social, collaborative nature of learning. Meanwhile, my studies abroad as an undergraduate and experience as a foreign correspondent taught me the importance of sustained inquiry, encouraging me to ask more informed, insightful questions as I proceeded. I am not sure how many countries I have visited, but I do know that their singular sensations and complex riddles have left an indelible mark upon me.

The multicultural nature of those experiences helped me as a teacher at international schools in Egypt, Ecuador, and Malaysia, where I had to adapt to distinct school cultures while finding a niche within the community at large. I realized that my own learning seemed greatest when I was suddenly destabilized, although capable of regaining my balance. I tried to approximate that experience for my students, challenging the status quo within respective institutions by becoming the first humanities teacher to: use computers for instructional purpose (Egypt); to use a computer lab as a classroom (USA); introduce an "electronic chalkboard" to the English classroom (Ecuador); and create global telecollaborative activities (Malaysia). Indeed, my personal vision has found creative expression in my classroom, which has gradually become a global learning environment.

Meanwhile, I have benefited from talented colleagues whose commitment to teaching rivaled their passion for learning. A brief stint as a secondary school administrator compelled me to write teacher evaluations and recommendations for a number of colleagues. The process of evaluation, however, quickly became a learning experience. Classroom observations taught me the value of silence following profound questions, the efficacy of a human voice and its inflection as an instructional tool, and the necessity of continual reflection and revision. I learned a great deal from observing educators, and I have drawn on those lessons while conducting professional development workshops in developed and developing nations.

As a teacher of teachers, my efforts have ranged from one-day workshops for the International Society for Technology in Education (ISTE) to week-long seminars sponsored by the World Links for Development program (WorLD). I shall draw upon these experiences to illustrate ways in which educators can integrate emerging technology to support their pedagogical and curricular goals. Whether improvising in my own classroom or helping others brainstorm innovative ideas, I enjoy the challenge of creating and sustaining an educational community of inquiry. The more varied my pedagogy, the better the chances that I can serve a diverse group of people and learning styles. My work in a networked classroom seems a logical progression in this regard, since the introduction of information and communication technology extends discussions beyond the class period, engenders a cross-pollination of ideas, and encourages intellectual adventures that nurture a fertile learning environment.

Finally, like many educators, I have learned the most about teaching from my students, particularly the ones who challenged me to find new ways of reaching them—while subjecting each innovation to an unflinching critique. This raises an important though oft-neglected point: Not all students wish to change the traditional classroom. Many have been conditioned by the conventional, detached relationship established when educators lecture, students produce work, and the work receives a cryptic grade and indecipherable scribbles in the margins. For students habituated to such routines, a teacher who demonstrates genuine interest in their lives and ideas may seem threatening. Students quickly recognize that a "community of inquiry" requires more commitment and effort on their part than the old dispensation. After all, it is easier to blame the teacher for one's personal failings if there is no personal relationship with that teacher. It is also easier to slight the learning process when one is not required to keep a process journal, produce an electronic portfolio, or engage in sustained discussions.

Eventually, however, most students appreciate the discipline of such activities and embrace the idea of the classroom as a community. It is gratifying to hear them speak of their learning in networked classes, but even more satisfying to learn that their interactions have inspired a human network. "This wasn't just another class," one of my students observed in a course evaluation, "it was like a small community." While a teacher's effort to engage students may plant the seeds for such transformations, they only flourish when students embrace learning as a collaborative process and season their inquiries with a generous spirit. I hope this book inspires that spirit as much as it inspires innovative classroom practices. For teachers are no longer isolated individuals confined within the four walls of a classroom. They now belong to a global network of educators, an intricately connected fraternity that has the ability to share ideas about teaching and learning in ways that were inconceivable just a generation ago. Nevertheless, new opportunities breed new responsibilities, for post-modern educators must find meaningful ways to re-invent themselves, their schools, and their educational systems. As we shall see, the process of personal and collective invention shares an intimate relationship with *literacy*.

R. W. Burniske

Introduction

The pleasures of reading itself—who doesn't remember?—were like those of a Christmas cake, a sweet devouring.

(Welty 1981, 486)

Literacy. Ask five people to define this term and you're likely to hear ten different answers. That's what happens, though, when a word develops a split personality. On the one hand, *literacy* conjures images of the technical skills required to "read and write," the denotation that the United States Army reinforced when it coined the term *functional literacy* during World War II. This line of thinking, as a number of literacy experts have noted, bred the ideas of "survival literacy" and "basic literacy" (Suzanne de Castell et al. 1989, 7). However, the second strain of literacy, *critical literacy*, vexes the conversation far more today because of its many connotations, most of which stem from the idea of what it means to be "educated." Where functional literacy lends itself to standardized tests that measure skills of one kind or another, it's clearly more difficult to determine when someone has acquired the critical literacy that describes "a liberally educated or learned person" (*The New Shorter Oxford English Dictionary* 1993, 1604). It's little wonder, then, that five respondents would hedge their bets, offering definitions that address both specific, technical skills and the more nebulous qualities that would fully describe the literate individual.

While functional literacy remains prerequisite for other types of literacy, it is not the primary focus of this book. Of course, educators still need to teach students how to "read and write" while incorporating new technology into their classrooms, but they also need to teach them how to interpret and "contextualize" the words and information they encounter in electronic mail, discussion forums, Web sites, and more. Unfortunately, many how-to books dedicated to technology in the classroom neglect this type of literacy, stressing technical skills that fail to help students find meaning through a truly "educated" approach to online reading and writing. Perhaps this explains why such books feel obsolete before the ink dries upon their pages. What educators need, therefore, is something more than a discussion of technical issues. To prepare themselves and their students for new types of literacy they must be receptive to new definitions of the term itself. This requires more than technical knowledge; indeed, it demands that they ask open-ended questions about the human condition, searching for more satisfying definitions and a deeper understanding of these matters.

With this in mind, it may prove helpful to think of literacy in terms of a taxonomy. The functional literacy required to read and write letters of an alphabet, and sound the words they form, serves as a stepping stone to more complex types of literacy. By embracing that notion one invites a more robust definition for literacy's most recent offspring, that troublesome fellow called *computer literacy*. This book encourages that move, purposely stretching *literacy* to invigorate discussions of computers in education. I shall consider a variety of literacies, all of which come into play when one talks about "literacy in the cyberage." Some of these terms are familiar; others are heuristics—which means I made them up! Though some may initially strike the reader as odd contrivances, all of these literacies apply to a networked classroom and the online environments in which students increasingly work.

Indeed, just as we must learn to read and write the alphabet to develop functional literacy, so too, we must learn how to "read" visual images, discursive practices, personal ethics, community actions, cultural events, global developments, and humanity in general. What's more, while learning to read others online we are also *composing ourselves*. This double *entendre*, which lends itself to the title of this book, suggests the need for composure as well as the desire for invention. We cannot achieve civil discourse online without composure, but neither can we satisfy our need for personal invention without giving full expression to a complex persona, the "saturated selves" that others must interpret through the pastiche of our words and images (Gergen 1991).

Unfortunately, competence with one form of literacy does not guarantee fluency with another. As a matter of fact, one of the more important questions is whether or not some forms of literacy are mutually exclusive. Consequently, educators need a far more robust definition for *computer literacy*, one that takes them well beyond functional literacy. Most schools have passed the stage in which computers are confined to a "keyboarding" or "computer applications" course. Thus, they can no longer view computer literacy in purely technical terms, nor as the province of a particular academic discipline. One's keyboarding skills are hardly a measure of computer literacy at a time when people speak of Netiquette, hypertext narratives, and virtual architecture. For classroom teachers to succeed with the integration of networked technology in pre-existing curricula, therefore, they must possess a theoretical foundation as well as technical skills. In fact, the former may prove more significant than the latter, since it will help classroom teachers determine which literacies they value and believe most significant for their students' development.

Cyberwriter at Work: The Design of This Book

Obviously, this is not intended as a "how-to" book, which will, hopefully, spare it the fate of those gathering dust upon the shelves of teachers' lounges and resource centers around the world. I would hope that it serves as a philosophical guide while providing practical ideas for classroom practitioners. Toward that end, each chapter begins with a brief discussion of the abstract concerns attending a particular type of literacy. From the question of definition I move to discussions of why teachers should be aware of such literacy and the skills students need to acquire it. A series of "literacy challenges," learning activities that encourage critical reading and writing online, will help classroom teachers synthesize theory and practice. In short, I look at ways to use networked technology and online learning environments to teach critical literacy skills. Here's a brief overview of what each chapter has to offer.

Chapter 1, *Media Literacy: Broadening the Definition of Computer Literacy*, identifies several shortcomings with impoverished definitions of computer literacy and the pedagogical and curricular approaches they inspire. As a corrective, I propose approaching computer literacy through a more traditional filter: classical rhetoric. By applying rhetoric, the ancient art of persuasion, and the rhetorical triangle of *ethos* (author's credibility), *logos* (message's logic) and *pathos* (emotional appeal to audience), educators will discover important concepts that help students "get outside" themselves and think of "the other"—the writers and audiences they will encounter via electronic mail, newsgroups, chat rooms, MOOs, web-based discussion forums, Web sites, and more. Ultimately, this forces a movement away from functional literacy, which has defined computer literacy for much too long, toward a critical literacy that requires far more than technical skills.

Chapter 2, *Civil Literacy: The CyberPilot's License*, emphasizes the fundamental need for students to take responsibility for what they say, how they say it, and the effect it will have upon others. This conviction has inspired an online tutorial that provides a forum where readers may conduct research and continue this discussion. The respective sections of the Web site provide the basis for this chapter, along with relevant literacy challenges. "Know Your Vehicle" presents resources that introduce the history, terms, and technology of the Internet. The "Rights & Responsibilities" section tries to clear the air(waves) and stimulate meaningful discussions in "The Pilots' Place," an online discussion forum. "Who & What Rules the Airwaves" introduces several resources on acceptable use policies (AUPs), state and federal laws, and the great debate over freedom of speech on the Internet. In addition, readers may visit "The Reference Desk" to add a link or visit online resources that others have recommended. "Piloting Skills & Netiquette," an interactive primer on the use of electronic mail, search engines, discussion forums, and more, focuses upon ethical concerns and definitions of acceptable use. Finally, "The Flight School" provides suggestions for cyberpilot trainers, suggesting ways to use "The CyberPilot's License" program for effective teaching and learning.

Chapter 3, *Discourse Literacy: Beyond the Chat Room*, assumes familiarity with the concept of *civil literacy* and a desire to consider online discourse in greater detail. I begin with a distinction between synchronous and asynchronous communication tools, focusing upon the former in this chapter. Whether teachers use software such as the Daedalus Integrated Writing Environment (DIWE), an Internet Relay Chat (IRC), or Multi-User Domain (MUD), they will find ample opportunities to establish healthy discursive practices locally before turning to asynchronous discourse on a national or international level. However, they must be aware that many students have established unhealthy discursive habits during unsupervised, recreational forays into cyberspace. I examine transcripts from classroom sessions, exploring ways to use synchronous, online discussions for instructional purpose. Of particular interest are role-playing activities that enable students to take the position of writers they have studied. This use of pseudonyms presents a singular opportunity for students to adopt the voice and viewpoint of another, stepping outside themselves as they acquire discourse literacy. The chapter concludes with student evaluations of these exercises, which provide candid insights about this type of learning activity.

Chapter 4, *Personal Literacy: Discovering Oneself Online*, reinforces the belief that we must take responsibility for our words and "actions" in an online community. Students need to realize the importance of how they present themselves and how others "read" them. In essence, *personal literacy* in an online environment compels readers and writers to fashion themselves in words while interpreting the selves they encounter. Teachers need to understand that "praxis doesn't make perfect." Experimentation and reflection are important, but insufficient if they allow students to practice slovenly habits—from poor grammar to an irresponsible flippancy—which frustrates genuine communication and renders students virtually "illiterate" because of their inability to read and write themselves. How might teachers help adolescents hear their own voice and understand how they are "coming across" to others via asynchronous media? I begin with exercises that help students discover what they think, looking at a "Why List" that helps them develop the *logos* of their arguments before stepping into asynchronous forums where they must use rhetorical strategies to persuade their audience through emotional *pathos* and a carefully constructed personal *ethos*. Variations on the "Why List" activity will help individual writers hear their own "voice," question their assumptions, and entertain alternative viewpoints to strengthen their personal literacy.

Chapter 5, *Community Literacy: Composing Ourselves in a Virtual Community*, acknowledges the transformation of classroom dynamics through the introduction of networked computer technology. To become an active member of an online community rather than a passive audience, students and teachers must conceive and conduct their work in new ways. They are no longer reading and writing within the vacuum of an isolated classroom. Instead, their coursework acquires a more authentic quality, engaging with a larger community of learners through telecollaborative endeavors. However, new opportunities also demand new responsibilities, from the "turn-taking" in online conversations to careful discretion between public and private messages. The literacy challenges and case studies in this chapter will help students and teachers discuss essential concerns and anticipate potential problems, culminating with the examination of a course Web site as a collaborative work-in-progress. I'll challenge the misconception that class Web sites are "products" constructed upon completion of a particular project. This requires a look behind the surface of a course Web site that provides interactive writing spaces that serve as communication media as well as an archive of student work. Ultimately, the Web site as a collaborative work-in-progress is both a creation and reflection of a particular community of learners and an opportunity for students to refine their collaborative skills and community literacy.

Chapter 6, *Visual Literacy: Web Sites, Rhetorically Speaking*, builds upon the preceding chapter's discussion of a class website, particularly the collaborative nature of that undertaking. By helping students understand the process of Web design from the inside out, teachers can de-mystify the Web and stimulate critical literacy. To develop their visual literacy, however, students need to understand the rhetorical strategies that Web designers employ. I'll present a case study in which students were asked to read and critique a satirical online article, considering how one can use the rhetoric of Web sites to inspire a critical *visual literacy*. The reader will gain important insights from an online, synchronous discussion of the satirical article, as well as student reflections on their misreadings. This will stimulate questions about how to "read" a Web site with a more critical eye, particularly when the *pathos* of graphical representations threatens to overwhelm the argument's *logos* and the writer's *ethos*. The chapter concludes with guidelines for the rhetorical analysis of Web documents and literacy challenges that ask students to apply visual literacy to the evaluation of hypertexts.

Chapter 7, *Global Literacy: Reading, Writing, and Dancing to a Global Beat*, assumes an understanding of the discursive practices necessary to sustain local telecollaborative activities. If such prerequisites are fulfilled, how might teachers design and facilitate a global telecollaboration? In essence, this chapter argues for broadening cultural literacy, taking it beyond national boundaries while asking the questions necessary for improvising a global dance. What does it mean, for example, to be good neighbors in worldwide communities and dance to the global rhythms of these social encounters? How does a classroom practitioner improvise within the constraints of curricula and technology while helping students discover their own Muse? How do we anticipate the challenges of working with telecollaborative partners in new learning environments, accommodating academic schedules and diverse cultures while fulfilling obligations to our own students and institutions? My line of inquiry will help teachers learn basic dance steps, anticipating the challenges of online venues as well as complications that arise while choreographing and conducting a global, telecollaborative dance. Educators interested in helping themselves and their students acquire *global literacy* through telecollaborative learning activities will also benefit from recommended Web sites that feature online tutorials and project ideas.

Chapter 8, *Evaluative Literacy: Peer Reviews, Electronic Portfolios, and Online Learning Records*, attempts to pull the disparate pieces together. It's often difficult for both students and teachers to keep track of online learning activities. Thus, it's important to reinforce the concept of a writing process, encouraging students to reflect upon the road taken to the final product of an essay. Toward that end, I begin with a literacy challenge introducing the concept of a "hypertext writing workshop." Then I examine electronic portfolios and a template that enables students to assemble the respective elements of an essay as a hypertext that includes a topic proposal, process journal, references, rough drafts, and final draft. This approach delivers privileged insights into the composition process, encouraging students to become more competent readers and writers. Finally, the Online Learning Record provides an alternative assessment method that engages the student as part of the evaluation process. The chapter concludes with a brief discussion of the respective sections of the Online Learning Record, which, as an extension of electronic portfolios, is consistent with a process approach to writing. This discussion will inspire teachers who seek alternative approaches to the "grading game," strategies that help students develop *evaluative literacy* skills, and better judgment of their own process and products.

Chapter 9, *Pedagogical Literacy: Plugging Into Electronic Pedagogy*, argues that professional educators must continually refine their ability to "read and write" pedagogical strategies, adapting them to suit their personal styles, curricula, and situations. They must learn how to "think through" emerging technologies, making informed decisions about which tool is most appropriate for a particular group of students and curricular objectives. Some devices are better as "push technology" (e-mail, mailing lists) while others require that they "pull" from them (newsgroups, discussion forums, Web sites). Classroom experience has taught teachers how to integrate texts, chalkboards, overhead projectors, VCRs—choosing a particular medium based upon their knowledge and understanding of what it affords and constrains. They must now develop a similar understanding of new media and the literacies they require and engender. This chapter provides a sense of closure by bringing educators back to the starting point: how do teachers use computer technology to teach literacy skills? However, it also extends the conversation by introducing the *Electronic Pedagogy* Web site, where readers will find archives as well as Web-based discussion forums that encourage further exploration of literacy in the cyberage.

How to Read This Book: A Linear Approach to Hypertext

One could approach this book in a *hypertextual* fashion, starting in the middle and randomly moving forward and backward through the text. However, I'd argue for a more traditional, linear reading. Readers will find that the chapters speak to one another, with earlier ones anticipating their successors, and later ones building upon their predecessors' lessons. Thus, each chapter contributes to the book's foundation, simultaneously drawing upon earlier points or learning activities while contributing something new to the discussion. Taken as a whole, the book's architecture takes the reader from the over-arching theme of computer literacy and the prerequisites of *civil literacy* to specific literacies that need attention while introducing networked computer technology to a classroom and curriculum.

One type of literacy may concern the reader more than another, but certain, fundamental literacies are required before students and teachers attempt complicated online learning activities. For example, the first chapter's discussion of media literacy and the importance of rhetorical traditions establishes a framework for the second chapter's concerns with civil literacy. This will, in turn, inform subsequent examination of discourse literacy, community literacy, and global literacy. Meanwhile, some of the concerns of visual literacy overlap with evaluative literacy, but a reversal of their chronology within this text might confuse readers unnecessarily. By gradually shifting from general to specific concerns the book argues deductively. However, the deliberate movement from personal literacy to community literacy and global literacy describes a trajectory from individual concerns to universal ones. I hope that this will stimulate discussion of local and global currents, simultaneously broadening and deepening our understanding of literacy. I would also hope that it helps a new generation of student learn how to read, write, and interpret their world while composing themselves online.

Media Literacy:
Broadening the Definition
of Computer Literacy

The electric light escapes attention as a communication medium just because it has no "content." And this makes it an invaluable instance of how people fail to study media at all.

(McLuhan 1964, 24)

What exactly does it mean to be *literate* in this world? Well before the 1988 Right to Literacy Conference, which hoped to "address an audience far beyond the bounds of Modern Language Association membership" (Lunsford, Moglen, and Slevin 1990, 1), educators paid a great deal of attention to the empowerment of students through literacy. More than a decade later, however, literacy remains a vexing issue, as illustrated by the keynote address at the 1998 Conference on College Composition and Communication. Cynthia Selfe's speech was a clarion call for humanists to bring previously neglected matters to the foreground because

> . . . we have a much larger and more complicated obligation to fulfill—that of trying to understand and make sense of, to pay attention to, how technology is now inextricably linked to literacy and literacy education in this country. (Selfe 1998)

When extended, this argument suggests that computer technology's impact on literacy also carries profound implications for the moral education of students. For when it comes to computer literacy, both the rights and responsibilities of those who acquire it must be considered, and attention must be paid to far more than the technical skills that would satisfy advocates of an impoverished definition. Just as words enlighten or deceive, serving moral or immoral purposes, so, too, computer literacy carries potential for good or evil. What is necessary is a more robust definition of this term, one that embraces rhetorical traditions as well as the exploration of human expression through emerging media.

Unfortunately, the repetition of terms such as *computer literacy* in the absence of thoughtful definitions and substantial concern encourages educational institutions to neglect the impact of terminology on students, teachers, and curricula. Contemporary rhetoric reveals an unhealthy preoccupation with a school's published curriculum and neglect of what Elliot Eisner describes as the implicit and null curricula. The *implicit curriculum* consists of everything a school's personnel teaches through the indirect media of assemblies, dress codes, detentions, and more; the *null curriculum* refers to neglected subjects, such as auto-mechanics, woodworking, and home economics. Often, what educators omit from the school's curriculum or fail to consider as a contributor to the school's ethos is just as important as what they self-consciously include (Eisner 1985).

It is worth thinking in such terms while examining the impact of the Internet gold rush on schools. To accommodate computer literacy in their K–12 curricula, many schools push to the periphery electives such as music, art, and physical education. This raises two significant questions: As schools introduce computer technology to their classrooms and endorse new expressions of the explicit and implicit curricula, how cognizant are they of their null curriculum's impact on students? While rushing to keep up with technology and placating vocal watchdogs of the explicit curricula, are school officials aware of the impact this may have upon the implicit curricula?

A fundamental anxiety, which shapes educational curricula more than it should, lurks behind the rhetoric of many computer literacy advocates: "If we don't do something to address this particular ignorance," they argue, "U.S. children will fall behind foreign children and the United States will lose its supremacy." No politician wants to be remembered for allowing the sun to set on the U.S. empire. Nonetheless, myopic definitions of terms such as *computer literacy* and the failure of schools and universities "to make a focused curriculum out of (their) contentiousness," impoverishes educational institutions in ways that few politicians understand (Graff 1990, 825). The end of the 20th century may well be remembered for the triumph of rhetoric that prompted enormous investments in technology as the panacea for all of public education's malaise. What is most remarkable, however, is how little clarity and substance has accompanied this experiment, which lacks basic definition and philosophical purpose:

> It is often asserted that one of the problems with computers is that too few people know how to use them. The population is accused of being computer illiterate. When calls are made for schools to provide better education in computers, it is not clear what is in mind. (Landauer 1996, 121)

What's more, preoccupation with what a new form of literacy enables may distract one from what it disables. It is naive to think computer literacy invites only positive change; implicit in the idea of integration, after all, is a quiet annihilation of that which preceded it. Yet, computer literacy advocates seldom acknowledge that one consequence of integrating technology into the classroom is that students will spend more time "interacting" with machines and less time interacting with "unmediated" human beings. Meanwhile, media critics point out that "technologies create the ways in which people perceive reality, and that such ways are the key to understanding diverse forms of social and mental life" (Postman 1993, 21). Thus, introducing the "boxes and wires" of telecomputing into schools is not merely a political or educational issue. It is a moral, philosophical, and cultural issue as well. To proceed with this experiment as if it merely alters a school's explicit curriculum without affecting the implicit and null curricula belies either a cavalier attitude or epistemological ignorance.

It would be unrealistic to expect classroom teachers to devote equal time and attention to all forms of literacy. So it is wise to ask at this point, as computer literacy gains momentum, what forms of literacy might be marginalized. Seymour Papert, emeritus member of the Epistemology and Learning Group at MIT's Media Lab, is representative of those who have little trouble "demoting reading from its privileged position in the school curriculum" because it would liberate children from the "early and massive imposition" of what he calls "letteracy." As Papert sees it,

> Literacy should not mean the ability to decode strings of alphabetic letters. Consider a child who uses a Knowledge Machine to acquire a broad understanding of poetry (spoken), history (perhaps relived in simulations), and art and science (through computer-based labs), and thus draws on this knowledge to conduct a well-informed, highly persuasive campaign to pre-

serve the environment. All this could happen without being letterate. If it does, should we say the child is illiterate? (Papert 1993)

Papert clearly favors a "translation/critical literacy" rather than the traditional "decoding/analytic literacy" taught in public schools (Myers 1996). Unfortunately, his immersion in computer culture often blinds him to its flaws. Similarly, computer science instructors, preoccupied with the syntax of programming language, seldom pause to consider the "rhetoric of the desktop," or to alert students to the ways in which a computer culture influences their language and perceptions. Nonetheless, students who create "documents" to be saved in "folders" and placed on a "desktop" are learning how to speak a corporate language. How many of them, while acquiring the skills that define computer literacy in myopic technical terms, will have the strength of character to resist the seductions of this metaphor or its impact on their perceptions of the world?

What is particularly disturbing about Papert's definition of literacy is its indifference toward human relationships with physical environments and peers. In *The Future Does Not Compute*, Stephen Talbott takes exception with Papert's vision of computer technology as the "primary instrument for overcoming abstraction, reintegrating education with life, and embedding the student in concrete learning situations" (Talbott 1995, 151–152). Talbott fears a distortion of reality and detachment from humanist concerns, claiming that:

> . . . it is a strange definition of "concrete" that places all its stress upon the student's active involvement, and none at all upon whatever it is he is involved with. The only fully concrete thing a computer offers the student is its own, perhaps enchanting presence. Beyond that it hosts a mediate and abstract world. . . . This makes it easier for the child to remain caught up in the computer's presentation of reality—and therefore inserts a more distracting, more comprehensive veil between him and the world into which he was born. . . .(Talbott 1995, 152)

The Curricular Conundrum

Given such pernicious possibilities, one may ask why educators should introduce computer-mediated activities to their classrooms. Why should humanities teachers, in particular, take part in shaping computer literacy if it poses a threat to the traditions they value? Such questions were largely absent from the Modern Language Association's Right to Literacy Conference in 1988, where "much of the debate focused on distinctions between functional literacy, cultural literacy, and public literacy" (Costanzo 1994, 11). Yet, a decade later, we stretch this attenuated term further by asking it to accommodate emerging technology and electronic texts. Whether the humanities teacher approves or not, "computers are altering the way many of us read, write, and even think. It is not simply that the tools of literacy have changed; the nature of texts, of language, of literacy itself is undergoing crucial transformations" (Costanzo 1994, 11).

Changes in literacy inevitably alter school curricula. Thus, humanists who retreat from the debate over computer literacy in schools may unwittingly invite the end of what they had hoped to preserve: a liberal arts curriculum. What is required, then, is the marriage of emerging technologies with the traditions of rhetorical education, a synthesis that would stimulate school curricula. However, this is not without risks, for the rhetoric and gadgetry of technology have the potential to overwhelm the subtler concerns of a humanities curriculum. One of the most eloquent advocates of such a synthesis is Richard Lanham, who notes that although computer literacy has encouraged an "extraordinary convergence" in university curricula, it also has the potential to displace a central fixture of the humanities curriculum. If allowed, the consequences will extend well beyond schools.

> Once you abolish rhetorical education, then you must ask, "How then, do I teach decorum. What else do I use for my behavioral allegory?" Property? Stuff? And what about the teaching of language? Once it has become simply instrumental, the clear, brief, and sincere transmission of neutral fact from one neutral entity to another, it loses [...] its power, as our present literacy crisis attests. If you pursue only clarity, you guarantee obscurity. And people lose their vital interest in language, as any composition teacher can attest. The "literacy crisis" is not only a social crisis, a crisis of instructional leverage, of educational policy, although it is all of those. It comes from the repudiation of the rhetorical heart of Western education, and its linguistic and behavioral education in decorum. (Lanham 1994, 83)

The Rhetorical Triangle: Ethos, Logos, and Pathos

If the abolition of rhetorical education invites such crises, what exactly can be done to revive "the rhetorical heart of Western education" while helping students acquire a more satisfying computer literacy? Clearly, this requires a delicate balancing act, merging rhetorical traditions with emerging technologies to arrive at a new synthesis called *media literacy* (see Figure 1.1).

Media Literacy

Media literacy is the ability to read and understand a communications medium by *looking through* the processes it enables, interpreting its signs and symbols, while also *looking at* the medium's impact on an author, audience, and message.

Figure 1.1

To succeed, we must adopt a holistic approach, establishing a literacy-across-the-curriculum program similar to writing-across-the-curriculum initiatives. Can we ask this of teachers who have not been formally trained in rhetoric? Are teachers of mathematics and science, let alone of the humanities, equipped to pose as rhetoricians? Yes, indeed, for all are engaged in rhetorical activities each day, whether seeking truth or trying to persuade someone to believe a story, cast a vote, buy a product, or take some other action. All of these activities require participation in the ancient "art of persuasion" that scholars of ancient Greece called *rhetoric*.

What this shift requires, more than formal training, is a reorientation in the way computers and computer technology are viewed. Until now, we've approved computer literacy as if it were just another form of basic literacy or a functional literacy necessary to succeed in the workplace. These forms of computer literacy required one to "look through" the technology and to learn how to manipulate hardware and software to accomplish certain tasks. However, it is now time to step back from the machinery and look at computers, networks, and the interactions they enable in order to learn how to "read" and "interpret" their impact. By looking at the machinery instead of constantly looking through it, one returns to the "rhetorical heart" of education while broadening the definition of computer literacy (Hass 1996; Lanham 1994).

How to begin? Like this: Return to the foundations of rhetorical analysis, which hold that every message has an author, an argument, and an audience. Rhetoricians speak of these three elements in terms of a "rhetorical triangle" (see Figure 1.2), employing the Greek terms *ethos, logos,* and *pathos,* which provide clues to the etymology of modern terms. *Ethos* speaks to the "ethics" or credibility of the author; *logos* addresses the "logic" of the message; and *pathos* relates to the emotional appeal (think of sympathy, empathy, apathy) and how it affects an audience. Whether one speaks of this as ethos, logos, and pathos or Author, Message, and Audience is a matter of personal preference. What is significant, however, is the way in which this rhetorical approach provides students—and teachers— with a vocabulary and tools for reading and discussing the signs and symbols they encounter both online and off.

Figure 1.2

Consider, for instance, television advertising. When a company hires a famous athlete, such as Michael Jordan, for endorsements, they do so with the knowledge that Jordan's ethos will reflect favorably upon their product. Furthermore, by using Jordan's athleticism to create a stunning visual image, accompanied by instrumental music and special effects, the advertisers find their way to the emotional heartbeat of their audience, drawing them in through an effective use of pathos. What is missing? What point on the rhetorical triangle may actually be blunt, compared to the sharp points of ethos and pathos used by this particular medium? In a word:

logos. Just because Michael Jordan, a tremendously gifted athlete, looks good in a particular pair of athletic shoes, drinks a particular soft drink, or endorses a fast food restaurant does not necessarily mean the product is right for everyone. Indeed, by scratching beneath the surface of these glittering advertisements, teachers can help students see that ethos and pathos are often used to distract the audience from a weak message, one whose logos does not hold up under close examination.

MEDIA LITERACY CHALLENGE # 1

The Rhetoric of Computer Advertising

One way to help students develop media literacy skills is by asking them to apply rhetorical analysis to another kind of advertising.

What to Do

1. To initiate this, ask students to find an advertisement for computer hardware, software, or accessories in a popular magazine. Have them examine the ethos, logos, and pathos used to sell the product to that magazine's intended audience.

2. Ask them to bring the advertisement and analysis to class. Have them form small groups, share the advertisements, and see if they can guess what type of magazine published them. Each group should list common images, themes, and methods used to express logos, establish ethos, and appeal through pathos.

3. In a subsequent discussion with the full group, create a list of rhetorical strategies that computer manufacturers use to persuade people that their product is "truly" the best and that a customer should act immediately by purchasing that product.

Is Everything an Argument?

Placing rhetoric at the heart of computer literacy not only broadens the definition of the latter term but also helps students cultivate critical literacy while engaged in recreational computer use. Consider, for example, the habit of browsing, or "surfing," the Internet, which has quickly become a diversion comparable to channel-surfing television programs. What is often missing from these activities is the kind of critical thinking teachers would like to instill in their students. Unless they're encouraged to think critically, students may simply acquire meaningless information that they fail to scrutinize or document in research papers.

This leads to an ethos problem. The student who borrows intellectual property without proper citations or uses inaccurate information gathered from a dubious source inevitably loses credibility. In such instances, the rhetorical triangle reminds students to consider all three fundamental concerns—ethos, logos, and pathos—before rushing to judgment. As a result, the rhetorical triangle furnishes a powerful means for analysis and articulation, serving as both an instrument of inquiry and a vocabulary for expression. Students who randomly pluck information from the Internet may not realize they have fallen prey to the salesmanship of pathos, which disarms their critical judgment by appealing to their emotions, distracts them with faulty logos, and leads them into the temptations that damage their ethos.

One may teach this lesson through the rhetorical strategies of daily life, since their prevalence alone helps students realize the importance of interpreting signs and symbols to develop media literacy skills. To emphasize a point, as well as start an argument, some rhetoricians claim that "everything's an argument" (Lunsford and Ruszkiewicz 1999). Although an overstatement, this is certainly a good starting point for discussion. While there is evidence of ethos, logos, and pathos in every statement read, seen, or heard, not all statements make the same kind of argument. Granted, this is not the kind of argument that adolescents have with their siblings, nor is it necessarily one in which the participants attempt to win a debate. Rather, it is the kind of argument that comes from either (a) an attempt to discover truth or (b) after having discovered that truth, attempting to persuade others to take an action (Lunsford and Ruszkiewicz 1999, 5).

When seen through this filter, a surprising number of statements—written, visual, musical, and virtual—acquire an argumentative quality. In other words, they can be viewed as rhetorical devices that attempt to persuade a particular audience. They may wish to share a truth, telling the audience that "Not marble, nor the gilded monuments/Of Princes, shall outlive this pow'rful rhyme" (Shakespeare 1964, 95); then again, they may wish to stir the audience to take action, submitting to the power of their persuasion.

MEDIA LITERACY CHALLENGE #2

Arguments 'R Us

This challenge helps sensitize students to a wide range of arguments they encounter on a daily basis.

What to Do

1. Divide the class into small groups and ask each group to consider one of the following questions:

   (1) Is a love letter an argument?

   (2) Is a grocery list an argument?

   (3) Is a restaurant's menu an argument?

   (4) Is a vacation itinerary an argument?

   (5) Is a birthday party invitation an argument?

   (6) Is a course syllabus an argument?

   (7) Is a standardized examination an argument?

   (8) Is a report card an argument?

   (9) Is a computer program an argument?

   (10) Is a Web site an argument?

2. Ask students how each item might present an "argument" and what media are used to express it. How do those media use ethos, logos, and pathos to convince an audience that their message is true or persuade them to take action?

Expanding the Challenge

To further develop students' understanding of rhetorical filters, ask them to write a brief rhetorical analysis of the promotional copy used in the packaging of computer merchandise. What evidence is there that the manufacturers have employed ethos, logos, and pathos to persuade the user that this is a quality product?

Suggested topics: the cover, table of contents, and blurb of a CD-ROM, computer manual, or software application. Help students discover dis-

Teacher's Tip

Although all of the items could be seen as arguments, students may have difficulty understanding this concept initially. Nonetheless, when they have begun to see their world through rhetorical filters, they should be ready to look at computer paraphernalia in new ways, subjecting it to similar critiques.

tinctions between advertisements for computer merchandise in various media and the promotional material found on the merchandise itself.

Questions for discussion: How is the imagery and text on the merchandise different from the imagery seen in the magazine ads? Is there a difference, or does it "echo" the persuasive tactics used in advertising campaigns?

The Technology of Writing

Ultimately, computer literacy needs to be considered as part of a larger discussion and placed within the context of significant cultural, historical, and technological developments. Just as typewriting classes gave way to keyboarding classes, computer application courses that isolate various software applications and treat the computer primarily in technical terms may also disappear. Until that happens, however, educators need to make a concentrated effort to situate computer literacy within the larger context of media literacy. This serves a number of purposes while calling attention to frequently neglected concerns. For instance, despite the attention that the Internet and computer technology have attracted, how often do people actually think about the impact of writing technology on their writing and thinking?

In his book, *Writing Space: The Computer, Hypertext, and the History of Writing*, Jay David Bolter describes writing as "a state of mind" while arguing for broader definitions of fundamental terms. In fact, Bolter not only argues that pencils, pens, paper, and computers are writing technology, but also that the skills themselves are technological inventions:

> There is good etymological reason to broaden our definition of technology to include skills as well as machines. The Greek root of "technology" is *techne*, and for the Greeks a techne could be an art or a craft, "a set of rules, system or method of making or doing, whether of the useful arts, or of the fine arts" (Liddell and Scott 1973, 1785). In the ancient world physical technology was simpler, and the ancients put a correspondingly greater emphasis on the skill of the craftsman—the potter, the stone-mason, or the carpenter. In his dialogue the *Phaedrus*, Plato calls the alphabet itself a *techne*. He would also have called the ancient book composed of ink on papyrus a *techne*; Homeric epic poetry was also a *techne*, as was Greek tragedy. All the ancient arts and crafts have this in common: that the crafts-

man must develop a skill, a technical state of mind in using tools and materials. Ancient and modern writing is a technology in just this sense. It is a method for arranging verbal thoughts in a visual space. The writer always needs a surface upon which to make his or her marks and a tool with which to make them, and these materials help to define the nature of the writing. Writing with quill and parchment is a different skill from writing with a printing press, which in turn differs from writing with a computer. (Bolter 1991, 35)

MEDIA LITERACY CHALLENGE #3

Musical Chairs and Writing Technology

This challenge will transform writing technology by turning what is usually invisible and common into something visible and extraordinary. In doing so, it raises questions to inspire further exploration of writing technology as well as classroom discussions about media literacy. As a result, this literacy challenge illustrates the need for broader definitions and a deeper understanding of the technology and media that students employ while developing literacy skills.

What to Do

1. Divide the class into groups of three or four students.

2. Ask each group to spend five minutes brainstorming a story idea about "a person in a place with a problem."

3. After they have established their outline, each group begins at one of seven workstations, each of which presents a different writing technology. By way of illustration, the workstations for this exercise could provide:

Station 1: Chalk and chalkboard.

Station 2: Crayon or charcoal and large, unlined poster paper.

Station 3: Pencil and unlined paper.

Station 4: Pen and lined paper.

Station 5: Markers and a whiteboard.

Station 6: Manual typewriter and typing paper with correction fluid.

Station 7: Laptop or desktop computer and diskette.

If any of these materials are unavailable, use comparable substitutes to approximate the evolution of writing technology from its simplest to most complex forms. Groups have five minutes to work on their story's narrative, using the writing technology at the station. Instrumental music provides a soothing background as well as practical purpose: When the music stops, so must the composition. Each group member must contribute at least one sentence to the narrative using the designated writing technology to write the sentence.

4. As soon as the music stops, each group steps back from its workstation and leaves its final sentence in a state of arrested development.

5. The groups rotate, moving to the next station in the sequence, where they read and continue their predecessors' narrative—beginning with that incomplete sentence—while using the new writing technology before them.

6. After the groups have completed a full rotation of the stations, so that everyone has had an opportunity to use each of the writing technologies, ask students to complete the survey form in Figure 1.3.

> **Teacher's Tip**
>
> When students have completed this survey, consider having them discuss it in their original small groups or in new groupings. Alternatively, it might be worthwhile to facilitate a full class discussion on "Writing Technology: Evolution or Revolution?" If addressed as an open-ended question, it helps students think about computers and computer literacy as both an evolutionary and revolutionary process. As a result, they should begin to see computer literacy in a new light, discussing it as part of a historical movement situated within the larger context of media literacy.

Civil Literacy

Once teachers have widened the parameters of computer literacy, enabling students to think of it in terms of media literacy, it is time to examine less technical matters. As already shown, there is far more to online learning environments than the "boxes and wires" that enable telecomputing. In many ways, the assembly of hardware and software presents fewer challenges than the creation of an online community of learners, particularly if the participants fail to behave in a manner conducive to educational endeavors. Having considered ways to restore the "rhetorical heart" of education to computer literacy, however, teachers are better prepared to cultivate *civil literacy* in cyberspace.

Media Literacy: Informal Study of Writing Technology

Name: _____

For each of the following, please use the space provided or write a brief commentary on the back of this sheet.

1. Which writing technology felt most comfortable? Briefly explain why you liked the "'feel'" of this combination most. Put another way, which combination allowed you to concentrate most upon the narrative you were writing?

   ___Chalk and chalkboard

   ___Crayon on large, unlined poster paper

   ___Pencil and unlined paper

   ___Pen and lined paper

   ___Markers on a whiteboard

   ___Manual typewriter and typing paper

   ___Laptop or desktop computer

2. Which combination called the most attention to itself, distracting you from the narrative, and how did it do this?

3. How did the respective "writing spaces" affect your sentence length or style? (In other words, how concerned were you with trying to "fit" your words/sentences into that writing space?)

4. If you had a choice of writing implement and 'writing space'—that is, the tool and the surface upon which it is used—which would you choose for the following activities, and why?

   Grocery list:

   Love letter:

   Diagram/map:

   Academic essay:

   A reminder (to yourself or family member):

5. Of these technologies, which do you think would be most useful to the writer who wished to emphasize the following, and why?

   —*Ethos* (the author's credibility)

   —*Logos* (the message)

   —*Pathos* (emotional appeal to the audience)

Figure 1.3

Civil Literacy: The CyberPilot's License

We must come to grips with various social issues as the network penetrates deeper and more broadly into the social and economic fabric of the community of nations.

Vint Cerf, Internet Society President (quoted in Miller 1996, 34)

Approaching computer literacy as a form of media literacy may help restore "the rhetorical heart of Western education," but to fulfill that ambition educators must help students consider the moral and ethical issues that attend their use of technology. This calls for a more enlightened approach to networked technology, one that realizes its potential to do both good and evil in schools and communities. For although this technology can be used to create a sense of community online, it can also be used to exclude or marginalize individuals and misappropriate intellectual property. At present, most school districts require that students and their guardians sign an Acceptable Use Policy (AUP) before granting Internet access to pupils. However, this proves to be a legalistic measure rather than an educational one. As an antidote, this chapter proposes a more thoughtful approach to what is commonly called *"netiquette."* This approach requires an essential literacy for children whose education introduces them to powerful, technological tools: *civil literacy* (see Figure 2.1).

In December 1994, one of the earliest guidelines for AUPs appeared on the Internet, advising policymakers to "make it clear that use of the Net is

---

Civil Literacy

Civil literacy is the ability to read, interpret, and respect the moral and ethical beliefs embraced by a particular social group and apply them in a responsible manner.

Figure 2.1

a privilege and not a right, and outline the penalties and repercussions of violating the AUP" (Classroom Connect 1994; see http://www.wentworth.com/classroom/aup.htm). Indeed, many school districts followed this advice, initiating students to the Web not through an educational program but through a legal document full of oblique warnings and ambiguous threats. Why is this such a pernicious development? If one thinks of an AUP as part of a school's implicit curriculum, then these documents could make schools less conducive to intelligent educational practice and less hospitable to the children they were designed to protect. This ought to make one ask a few troublesome questions. For example: Is an AUP designed to protect children from pornography on the Internet or to defend schools from civil suits? Ultimately, whom does the AUP serve? Whom does it protect?

Defendants of these litigious documents speak in fatalistic terms when they ask, "How else can we protect children and establish the rules?" This, however, exposes the flawed thinking, and disingenuous character, of an AUP. A school that distributes such documents without an introductory course to accompany them is more concerned with legal issues than education. What's more, these AUPs reveal an unhealthy preoccupation with a school's published curriculum and neglect the implicit and null curricula that influence children.

The CyberPilot's License

Draconian threats have seldom taught students how to drive cars or prevent unwanted pregnancies. Certainly, educators need to offer children guidance for telecomputing as well as other activities, but AUPs, as presently conceived, are legalistic and threatening when they ought to be instructive. As a corrective measure, faculty representatives from all disciplines ought to develop a program that addresses the concerns attending computer literacy, teaching what is meant by the responsible use of computer technology. This proposal should not be confused with a number of commercial ventures promoting an "Internet driver's license" that stresses technical skills. Instead, *The CyberPilot's License* focuses upon the civil literacy that must accompany technical skills so that students give more thought to the moral and ethical issues raised by networked technology. AUPs are a component, although not necessarily the centerpiece, of such a program, just as driver's education is a requirement for anyone who wishes to obtain permission to operate an automobile on public roadways. Meanwhile, readers primarily interested in devising a computer literacy course that stresses functional literacy would do well to visit the Web site for the *European Computer Driving License* (http://www.ecdl.com/). Established by a nonprofit organization in Ireland, this program offers a complete syllabus featuring seven learning modules and a scope and sequence designed to create international standards.

As for *The CyberPilot's License*, an online prototype has been created with the hope of attracting students, parents, and educators who wish to collaborate in the development of a progressive educational tool, constructing a thoughtful antidote to AUPs. *The CyberPilot's License* Web site (http://www.cwrl.utexas.edu/~burniske/cpl) offers links to useful online resources concerning civil literacy in cyberspace, along with interactive tools that enable investigation of the social, moral, and ethical issues that computer technology introduces (see Figure 2.2). Its design is informed by the belief that "the 'one-size-fits-all' approach rarely fits more than those who created it" (Burniske 1999).

Critics of this proposal may consider it an unnecessary encroachment upon academic curricula. Others will quarrel over the appropriate place for it within the curriculum. Both responses, however, produce the kind of myopic and evasive stances that perpetuate the "overly-narrow, official version of literacy practices or skills" that Selfe (1998) has admonished language arts educators to resist. Educators cannot dismiss "netiquette" as irrelevant, banishing it to the null curriculum. Nor can they allow disputes over its proper place in the curriculum to stall its introduction. Traditionally, few computer science courses have given "Web ethics" more than a peripheral glance. Meanwhile, humanities teachers complain they already have too much to do, too little expertise with telecomputing, to accept such responsibilities. However, emerging technologies blur the distinctions between disciplines, compelling simultaneous instruction of skills and the

Figure 2.2   Reprinted with permission of R. W. Burniske. © 1999. All rights reserved.

responsibility inherent in their exercise. "Computer ethics" must, therefore, be an integral part of *any* class that uses computers—and a prerequisite for computer literacy.

In its present form, *The CyberPilot's License* offers five sections for students, teachers, parents, and policymakers to explore and develop, offering both an archive of useful Web sites as well as Web-based discussion forums. What follows is a more detailed discussion of the respective sections, including a rationale for introducing students to these concerns, Web addresses of pertinent sites on the Internet, and civil literacy challenges. None of this should be interpreted as a prescription, but it should whet appetites for discussion of provocative issues, assisting teachers interested in adapting such a model to suit a particular curriculum and age group.

Know Your Vehicle

Despite a century's experience with automobiles, a significant number of drivers still operate a vehicle without understanding its mechanics. Nor do they believe it necessary to acquire such understanding. Although this may be true, it betrays an alarming and willful ignorance that merits a qualifier. Such ignorance may not prevent one from operating a vehicle, but it could eventually lead to significant problems. Failure to understand why an automobile engine needs clean engine oil, a functional radiator with coolant, or balanced tires and proper alignment, may not prevent one from driving a vehicle (for a while). However, it's just a matter of time before something breaks down, forcing the operator to consult someone who does understand the vehicle. The same applies to networked computers and the "cyberpilots" who use them to navigate through cyberspace. What one doesn't know may not prevent one from making these vehicles work, but it could ultimately do harm.

Students may protest that studying the history, terminology, and technology of the Internet is boring or unnecessary, but teachers should explain that one cannot achieve computer literacy without the knowledge necessary to place all of this within a larger social and cultural context. With that in mind, the "Know Your Vehicle" section of *The CyberPilot's License* focuses upon the vehicle itself. What does this have to do with civil literacy? As with driver education, networked computers present opportunities that didn't previously exist. They have, however, evolved out of traditions that adolescents cannot fully appreciate without greater historical perspective. Thus, it helps to know a little about the history of the Internet, as provided by a resource like *Hobbes' Internet Timeline* (http://pollux.com/compuweb/timeline.htm), or to have knowledge of a *Glossary of Internet Terms*, like the primer from the Internet Literacy Consultants (http://www.matisse.net/files/glossary.html). A brief introduction to the history and terminology helps students see that although "cyberspace" offers new possibilities, many of the activities they encounter there have historical antecedents. Also, familiarity with the terminology is an integral part of literacy and is critical to the kind of civility educators wish to inspire. Before students reach for the slang terms used to describe online activities, it's worthwhile to identify the formal terms that help define the language of this culture.

Background knowledge of this sort proves useful when students turn to primers that will help them understand how the Internet works and how they can harness its power for educational purposes. There are many online tutorials to choose from, including the Public Broadcasting System's *Using and Understanding the Internet* (http://www.pbs.org/uti/) and Paradesa Media's multilingual introduction, *Learn the*

Net (http://www.learnthenet.com/english/index.html). A number of educational institutions also provide directories to online tutorials: Robert Gordon University in Aberdeen maintains one of the best; *NetLearn* (http://www.rgu.ac.uk/~sim/research/netlearn/callist.htm) is a veritable encyclopedia of resources for learning and teaching Internet skills. The site offers a wealth of hyperlinks to carefully selected resources, presenting thoughtful annotations that include brief reviews. With such an embarrassment of riches to choose from, teachers might wish to arrange a scavenger hunt for students to find the "best" online primer. However, it helps to establish criteria first, so that an online "search" doesn't deteriorate into casual "browsing" or random selection of mediocre or misleading resources.

As students gain familiarity with the "vehicle," they may want to know more about *All Search Engines* (http://www.allsearchengines.com), listservers, newsgroups, and more. And what of the students who come to class with a fairly good understanding of the vehicle? If they already know the vehicle, should they take part in exercises such as this? Absolutely! In fact, they should be deputized to assist their teacher and classmates. This is a good opportunity to model a collaborative approach to learning, which sits at the core of civil literacy.

Rights & Responsibilities

As mentioned earlier, the flaws in AUPs for technology stem from a preoccupation with legal concerns rather than educational ones. As a result, these policy statements typically focus on the rules and regulations that govern student behaviors and the consequences for disobeying them. What's missing from this equation? How about an understanding of why these rules and regulations exist? Imagine approaching student questions as an educational opportunity rather than a disciplinary threat. Perhaps what adults interpret as sarcasm or insolence actually reveals relative inexperience ("Why can't we use each other's personal accounts?"), fundamental ignorance ("Why should we refrain from flame wars?"), or a first amendment challenge ("Why can't we view pornography in school if it's protected as free speech?").

Schools often rely upon threats, like those featured in the AUP, to force student compliance rather than appealing to the better part of human nature. As a consequence, schools neglect or inhibit a child's natural curiosity, which often expresses itself through a desire to understand why certain actions and activities are prohibited. To repair some of the damage done to their students' intellectual curiosity, teachers may wish to have them visit the *Center for Democracy and Technology* (http://www.cdt.org), a nonprofit organization that develops and advocates public policies that support constitutional civil liberties and democratic values in new computer and communications technologies. Students would also benefit from learning about the *Computer Professionals for Social Responsibility* (http://www.cpsr.org/) who seek to raise awareness of the forces involved in the development of cyberspace while promoting civil liberties through the *Cyber-Rights Homepage* (ftp://www.cpsr.org/cpsr/nii/cyber-rights/index. html). This could, in fact, inspire discussions about distinctions between privileges and rights; a student's computer privileges may be revoked, but what about his or her civil liberties?

Meanwhile, *The CyberPilot's License* Web site features interactive spaces where pilots of all ages may raise questions and seek answers about their rights and responsibilities. Visitors are encouraged to contribute to a collection of case studies. As the collection grows, students and teachers will have an opportunity to learn about important legal cases involving students whose actions have challenged conventional ideas about online "rights and responsibilities." *The Pilots' Place*, a Web-based discussion forum, will serve as both a virtual meeting place and a digital archive of landmark cases (http://www.cwrl.utexas.edu/~burniske/cpl/students/index.html).

Who & What Rules the Airwaves?

It seldom hurts to understand the context within which an individual operates. Therefore, this section of *The Cyberpilot's License* addresses a quintessential problem of the human condition: How can a part survey the whole? The Internet is a vast, collaborative work in progress. As such, it may seem as though no one is in charge of it. That may have been true once, but as more people have gone online and as celebrated cases have called attention to the need for rules and regulations, a whole new genre of legislation has arrived. In order to reach an understanding of AUPs, state and federal laws, and the great debate over freedom of speech on the Internet, one must investigate civil literacy in cyberspace. Students and teachers can also locate definitions of important terms, laws, and cases concerning censorship on the Internet, as well as various opinions on the question, by visiting *Ohio University's Censorship* site (http://www.tcom. ohiou.edu/OU_Language/project/censorship.html).

Meanwhile, how do educators distinguish between acceptable use and unacceptable abuse? A text-based "gopher" collection at *Rice University* (gopher://riceinfo.rice.edu:1170/11/More/Acceptable) provides good material for in-class debates that may help participants reach satisfying conclusions. While they're at it, students and teachers are encouraged to visit *The Reference Desk* (http://www.cwrl.utexas.edu/~burniske/cpl/reference.html), an interactive archive that enables the telecollaborative construction of an online library. Visitors may add annotated hyperlinks to Web documents related to civil literacy or follow links to resources that others have recommended.

Piloting Skills & Netiquette

By now, it should be obvious that there's far more to civil literacy than technical skills. However, teachers seeking concrete exercises that "show" what the previous sections "tell" will find what they're looking for in "Piloting Skills & Netiquette." This section of *The CyberPilot's License* introduces students to several problematic issues they'll encounter while flying through the information skyway. Hopefully, by the time they've completed these exercises they will never again think of computer literacy as a purely technical skill. Nor will they suffer the delusion that online activities can be divorced from social and cultural concerns.

Print limitations do not permit a full sampling of the learning activities available in this section of *The CyberPilot's License*. For more exercises and the complete text of the ones offered here, visit *"Piloting Skills & Netiquette"* online (www.cwrl.utexas.edu/~burniske/cpl/skills.html). For now, this limited sampling should reinforce the significance of civil literacy in cyberspace, stimulating class discussions while providing a glimpse of learning activities that facilitate further inquiry. The following, abbreviated versions will enable classroom teachers to review learning activities without sitting in front of a computer screen. Later chapters will present further selections, but this section begins with two fundamental concerns of civil literacy in cyberspace: intellectual property and human rights.

Intellectual Property in Cyberspace: An Overview

One of the most important distinctions for a scholar, both online and off, is the difference between borrowing information and stealing it. This applies not only to the physical world, but also to the intellectual one. Unless students understand this distinction, they may harm others or themselves in cyberspace. This overview should help cyberpilots-in-training gain respect for what's known as *intellectual property*. It introduces general principles and specific guidelines for refraining from the misuse or abuse of intellectual property. The entire exercise is, in fact, guided by the notion that safe cyberpilots learn how to borrow without stealing.

Private E-mail

Private e-mail is, first and foremost, private material. Before one considers using a quotation from private e-mail, be sure to ask permission from the author. If the individual isn't comfortable with another's use of the message, then the writer is ethically bound to omit that document from his or her essay. However, if the author does grant permission, the document must be cited properly. Here's why and how to do that.

Why to

Tell students to resist the temptation to simply "cut and paste" a passage from e-mail into an essay. Why? Because the ideas, and their expression, belong to someone else. Respect other people's property, whether it's intellectual or physical. Also, writers could find themselves in very deep trouble if the individual from whom they are borrowing this passage should decide to use the exact same one in the report he or she is writing for the same class. So, give credit where credit is due: Document that e-mail message! Otherwise, writers risk damaging their ethos, which means their credibility and reputation will suffer.

How to

There is still debate over the issue of how to cite electronic sources, so, if something seems odd to you, investigate the Web or printed handbooks to see if better alternatives have emerged. For the sake of consistency, let's adopt the Modern Language Association (MLA) guidelines for citing electronic sources. The MLA would cite itself as follows:

Gibaldi, Joseph. *MLA Handbook for Writers of Research Papers*. New York: Modern Languages Association of America. 1999.

Depending upon the academic discipline and the teacher's preferences, writers may wish to use a different reference style, such as the American Psychological Association (APA) guidelines or *The Chicago Manual of Style*. What matters most is consistency, so choose one set of guidelines or another, but make certain to stress the need to provide complete bibliographical references. For further information on bibliographical information, consult a handbook or visit a reputable online source such as the Internet Public Library's guidelines for *Citing Electronic Resources* (http://www.ipl.org/ref/QUE/FARQ/netciteFARQ.html). For now, here is what the MLA Handbook suggests for citing electronic mail messages:

> . . . give the name of the writer; the title of the message (if any), taken from the subject line and enclosed in quotation marks; a description of the message that includes the recipient (e.g. "E-mail to the author); and the date of the message. (Gibaldi 1999, 199)

For example, let's say that Penelope Jones received an e-mail message from Josephine Smith. The subject line of the message was "Yikes, how do I do this?" Penelope received it on April 1, 1999. If Penelope wanted to use this item in an essay, how would she cite it? According to the MLA conventions, the bibliographical citation would look like this:

> Smith, Josephine. "Yikes, how do I do this?" E-mail to Penelope Jones. 1 April 1999.

Mailing List Messages

What is a "mailing list" (or *listserver*), anyway? Think of it as a public forum that distributes messages through an "electronic mailbox in the sky." People from all over the world subscribe to this mailbox so that whenever someone puts a message in it, they, along with all other subscribers, automatically receive a copy of that message. So, unlike "snail mail" or even faxes, messages sent to a listserver allow for "one-to-many" correspondence without the writer sending more than one copy through the airwaves. Pretty amazing, huh?

Cyberpilots are sometimes tempted to borrow ideas or information from interesting messages encountered on electronic mailing lists, as though these items are "free" for the taking because they appear in a "public" forum. This is an unethical practice, however, and one that must be avoided. Here's why.

Why to

Building a community of learners is like building a house: Both need a solid foundation. The foundation for the community of learners is personal integrity. If cyberpilots steal ideas and information from strangers they've encountered on electronic mailing lists, without noting the source, can you imagine the difficulty future scholars will have in trying to locate the origins of this information? Do not borrow material from mailing lists without citing it properly. On the spur of the moment this may save time, but in the long run it could damage reputations, spoil integrity, and confuse individuals who rely upon a community of scholars to assist their research.

How to

The Modern Language Association (MLA) guidelines offer the following advice:

> To cite a posting to an e-mail discussion list, begin with the author's name and the title of the document (in quotation marks), as given in the subject line, followed by the description Online posting, the date when the material was posted, the name of the forum [...], the date of access and, in angle brackets, the online address of the list's Internet site or, if no Internet site is known, the e-mail address of the list's moderator or supervisor. (Gibaldi 1999, 200)

So, imagine this: A student named Nicky Murrieta posted a message entitled "Communication in Cyberspace" to a listserver for a project called *The Media Matter* on September 2, 1999. You have this e-mail message because you were subscribed to the project mailing list (mediamatter @jaring.my) and received the message on September 3, 1999. The project had no Web site then, nor does it have one now, but the moderator's e-mail address was (buddyb@iskl.po.my). What to do? Try this:

Murrieta, Nicky. "Communication in Cyberspace." Online posting. 2 September 1999. The Media Matter. 3 September 1999. (buddyb@iskl.po.my).

Newsgroup Messages

What is a "newsgroup" and how would you know one when you saw it? Well, perhaps it would help to think of newsgroups as discussion groups arranged by theme with technology keeping the "minutes" of their conversations. There are literally thousands of newsgroups on virtually every topic one can imagine. Before the World Wide Web made it possible to access information through Web sites with graphic images, "Usenet newsgroups" were one of the most popular ways of sharing information online. They are still quite popular, perhaps because, unlike a mailing list, a user doesn't need to "subscribe" to a newsgroup. The user goes to it, rather than having its messages automatically come to the user. In time, one is grateful for this!

Newsgroups are not necessarily about news. Rather, they bring together people interested in a particular topic, ranging from politics to recreation, activism to alternative lifestyles. Within these groups, one might hear eyewitness accounts of social protests, natural disasters, and other historic events. One can also join discussions about film, music, sports, and other recreation. To learn more about the possibilities, visit the Deja News archive (http://www.deja.com/). However, before flying into a particular newsgroup, cyberpilots should make sure they know what they are getting into. Upon arrival at a newsgroup forum, its often wise to "lurk before you leap" into a discussion, getting oriented within the conversation by first making certain this is the right place. If it's not, then exit and check out another newsgroup. You're bound to find one of interest, because there are tens of thousands, but finding a niche may seem rather intimidating at first.

After finding the right newsgroup, it's still important to remember the context of the conversation and always consider sources. Before snatching an interesting quote from a newsgroup, one needs to learn something about the individual who made the statement, especially if it presents obscure "facts" that need verification. Good scholarship depends largely upon good, reliable sources of information. So before using a newsgroup message in an essay, it's a good idea to do a little homework on the source itself.

Why to

As with messages from a mailing list, it's essential that one gives credit where credit is due, providing a "source" that other scholars can locate.

This demonstrates that one has done the necessary homework instead of shooting from the hip, tossing words and ideas around carelessly.

How to

According to the MLA, here's how to handle newsgroup sources:

> To cite a posting to a Usenet news group, begin with the author's name and the title of the document (in quotation marks), as given in the subject line, followed by the description Online posting, the date when the material was posted, the date of access, and, in angle brackets, the name of the newsgroup with the prefix *news*. (Gibaldi 1999, 201)

For example: Imagine that someone named I. M. Patriotic posted a message entitled "Big Bend Is Awesome!" on the "National Parks" newsgroup (rec.outdoors.national-parks) on July 4, 1999. Because newsgroup messages are automatically archived, a student might discover this posting on October 31, 2000. Following MLA guidelines, the citation would look like this:

> Patriotic, I. M. "Big Bend Is Awesome!" Online posting. 4 July 1999. 31 October 2000. (news: rec.outdoors.national-parks).

Synchronous Communication (MUDS, MOOs, IRCs)

"Context is everything," they say, for a writer must always bear in mind the situation from which a comment is taken. Quotes taken "out of context" are often misleading, delivering either a half-truth or a complete distortion. This is especially true when it comes to synchronous online communications. In these conversations, the speakers are individuals typing at their own keyboards, often separated by distance, yet connected through the Internet in a conversation that materializes upon their respective screens at nearly the same moment. Before using material from such conversations in an essay or report, it's absolutely critical that one consider the context of the remarks, then make sure to properly acknowledge the author(s) of those remarks.

Why to

As with private e-mail, the author of the message may not be comfortable with its use in another medium. Secure permission before using quotations.

If permission is denied, look for other sources of information. If permission is granted, be sure to give full credit and provide sufficient information to allow the reader of the essay to understand the context of these remarks. If not, the work will lack credibility and the report will sound more like gossip than research. Students need to be careful because their reputation is at stake as well as their relationship with the individual(s) they chose to quote. Also, their ethos, the credibility that they need to persuade an audience, suffers whenever they cut corners or employ unreliable sources of information. Chat rooms may be entertaining, but one should never select material from them without first considering the source, the context, and its appropriateness within a scholarly work.

How to

There are a number of ways in which synchronous conversations take place online. However, the MLA guidelines seem broad enough to encompass most variations within this genre. Here's what they have to say:

> To cite a synchronous communication posted in a forum such as a MUD (multiuser domain), or MOO (multiuser domain, object-oriented), give the name of the speaker (if you are citing just one), a description of the event, the date of the event, the forum for the communication (e.g., LinguaMOO), the date of access, and the network address, with the prefix telnet://. (Gibaldi 1999, 201)

It's worth noting that the MLA encourages writers to provide "an archival version of the communication" whenever possible (Gibaldi 1999, 202), but it is often not possible. Also, in order to provide a "context" for the discussion, a writer may wish to cite more than one speaker. So, let's imagine that a student wants to cite a conversation between two speakers, Justin Brownie and Kiki Buttafucco, involved in a MOO session discussing the merits of synchronous writing environments for educational purposes. The discussion took place in Cheshire MOOn, a MOO maintained at the University of Texas, as part of an interactive panel discussion entitled "Can You MOO?" during a conference held on January 31, 2000. If the student discovered a transcript of this discussion on April 20, 2000, the citation would look like this:

> Brownie, Justin and Kiki Buttafucco. Conference panel. Can You MOO? 31 January 2000. CheshireMOOn. 20 April 2000. (telnet://cheshire.cwrl. utexas.edu:7777)

World Wide Web Discussion Forum Messages

A "discussion forum" (or "message forum") is a place within a Web site where one finds asynchronous conversation (conversations between people who are not online at the same time). Similar to newsgroups, a discussion forum may be dedicated to a particular topic; unlike many newsgroups, however, discussion forums are usually situated within the context of a Web site. For example, a Web site for a professional football team might include a discussion forum where fans gather to discuss the team's performance. Thus, the information one finds in a discussion forum is the collection of messages produced by cyberpilots with a common interest. If a student should "borrow" information from a Web-based discussion forum, he or she would need to cite its location on the Web.

Why to

Inexperienced cyberpilots make the mistake of thinking "no one will notice if I borrow just one quote from a discussion forum." However, the moment writers steal intellectual property and introduce it to an essay or report, presenting it as if it is their own, they have compromised their integrity. If the idea or information that is stolen proves especially interesting, and others wish to learn more about it, how does one direct them to its source? By failing to keep track of sources, and committing plagiarism by stealing thoughts from discussion forums, a writer will do considerable damage to the community of learners who depend upon each other.

How to

Here's what the MLA advises:

> ...begin with the author's name and the title of the posting (if there is one), in quotation marks, followed by the description Online posting, the date when the material was posted, the name of the forum, the date of access, and, in angle brackets, the network address. (Gibaldi 1999, 200–201)

How might this work? Imagine that someone named Jacqueline Sue Wines posted a message entitled "Te Amo!" on August 14, 1999, in a discussion forum on the *Utopian Visions'* Web site (http://www.en.utexas.edu/uv). If a student discovered this on February 27, 2000, and used an excerpt from it in an essay, the citation would look like this:

Wines, Jacqueline Sue. "Te Amo!" Online posting. 14 August 1999. Utopian Visions. 27 February 2000.(http://www.en.utexas.edu/uv).

Web Sites and Databases

All of the electronic resources considered thus far have come from rather informal sources. Indeed, it is their informality that leads some students to think excerpts can be "borrowed" without formal citation. Clearly, this leads to problems, particularly when more than one student uses the same quotation from an e-mail message, discussion forum, newsgroup, mailing list, or synchronous chat. The same is true for information "borrowed" from Web sites that do not present the name of a specific author. The temptation to take intellectual property from these sources without proper attribution is strong, but unless students resist that temptation they'll contribute to a breakdown of the rules that bind and maintain a community of learners. Before leaving this discussion, therefore, it's important to consider some of the formal publications encountered on the World Wide Web.

Chapter 6, *Visual Literacy*, looks more closely at Web sites and how to subject them to a critical "reading." For the time being, though, the reader needs to distinguish between Web documents (everything from articles and essays to film clips and sound bites), Web pages (individual pages of a site), and the Web sites themselves (the sum of all these parts). An entire chapter of this book could be dedicated to the proper citation for various Web documents; however, what's most important is to establish the basics that students can apply to a wide range of Web resources. They will quickly note parallels between the citations for print and electronic books, essays, and articles. However, what they may overlook is the need to cite photographs, illustrations, song lyrics, and other documents they find on the Web. In all cases, students should secure permission for using these items before integrating them into their work. Citations alone are not sufficient. When in doubt, it's best to ask for permission and footnote that source. And that brings up the matter of the source itself.

Before writers snatch something from the World Wide Web, it's essential that they determine the source of that information and whether or not its creators would want them to borrow it. Just because it is technically possible to do something, one shouldn't assume it's a moral, legal, or ethical practice. This is where the analogy between physical and intellectual property is important for developing civil literacy in cyberspace. Many students use the "copy/paste" functions on their keyboard to import documents without subjecting them to close scrutiny first. (This is the equivalent of photocopying articles from microfilm and microfiche in the library without first checking to see if the article will be useful.) It's important to understand the distinction between Web sites, Web pages, and Web documents. After students understand that everything on a Web page within a Web site should be considered a "document" created by another person, they'll be more sensitive to the concerns of intellectual property. It's in their best interest, after all, because most consumers of information on the Web eventually become creators of intellectual property themselves. "What goes around, comes around," and in this case that makes civil literacy a necessity. Students must, therefore, learn to place a Web document within its proper context, determining who is the owner of that property.

For starters, students should learn how to read the "uniform resource locator" (URL), or Web address, for a site. Let's take a look at one. The Computer Writing and Research Lab (CWRL) at the University of Texas has the following URL: (http://www.cwrl.utexas.edu). What does each part mean? Here's a breakdown (with parenthetical explanations):

http—hypertext transfer protocol (the "language" computers use to transfer Web documents)
www—World Wide Web (the medium in which we're working)
cwrl—Computer Writing and Research Lab (the computer "server" that holds Web documents)
utexas—University of Texas (the larger organization within which the 'cwrl' resides)
edu—educational (the "domain" or classification of this organization)

Perhaps the first thing for students to look at is the final item in the URL. The domain gives the first clue, providing an institutional context. If ".edu" appears in the address, the site was created at an educational institution. The documents one finds there might be "free" for the taking, but they would most definitely require proper citations and, in many cases, permission. Similar rules apply to documents found on government Web sites, which typically feature ".gov" at the end of their address. Commercial sites, which end with the suffix ".com," might not allow access to documents without payment. Even then, however, a writer ought to provide full and proper citations. Whether .edu, .gov, or .com, as always, it's important to know the source of information before relying too heavily upon it in research. Otherwise, one could mistake propaganda for objective information.

Why to

Web documents did not fall from the sky, nor were they created for cyberpilots to pillage. One must respect intellectual property, giving full and proper reference to the authors, organizations, and Web sites that have provided information. Even the simplest sites deserve this treatment. Think of the World Wide Web as the product of electronic publishing. Every Web site is essentially produced by a "publisher," be it an individual in Ecuador, a nonprofit organization in Egypt, a multinational corporation in Malaysia, or a state university in the United States. Each of these publishers deserves the same respect and courtesy that one would offer a print publisher. Translated: Writers can "borrow" some materials, but they had better not steal.

How to

As already indicated, to provide the "how-to" for every variety of Web documents would require a separate handbook. The best advice is to consult a resource such as the *MLA Handbook for Writers of Research Papers*, which was updated in 1999 to include every electronic resource one could imagine as of that date. For now, what's most important is to emphasize approaching all Web documents as if they are "texts" of some kind. Although it may initially seem strange, think of a clip from a song or movie, a photograph from an online exhibit, a cartoon from an online magazine, as well as personal and professional essays as "texts." As such, they deserve fair treatment; writers who borrow them are responsible for giving credit where credit is due. Perhaps the most effective way to "teach" this is by asking students to make a list of Web documents and see which of them they think need to be cited. Although they may quickly list online books, articles, and essays, they may not think of the previous items. They might also overlook the need for citing databases or "collections" that don't seem to have an "author." This should prompt an important discussion about intellectual property and online resources.

Rather than focus on individual Web documents, it is helpful to consider larger sources of information on the Web. The MLA guidelines for citing information databases and scholarly projects offer the following checklist:

1. Title of the project or database (underlined)
2. Name of the editor of the project or database (if given)
3. Electronic publication information, including version number (if relevant and if not part of the title), date of electronic publication or of the latest update, and name of any sponsoring institution or organization
4. Date of access and network address (Gibaldi 1999, 180)

It's worth noting that the MLA guidelines end with this clever bit of counsel: "If you cannot find some of this information, cite what is available." In other words, a student who discovers information published on March 10, 2000, from the Cable News Network's collection, "CNN Interactive," may not find an "author" or page numbers. However, if that student downloads the information on July 9, 2000, he or she can, at the very least, help readers locate the source with a notation like this:

CNN Interactive. 10 March 2000. Cable News Network. 9 July 2000. (http://www.cnn.com).

CIVIL LITERACY CHALLENGE # 1

Borrowing Without Stealing

What to Do

1. Give students the information in Figure 2.3 about physical and intellectual property.

2. Present this scenario to students:

When in Doubt, Document That Source! Let's say you're writing a short research paper for class. You go to the library and discover some useful information in an encyclopedia. It's perfect for your essay, but you want to provide proper references. No problem. You know how to cite information from an encyclopedia, right? Good. However, what if that's the only information you can find on your topic in a printed source? What if the rest of your sources are all electronic ones? What if you want to use one or more of the following, which are among the most common sources of information available to online researchers?

- Private e-mail
- Mailing list messages
- Newsgroup messages
- Synchronous communication (MUDS, MOOs, IRCs)
- World Wide Web discussion forum messages
- Web sites and databases

3. Give students a few minutes to think about the following questions. Then ask them to write a response to each for the electronic sources listed, and prepare to discuss their responses with classmates.

   a. WHAT special considerations should you give to these electronic sources? In other words, what's unique about these sources? What defines them?

   b. WHY must you provide documentation for these sources?

   c. HOW should one cite each of these sources?

4. In small groups or as a full class, ask students to discuss what they have written and make a list of other electronic resources that require proper documentation when used as secondary sources. Finally, encourage students to identify parallels between print and electronic sources while investigating different approaches to the citation of online sources. To arrange the latter, have them consult different style manuals and handbooks, including online reference material like the Internet Public Library's guidelines for *Citing Electronic Resources* (http://www.ipl.org/ref/QUE/FARQ/ netciteFARQ.html). Discuss the variations in these guidelines, noting the patterns that emerge as well as the differences that exist. As is often the case, establishing the conceptual framework—a rationale for documentation of electronic sources—encourages students to obey what often feel like unwritten rules, but which remain a fundamental requirement for scholarly communities.

Teacher's Tip

Although limited in scope, this exercise helps students understand the significance of respecting intellectual property. The items selected for discussion are some of the most frequently used without proper documentation. Because some sources are less formal and are not considered "published," students may overlook the need for citations. However, if teachers return to the rhetorical heart of computer literacy and reiterate the need for civil literacy, students will learn that borrowing ideas from informal and unpublished sources can damage one's ethos just as much as borrowing from formal, published sources. Although students should have fewer problems understanding the need for documentation of online books, magazine articles, and essays, it is the "gray area" of these interpersonal messages that teachers need to address in order to strengthen students' civil literacy skills.

Physical and Intellectual Property

Physical Property: Imagine spending several hours each day, over the course of several weeks, creating something unique. Perhaps it's a small, wooden cabinet with specially designed shelves and drawers. You design it to suit a particular space in your house and fulfill a specific purpose. You do the best you can to make it both functional and handsome, trying out different finishes before you get it to match the room it will occupy in your house. It may not be the finest piece of carpentry you've ever seen, but it is yours, and you are justifiably proud of it. How would you feel if someone came along and "borrowed" it without asking your permission?

Intellectual Property: Now imagine spending just as many hours, over the course of several weeks, creating a Web site. It's your first Web site, with links to original pictures you've drawn and essays that you've written. You've spent countless hours refining those essays, scanning the pictures, and creating a "look" that is both visually appealing and helpful. You admit it's not the finest Web site on the Internet, but it is yours, and you are proud of it. How would you feel if someone came along and "borrowed" those pictures and essays without asking your permission?

"Borrowing" intellectual property without the creator's permission is a serious matter. In fact, it is *theft*. What's more, it's a violation of your school's policies on academic honesty, and it could lead to serious problems. Perhaps you've discussed the issue of plagiarism (presenting other people's words or ideas as if they're your own) with respect to print materials. If so, you've learned to document sources of information, giving credit where credit is due. It should come as no surprise, then, that you must do the same thing for sources of information on the Web.

For example, while no one owns the "idea" of a Web site, individual creators own the rights to their creation. *The CyberPilot's License* Web site, for instance, is a unique expression of relatively common ideas and principles. So while "linking" to this site is not a violation of intellectual property rights, "borrowing" the original exercises you find there without giving proper credit would most certainly be a violation. Make sense? If not, take a moment to discuss the ideas of plagiarism and academic honesty with your teacher, then proceed to the next section.

Figure 2.3

**CIVIL
LITERACY
CHALLENGE #2**

Putting Out the Flames

Although intellectual property rights remain controversial and ambiguous, the second major concern of civil literacy depends largely upon common sense and respect for individuals rather than for their property. As everyone knows, in real life there are many ways to offend, humiliate, and hurt others. The same is true online. However, what's different in this environment is that participants cannot see the physical reaction of their audience. Without the visual cues that people have learned to "read" on human faces—the blushing of embarrassed cheeks, the furrowing of an angry brow, the widening of offended eyes—how can young writers determine whether or not their words have given offense? If offended, what should an individual do? How do participants communicate wounded feelings without escalating tensions? Perhaps a civil literacy challenge dedicated to online "flame wars" will help.

What to Do

1. Present this scenario to students:

   Imagine this: After many hours of researching, composing, and revising, you've filed your first online report for a school telecomputing project that asks you and your classmates to correspond with students around the world. You've put a lot of yourself into this work, and you are proud of what you've accomplished. You're eager to hear what other participants think of the report, although you're a little nervous as well. So the arrival of an e-mail response the very next day leaves you breathless. The message reads as follows:

   > I just read the report you submitted to the discussion forum. I thought the first paragraph was kind of informative, but the rest of the report is dull and useless. You base most of what you write on observations and personal experience, which makes it pretty egotistical and boring. To tell you the truth, I didn't see the point. If this weren't a school project I would've quit reading after the first paragraph. I think you should back up your opinions with facts; it would make your report more believable and interesting. I don't have any questions because there wasn't anything there that I didn't already know.

2. Ask students how they would reply to this message. Perhaps the best way to answer that question is to have students ask another one: What sort of dialogue would they like to have with this individual? A message of this sort often leads to what's called a "flame war" in cyberspace, the equivalent of a "put-down" session on the playground. The "cyberbullies" who thrive on this activity are cousins to playground bullies and often are just as cowardly, insensitive, and irresponsible. So how does one defuse the situation? What strategies might put out the flames in cyberspace before the possibility of meaningful discussion is destroyed?

3. To help students consider a range of possibilities, have them consider four fairly common reactions to a message of this sort. They are not the only possible reactions, just four of the most common. Ask students to have a sheet of paper and pen or pencil at hand, so they may respond to each of the options as they are presented. Give students each option in turn.

   a. **Option 1: Fight Fire With Fire.** In this option, the recipient of the original message adopts a confrontational approach:

   > What gives you the right to speak to me like that? To tell YOU the truth, 'Egotistical' doesn't begin to describe your response to my report. OK, so maybe it didn't have enough facts to please you, but I put a lot of time and effort into that report, and I don't think anyone has the right to call it 'dull and useless' or even 'boring.' I can't wait to see your report. It's probably full of 'dull and useless' facts that really bore the life out of a reader. You just wait, Mr. Egotistical. You'll get yours!

   ### Student Preparation

   Have students write, on a separate sheet of paper, what they think would happen if they sent a reply like this. Will their correspondent meet "fire with fire" or take a different approach? What will they, in turn, do after they've heard the response?

   ### Responses to Fire

   When students have finished, ask them to share their "Responses to Fire" reactions. Unfortunately, hostile replies are an all-too-common response to inflammatory messages. It's unfortunate, because they seldom resolve conflicts. Nonetheless, we're all human, and sometimes emotions get the better of us. So, let's consider three potential reactions to a message like this and prepare to discuss them with students.

Flame on! There's a good chance your "Fire" reply will invite a similar one, which means you're about to get caught in a nasty verbal exchange commonly known as a "flame war." Is this what you really want? Is it worth expending time and energy on potentially destructive ends? Be prepared for those flames to climb even higher, and decide whether you intend to toss gasoline or water onto them in the next round.

Apology/Clarification If you receive an apologetic message, clarifying the previous remarks, then it's your turn to eat humble pie and apologize for your fiery response! Who knows, that first message may have been written by a bored, distracted, or lazy writer who forgot that a human being would take offense to it. Now then, shouldn't you douse the flames and start anew?

Silence Hmmm... always a hard one to "read," particularly when you don't know your correspondent. Perhaps he's ignoring you? Perhaps he didn't even see the message? Or perhaps this indicates thoughtful reflection, which is seldom a bad thing. Regardless, if the silence continues, and you feel somewhat guilty for your strong response, then you may wish to send a follow-up message in a few days' time. If this, too, meets with silence, it's probably best to move on and let bygones be bygones.

b. **Option 2: Dousing the Flames.** In this option, perhaps you would rather not fight fire with fire. After all, your correspondent may not realize the tone of that first message was offensive. What if this person isn't a good writer or lacks the vocabulary and skills necessary to communicate in a tactful, sensitive manner? If so, this could be your chance to educate that individual, express a candid reaction to the offensive message, and initiate a more thoughtful dialogue. So, imagine that you try to "douse the flames" by sending a response like the following:

```
I was upset by your response to my report. Perhaps I took it
too personally, but I think you overstated things a bit, and
it hurts to have someone call my work 'dull and useless.' I
```

admit it wasn't the best report in the world, but it was the best I could do the first time around. I'd appreciate it if in the future you'd refer more specifically to the report. Which facts did you find 'informative' and useful? Where did you find it 'egotistical and boring?' We're all trying to learn from our mistakes, aren't we? So I'd appreciate it if in the future you could 'show, not tell' what you mean—as well as use a kinder, gentler tone.

Student Preparation

Have students write, on a separate sheet of paper, what they think will happen if they send this reply. Will their correspondent respect their attempt to "douse the flames" like this? What will they do after they've heard a response?

Responses to Dousing the Flames

When students have finished, ask them to share their hypothetical reactions. This type of response to an inflammatory message is more effective if the goal is "communication" rather than revenge. Once again, there are three fairly common responses to a message like this; students should be prepared for each of them.

Flame on! If a response this genuine and heartfelt meets with another offensive statement, you're obviously dealing with someone who *wants* to incite a "flame war." You should consult with your teacher about this matter and refrain from further attempts to communicate with the individual until there's a significant change in tone and treatment. Until you've established mutual respect there can be no genuine communication with this individual. And until there's genuine communication there will be no educational discourse. So why bother? Devote your energies to more productive discussions. Don't let yourself be dragged into a nasty flame war.

Apology/Clarification More than likely, your response will invite some form of apology or clarification. Perhaps your correspondent was just going through the motions of a homework assignment, typing a flippant reply without thinking of its impact on you. Perhaps he or she didn't give much thought to the "tone" of the words or your interpretation of them. If that's the case, and the reply to your message at least tries to clarify the cause of the original one (if not apologize for it), then it's wise to move on. You can establish a healthier discourse by acknowledging their clarification, saying that you're grateful for their consideration, and then demonstrating the kind of discussion you'd like to have.

Silence This is often an indication that the other party needs time to think about things. Let them. If a reply comes, it will probably be one of the previous types. If there's no reply, however, you may wish to send a one-liner after a few days. Your correspondent may choose to ignore that as well, but at least you will have defended yourself and your position without adding to the flames. If the silence becomes permanent, you're probably right to "read" this as confusion on the part of your correspondent. Perhaps they're not accustomed to being confronted in this manner. Perhaps they're too proud to admit they were wrong and apologize. Or perhaps your tone was so disarming that it left them confused. It's best not to rub anyone's face in his or her past mistakes, but if and when this individual surfaces, take note of his or her tone. If it's still nasty, then he or she probably has not learned from this encounter and will need another dose of *civil literacy*. However, if he or she is deferential, offering thoughts in a more polite and respectful manner, take that as a sign that your effort to douse the flames not only succeeded, but helped alter the discourse as well.

c. **Option 3: The Silent Treatment.** Actions, they say, speak louder than words. Yet what is an "action" in cyberspace? What constitutes an "action" in an online discussion? In a virtual community of inquiry where one can only act through written statements, there are only two ways in which to make a statement. These statements are the actions that will define a writer in the community of inquiry. What are they? The obvious action is a written message, but there is another way to make a statement—one that is subtler but may prove very effective in "putting out the flames." The "silent treatment" requires that a writer do nothing more than listen and refrain from the active responses described by the first two options (fighting and dousing). So, imagine the response to the original, offensive message looks like this:

Student Preparation

Have students, on a separate sheet of paper, write down what they think will happen if they simply ignore the original message. Will their correspondent meet silence with silence or send another message? What strategies might students adopt if another fiery message comes their way? What if an apology follows? What if nothing comes their way?

Responses to Silence

When students have finished, ask them to share their hypothetical reactions to "Responses to Silence." Yes, silence is a response. It is often an eloquent one, too, full of meaning. Sometimes the most effective way to deal with cyberbullies is to simply ignore them. Easier said than done? Perhaps, but when one is pondering what to "do" about a nasty message, don't forget that silence is an "action" in cyberspace, and sometimes the most appropriate one. Once more, consider three common responses to a "statement" of silence, and discuss them with students.

Flame on! In rare cases, involving the most jaded or immature cyberpunks, your silence could incite another hostile remark ("What's the matter? Did I hurt your feelings or something?"). You could choose to ignore that as well, or else state your position as firmly and carefully as possible, indicating that you do not wish to engage in this kind of discourse. Ultimately, if you want to build a "dialogue" you have to devise strategies for dealing with people who are brusque, insensitive, or offensive. Fighting fire with fire may provide immediate gratification, but it may ultimately come back to haunt you. Tread carefully.

Apology/Clarification If your silence invites an apology or clarification, you're most likely dealing with someone who didn't mean offense in that first message, but who now senses that you took it. So, if "The Silent Treatment" is met with a brief message, perhaps a "hello" or "hope you didn't take that the wrong way . . ." then it makes sense for you to reply, stating the reason for your silence and establishing the kind of dialogue you wish to participate in.

Silence If silence begets silence, you must now determine what it is that you want. How is one to interpret a silent response to one's own silence? As this is your first "interaction" with this correspondent, perhaps you were premature in judging those remarks? What if no malice was intended? Perhaps now that you've allowed your emotions to calm themselves you can send a brief message, stating your initial reaction and establishing a 'kinder, gentler' dialogue. Then again, if you found the original message truly offensive or obscene perhaps it's best to just let the flames die without stirring the embers.

d. **Option 4: Full Group Discussion.** Clearly, this scenario describes more than an isolated incident between two people. Indeed, episodes like these involve an entire community. The moment a personal message enters a public discussion forum it becomes everyone's concern. Depending upon the situation, students may wish to discuss this matter with their classmates before taking action online. Rather than taking it personally, present it to the class as a community issue. What sort of action would they recommend? What kind of discourse do they wish to encourage? What should others do if an unwanted "flame war" arises and, in spite of their efforts to douse or ignore the inflammatory messages, it persists?

Ultimately, one of the challenges of communicating through electronic words is learning how to read messages from virtual strangers, interpreting the meaning of the message as well as the intent of the messenger. Without the aid of facial expressions, body language, or tone of voice, it is sometimes difficult to determine a writer's intention. Did the author mean to be rude, or was he or she simply insensitive to the audience? As a general rule, it's best to give people the benefit of the doubt, but if students encounter someone who wants to engage in a "flame war" it's best to consider where that might lead. If attempts to "Douse the Flames" don't succeed, "The Silent Treatment" might be the best course of action. Consider a variation on the golden rule as it's applied to cyberspace interactions: "Write unto others as you would have them write unto you." Unfortunately, not everyone shares this belief—and even those who do often forget to live by it. So students need to devise strategies for dealing with people who wish to incite a flame war and provoke a strong reaction. Rather than fleeing from such problems, advise students to approach them as opportunities to discuss the "rules and regulations" an online community should establish. How, for instance, does a group maintain civil literacy while discussing controversial issues? Chapter 5 returns to such questions, when it broaches the concerns of *community literacy.*

The Flight School

How might one use a program like *The CyberPilot's License* for effective teaching and learning? "The Flight School" offers suggestions for teachers who are just starting out as well as counsel for young cyberpilots who wish to acquire the civil literacy necessary to succeed in an online learning environment. A brief handbook responds to frequently asked questions in an informal voice that speaks directly to classroom teachers.

The CyberTrainer's Handbook

Experienced educators know that good teaching relies upon creativity, inspiration, intuition, and preparation. Prescriptive formulas seldom work because a particular course and group require more than generic recipes. With this in mind, the following dialogue provides insights from experienced cyberpilots who wish to help.

By all means, if you find better ways to use *The CyberPilot's License*, or have ideas and activities you wish to share, please submit them to the "Flight School Forum" (http://www.cwrl.utexas.edu/~burniske/cpl/teachers/index.html).

Q. In what "order" should I use The CyberPilot's License's sections?

A. Although no strict chronology is intended, you should acquaint yourself with each section of the Web site to consider how it would work best in your particular course. As stated in the introduction of the *CPL*, the primary objective here is to help students think about the moral and ethical issues that accompany the acquisition of cyberpilot skills. Students just beginning to use the Internet need to learn what it is and how it works, which is why the "Know Your Vehicle" section appears at the top of our list. However, teachers should use this section in tandem with "Piloting Skills & Netiquette," so that students don't perceive the skills and ethics as separate issues. What's more, the order of activities within the "Piloting Skills & Netiquette" section is by no means formulaic. The first section, "Web Ethics," provides an "umbrella," covering the global concerns of intellectual property and "netiquette." From there, choices are left to the teacher's discretion.

Q. Should one begin with e-mail activities or Web browsing?

A. So much depends upon your situation. If your school doesn't provide individual e-mail accounts, and you think activities dedicated to that topic are not relevant to your students, skip those sections in favor of the ones devoted to the Web.

Q. Where might other sections fit into my curriculum?

A. Two sections, "Rights & Responsibilities" and "Who & What Rules the Airwaves?," would seem ideal for teachers who wish to encourage further research. These areas put students in touch with the greater context of the Internet. Although it may be best to wait until students become familiar with online research and communication tools, one could easily integrate these sections of the *CPL* from the outset—depending, once again, upon the course and students you teach. It should be noted, too, that students will find a discussion forum within the "Rights & Responsibilities" section. "The Pilots' Place" enables them to speak with peers about mutual concerns or raise issues to hear how other schools handle problems related to online activities.

Q. Is "The Flight School" section a "virtual lounge" reserved solely for teachers?

A. Although "The Flight School" is designed for teachers, students are not forbidden to enter. Here you'll find teaching tips, an AUP template, and a discussion forum where teachers may share strategies, ask questions, and collaborate with distant colleagues. Feel free to drop by at any time and offer your suggestions. Ultimately, the more viewpoints on these matters the better. Because "netiquette" is still evolving and the Internet is such a new educational tool, one of the best things we can do is to help one another find solutions to new challenges.

Q. What if I have questions no one at my school can answer?

A. Head to the "Flight School Forum," and post your question or concern. We're all in this together, aren't we? So let's help one another navigate the airwaves safely and ask the difficult questions that may help us discover more effective ways to use the Internet for educational purposes.

The CyberPilot Journal

One highly recommended exercise for all cyberpilots is a process journal. This should be used at the discretion of the teacher and student. Students may wonder why they're being asked to keep a journal, so "Why to Keep a Journal" (Figure 2.4) is written with them in mind. Teachers should feel free to adapt this to suit their needs, thinking of ways in which The CyberPilot Journal could assist students while serving a practical purpose within the curriculum.

The CyberPilot's Permit

Initially, a school may issue a cyberpilot's permit that must be presented at designated Internet stations (library, computer lab, etc.) before a student may log on during the school day. Misuse of the permit could result in the suspension of privileges. Remind students that they may refresh their memory by taking another look at the "Rights & Responsibilities" that are involved.

Acquiring the License

Depending on a school's policies, students may be required to complete classwork and pass a written test, sign an agreement promising responsible conduct, or acquire parental consent on a standard waiver before they're allowed to use the school's network to access the Internet. If a signature from the student (and the student's guardian) is required upon a lengthy AUP, remind them that it's a good idea to study that document carefully before signing. Read through it carefully with their parent/guardian. Ask questions to clarify what they don't understand. In essence, that document may be boiled down to the short form shown in Figure 2.5. If a school does not have such a form, consider modifying the one in Figure 2.5 and using it so that students can declare their intention to be courteous and considerate cyberpilots.

The CyberPilot's Caveat

Just as driver's education does not prevent the abuse of an automobile license, *The CyberPilot's License* will not provide a panacea for the abuse of computer privileges. However, such a program would help schools create an AUP that makes a meaningful contribution to their curriculum. The

---

Why to Keep a Journal

Dear Student,

Perhaps you've never kept a journal before, or you're wondering why anyone should keep one while learning how to fly through cyberspace. Here are a few of the more common questions that this activity prompts, along with some thoughts in response to them.

Q. Why should I keep a journal?

A. There are many reasons to keep a journal, but perhaps the best one for the CyberPilot Journal is that it will serve as a place to record your questions and observations, as well as your notes, to help limit confusion. Also, this exercise may be especially useful for students who lack regular online access and wish to refresh their memory between visits to the computer lab. At times we can forget just how much we're learning, but if you keep this journal faithfully it will remind you of all that you've covered and help make your next encounter with the World Wide Web a successful one.

Q. What should I write in my journal?

A. Think of the journal as a place where you can record thoughts and ideas. These may take many forms, depending upon the individual, but might include:
  - Instructions for logging on to your account
  - E-mail addresses
  - URLs for interesting Web sites
  - Ideas for Web site construction

Q. How often should I write in the journal?

A. This is a personal decision, but keep the journal with you whenever you're working on activities related to the CyberPilot License. You might use it to take notes during online sessions and write reflections immediately thereafter.

Q. Should I keep it as an electronic or handwritten document?

A. This will depend upon your situation and comfort level. If your access to computers is limited, it makes sense to keep the journal in handwritten form. Just be sure to use a sturdy notebook, one that will hold up over the course of a year (or more), and take good care of it. If you *do* have frequent access to computers you might consider keeping the journal in an electronic form. This could be a simple folder with a list of files containing dated observations/reflections. Once you've gained online experience, though, you might attempt this as a Web page, creating separate pages for each category. Who knows, with time your journal could become an important resource for others!

Figure 2.4

program should provide in-service opportunities for faculty and elective courses for students, introducing the terms and technology, the ethical issues attending them, and the rights and responsibilities of cyberpilots. Upon completion of this course students should acquire signed letters of consent from legal guardians, assuming responsibility for their online actions. This would address the legal and parental concerns cited by defendants of current AUPs, while employing an acceptable use policy as an instructional tool rather than as a vague threat.

The CyberPilot's Agreement

I agree to follow the 'rules of the airwaves' as I fly through the Information Skyway. I understand that failure to comply with the rules, abusing this privilege by engaging in obscene or hateful language, distributing offensive material, or harming others will lead to the immediate forfeiture of my CyberPilot's License. However, while I acknowledge this privilege and the responsibilities that go with it, I also maintain the right to use the Internet for research and communication purposes. I understand that this right cannot be revoked without due process and confirmation that I have violated the rules and regulations that govern the use of networked technology within our school.

Full Name: _____ Home Phone: _____

Address: _____

Student's Signature: _____ Date: _____

Guardian's Signature: _____ Date: _____

Teacher's Signature: _____ Date: _____

Figure 2.5

SkyLight Professional Development

It is difficult to speak to these issues, and articulate proposals like *The CyberPilot's License*, without sounding self-righteous or hysterical. However, the suggestion of *The CyberPilot's License* comes as a progressive measure, not a reactionary one. To succeed, it must bring human concerns to the foreground of computer literacy, encouraging a thoughtful approach to technological narratives without neglecting human narratives. That basic tenet is the best hope for ensuring that computer technology serves humanity, rather than humanity serving technology. Hysteria? Perhaps, but wouldn't educators rather be charged with that, and preserve a humanist curriculum, than be guilty of an indifference that renders humanism null and void?

After all, without civil literacy, online interactions will deteriorate. Thoughtful "arguments" could turn into shouting matches, and participants may forfeit opportunities to learn from alternative views and conflicting opinions. What good could possibly come from an environment that enables such behavior and discourse? Consider the ramifications. The breakdown of civil discourse engenders distrust, confusion, and cynicism, reducing the chances that a reader will understand another writer. With time, it becomes difficult to read and interpret the words and intentions of online counterparts. In such environments no gestures seem genuine or unconditional. Rather, they produce a cacophony of words, shedding more heat than light. Clearly, the concerns of civil literacy must remain central to the pursuit of *discourse literacy*, which is the next chapter's theme.

Discourse Literacy:
Beyond the Chat Room

. . . to speak a true word is to transform the world.

(Freire 1997, 68)

By the time students enter a networked computer classroom, many have already experienced online chat rooms, newsgroups, and discussion forums on their own. For the classroom teacher this can be both a blessing and a curse. The blessing? Such students may understand the technical concerns, bringing a comfort level and familiarity to class sessions that makes it easier for teachers to introduce new learning activities. The curse? This could also mean that students have acquired some unfortunate discursive habits. In other words, teachers have their work cut out for them if they wish to encourage inquiry and dialogue, the prerequisites to a healthy learning environment. What has to happen, ultimately, is that the teacher must address the importance of discourse literacy, reminding students that often what matters most is "not what you say, but how you say it." Just as teachers remind students that the language of the playground is inappropriate in a classroom, students must now distinguish between the discourse of informal chat rooms and that of online discussions in class.

In some cases, using inappropriate discourse is harmless and unintentional, the kind of problem that teachers of adolescents come to expect. Just as they sometimes drag playground discourse into the classroom, students are likely to carry chat room discourse into educational online discussions. This reveals an important distinction, however. When teachers conceive online learning activities—whether conducted via e-mail, discussion forums, newsgroups, or some other medium—they tend to think of them as writing activities. Thus, the rules of grammar, along with the decorum one expects of written correspondence, apply. However, adolescents who have spent time in chat rooms or in a multiuser domain (MUD) have a very different orientation. They often think of these activities as conversations, attaching to them the less rigid rules of spoken language. Thus, a potential conflict exists between the expectations that students and teachers bring to these activities, particularly when there is confusion over the type of discourse in which they are engaged. This is especially true when teachers arrange informal, brainstorming activities that use online tools for *synchronous* rather than *asynchronous* discussions.

These types of discussions are fairly common now, but that does not mean that the tools or the rules for playing with them have been mastered. *Synchronous* conversations are those that take place in "real time." That is, participants are able to contribute at the same moment in time, allowing for interruptions and dialogical discourse. Examples of synchronous conversations are face-to-face discussions in a conventional classroom, telephone calls, Internet Relay chats, and a variety of synchronized discussions arranged through a networked computer lab. These activities encourage a less formal discourse, drawing as they do on cultural expectations of spoken language. However, *asynchronous* conversations present different connotations and expectations. One tends to think of these as descendants of written language, obeying the rules and regulations of a more deliberate and formal discourse. Electronic mail, discussion forums, newsgroups, and electronic bulletin boards fall into this category, because they allow the writer/speaker to compose statements in the absence of an audience. The "turn-taking" here does not allow for interruptions, which means each participant has an opportunity to speak without pause, inspiring declamations as well as dialogues.

Perhaps the greatest challenge for classroom teachers, however, is deciding what to do when students confuse these two discursive styles. Students may think they have expressed themselves in an appropriate manner, only to discover that others find the form and substance of their remarks offensive and inappropriate. If this is especially true of synchronous online discussions, does it mean that classroom teachers should simply avoid them? Is it possible to use such activities for learning purposes? Is it im-

> ## Discourse Literacy
>
> Discourse literacy is the ability to read, understand, and abide by norms that govern the discursive practices of a particular social group.

Figure 3.1

possible for students to break the bad habits acquired while speaking under the cover of anonymity in chat rooms that may breed irresponsible behavior and discourse?

These are difficult questions, but perhaps the answer to them lies within the study of a literacy that goes to the "rhetorical heart" of this book. A fundamental prerequisite for reading and interpreting online discourse as well as composing and presenting ourselves in a manner consistent with our intention is *discourse literacy*. By no means confined to online activities, it is nonetheless essential for communication and learning within these environments.

Before answering some of the questions concerning synchronous online discussions, let us first address rhetorical concerns that challenge students in any writing environment. One of the most difficult concepts for young writers to comprehend is the idea of "voice." They often reveal both ignorance and naïveté when encouraged to use a more natural voice in their writing. "How can I have a voice when I write?" they ask. And yet, all writers most certainly have a voice. But how can teachers "show" what they would otherwise "tell" ineffectively? How can they "hold a mirror up to nature," as it were, and help students see themselves in their own prose?

DISCOURSE LITERACY CHALLENGE # 1

Hearing Voices

One way to introduce voice is to examine various authors' writing styles, taking note of the diction, sentence structure, and qualities that identify them.

What to Do

1. For this exercise, teachers should select four different authors with distinctive writing styles.

2. Divide the class into eight small groups (three to four students per group). Each group draws the name of an author from a hat; two groups focus on each of the respective authors.

3. Ask each group to type a representative paragraph from their author (250 words or less).

Teacher's Tip

Ask students if they can see how one creates a voice as a writer and why each word and phrase must be carefully considered because of its contribution to the writer's style and the impact of that voice on an audience. In other words, bring them back to the rhetorical heart of this matter. What the students did, essentially, was to alter the pathos of their paragraph, beginning with all the words and phrases that produce an emotional reaction. This would affect the writer's ethos in some way, because credibility is earned one word at a time, and it would perhaps even alter the logos of the message. The point? Words and expressions define the writer. As the discussion of civil literacy revealed, words are actions in cyberspace. Writers are responsible for those actions and their impact on others. So before jumping into chat rooms and discussion forums, it is a good idea to gain greater control of one's writing voice. Unless students understand that they have a voice as a writer and that it can affect others deeply, they will lack the discourse literacy necessary to temper that voice.

4. After they have saved the original file on diskette, each group italicizes modifiers, underlines figures of speech, and counts the average number of words per sentence. They save this file as the "original."

5. Then, each group rewrites the paragraph by replacing each of the modifiers with a synonym, selecting different figures of speech, and altering sentence lengths to see how this affects the writing style and voice of the piece.

6. When the groups have finished, ask them to give an oral presentation of the original paragraph, followed by an analysis of it and an oral presentation of the revised passage.

When students begin to "hear voices" in writing, they are ready to experiment with different writing styles and refine their discursive practices. The ability to distinguish various writing styles enables students to discover their own personal voice, which will serve them well in online discussions. Until they do so, however, their protests of poor grades recite a familiar chorus: "I know the writing style's weak, but what about the content?" What they fail to understand, due to limited discourse literacy, is that style and content cannot be separated.

Imitating Voices

The following literacy challenge helps students see how style shapes content, altering the reader's experience of a story.

What to Do

1. To begin, ask students to imagine an incident that involves three or four people. It should be a minor incident, one that can be told in 250 words or less. This will help them focus upon writing style more than on plot or character development. Give the students part of one class period to write the story.

2. If possible, locate a copy of Raymond Queneau's *Exercises in Style* to see how his playful approach to style shapes his story and to pick up ideas on different stylistic approaches that students might adopt. In his book, Queneau provides ninety-nine variations on a simple theme:

   > The narrator is on the S bus at rush hour.
   > He notices a young man with a long neck wearing a hat.
   > The young man is annoyed with someone beside him; says he's bumping into him.
   > Finally, the young man sees a vacant seat and takes it.
   > Two hours later the narrator sees the same man at the Gare Saint Lazare. He's with a friend who says, "You ought to get an extra button put on your overcoat." The friend shows him where and explains why. (Queneau 1981)

3. Share a few of Queneau's styles with students, then instruct them to write a second version of their story, this time using an entirely different voice. If they are at a loss, encourage them to tell the story from a different point of view or a different frame of mind. What if the narrator were agitated? Amused? Bewildered? Horrified? What if the story were told by someone other than the narrator? In Queneau's story, one could have fun telling the incident from the perspective of the bus driver or the young man wearing the hat.

4. After this retelling, students play "musical chairs" and shift to adjacent computer terminals at short intervals to analyze their classmates' stories, applying some of the techniques acquired from Discourse Literacy Challenge #1 to examine the voice of the original as well as the revised version.

Expanding the Challenge

Ask the students to return to their own narrative and write yet another version, employing yet another voice. Depending upon the age group, one could ask that they adopt a particularly bad writing style—passive voice, redundant and verbose language, sentence fragments, and so forth—to help the students see how such poor practices interfere with communication. In a networked classroom, one could also ask students to continue a classmate's narrative, similar to Media Literacy Challenge #3 in chapter 1. By purposely adopting different styles, and by increasing their sensitivity to language and voice, students will begin to develop the discourse literacy necessary for successful interactions in online writing environments.

Teacher's Tip

This exercise can be conducted in a computer lab without network capabilities. In such instances, students can play musical chairs by shifting to the terminal on their left (or right) to read what a classmate has written. If network capabilities exist, students can post their writing to a class folder or bulletin board, where others may read and respond to the pieces.

Greater Expectations: Synchronous Online Discussions

The previous exercises could be conducted in a conventional classroom, but a networked computer class enables activities that are cumbersome in a traditional setting. If teachers manage this learning environment properly, and students bring a collaborative spirit to the activities, the class will enjoy writing workshop exercises that were often difficult with slate chalkboards and overhead projectors. To illustrate this point, consider student interaction in a new medium—synchronous, online discussions. In order to succeed in this environment, students must understand that their voice affects the tone of the discourse. For discourse to remain civil, even amid discussion of controversial subjects, they must be sensitive to word choice, writing style, and the tone of voice engaged in the conversation.

At this point, the reader might wish to raise a few important questions. Why bother? What can be accomplished with synchronous, online discussions? Are they really worth the trouble? In response, one could argue that this type of activity improves the chances for student participation in class discussions while decentralizing the discourse. In other words, the teacher and impulsive speakers no longer dominate the discussion. This can be exciting and intimidating for teachers as well as students, so comfort levels should dictate one's approach to the activity. If done well, synchronous discussions facilitate small group discussions and help students refine their reading, writing, and discourse literacy skills. Nonetheless, do not overlook the challenges, which begin with technical concerns but quickly turn into questions about healthy discursive practices and pedagogical strategies. What is acceptable in this environment? If students begin to disparage one another or engage in the rough-and-tumble rhetoric of online chat rooms, what can teachers do besides pull the plug on the exercise?

As with many classroom activities, the teacher sets the tone and models the desired behavior. Before introducing students to synchronous discussions for brainstorming or exploring ideas, it is important that teachers establish greater expectations than students bring to informal chat rooms. With this in mind, it is a good idea to write a prompt in advance, something that will focus the discussion. If the teacher says, "Okay, let's log on and talk about last night's reading," students may think anything goes. Unless tightly focused, the exercise may deteriorate into a social gathering where flippancy and digression become the norm.

Consider the following example, taken from the start of an actual synchronous exchange in a classroom. In this instance, students were asked to discuss whether they thought of writing as a private or a social act. What the reader sees is precisely what the participants in this online discussion saw scrolling up their computer screens at the start of this synchronous session. Because they were simultaneously composing, reading, and submitting messages, the conversation forfeited the linear qualities of a reciprocal, face-to-face discussion as indicated by delayed responses to certain threads of the conversation. Notice that a casual approach to grammatical concerns—punctuation, spelling, capitalization, and so forth—accompanies a casual approach to the discourse and exercise.

```
Howage S.: hey
Paul M.: hello all
Lauren G.: writing is communication, and communication is
social
Howage S.: thats deep
Paul M.: who thought denver would win?????
Liz E.: how can thinking be considered social? talking is
social, but thinking is personal
```

```
Hee L.: how was the super bowl?
Samuel F.: It is my belief that writing and espescially
thinking are personal acts.
Howage S: it did not suprise me
Liam F.: i think one way writing is a social act is that we
share ideas in either a classroom or with our friends
Wayne: ok.... I didn't read the assignment, so can yall fill
me in?
```

Notice the mixture of discourse styles and subject matter. In many ways, this discussion sets an unfortunate precedent, one that this particular session may not overcome. The teacher not only has forfeited control of the conversation but also may have invited discourse habits that mirror online chat rooms more than thoughtful classrooms. An intelligent prompt with guiding questions would have helped to establish a sense of purpose and to illustrate the kind of inquiry and discourse the teacher wished to inspire. Although it cannot ensure that students will stay on task, a good prompt can at least give them a sense of direction, a purpose that helps define expectations and boundaries. The inaugural session should place the concern of discourse literacy and the creation of a community of writers at the foreground. Thus, the following prompt for a synchronous discussion using "Interchange," a feature of the Daedalus Integrated Writing Environment (DIWE), encouraged students to reflect upon their reading and share their reactions to it by addressing open-ended questions.

```
I'd like to use this first Interchange session to discuss
some ideas that your readings have introduced. In "The Writ-
ing Community" Ramage and Bean made the following claim:
"Behind the notion of the writing community lies the notion
that thinking and writing are social acts" (Writing Argu-
ments, 1998, p. 435). Did this claim surprise you in any
way? Have your own experiences encouraged you to conceive of
thinking and writing as "social acts" or private, personal
acts?
```

If the inaugural session establishes good discourse practices, it will be much easier for future sessions to stimulate healthy discussions, allowing students to "think out loud" and explore ideas in a more open-ended manner. The following prompt is a good example of how one can use synchronous conversations to continue previous discussions, especially ones that failed to open the inquiry and inspire students to question their assumptions. In this instance, the teacher wanted students to reconsider some of the positions they had previously taken. The teacher hoped that by doing this in an online, synchronized forum students would explore their positions more openly than they had during face-to-face discussions.

```
In class on Monday one of you claimed that a definitional
argument could become a "boring" discussion of "semantics."
I'm not sure what was meant by "boring" or "semantics," nor
am I sure the speaker had clear definitions in mind, so I
thought we'd use this session to brainstorm a little, helping
one another consider terms worth investigating. You're free
to pursue this in whatever manner you wish, but it might help
to begin by offering a term that you think needs to be de-
fined more clearly. Why is it important to define that term?
It may help to reflect on the following passage from your
text before you begin: "For some people, all this concern
about definition may seem misplaced. How often, after all,
have you heard people accuse each other of getting bogged
down in 'mere semantics'? But how we define a given word can
have significant implications for people who must either use
the word or have the word used on them." (Ramage and Bean
1998, 204)
```

After an inaugural session, it is often wise to print out the transcript and ask students to "perform" the text as if it were a script. This reinforces the importance of civil literacy, holding everyone accountable for his or her words. Although the decentralized discourse of a synchronous discussion is liberating and often enables shy students to speak more than they would in conventional class discussions, teachers should not allow students to indulge in discursive habits that would not be tolerated in face-to-face sessions. The following prompt was offered at the start of a synchronous discussion immediately after the previous one. In this instance, the teacher merges both the medium for this conversation and its topic, asking students to question the medium while using it to facilitate their conversation.

I thought we'd conduct our "definitional argument" on Interchange today. This seems appropriate, since we'll argue the following: "Interchange is/is not communication." Now that you've had a chance to review your group's previous Interchange session, discuss the meaning of "communication" in our discussion forum, and reflect on various issues, what's your opinion? Does an Interchange session meet your definition of "communication" or not? Please take a position, presenting an "enthymeme" as well as the warrant, backing, and grounds of your argument. You should also be prepared to discuss the conditions of rebuttal, qualifiers, and questions.

Obviously, curricular obligations do not allow teachers to dedicate all of their time to discussions of instructional technology. In most instances, teachers need to use computers as a vehicle for the study of other topics, not as the subject itself. How might teachers stimulate thoughtful, topical discussions in synchronous online sessions? Often, it is simply a matter of asking questions that encourage students to take their own ideas and questions seriously. The following prompt tries to do just that, asking students to generate their own questions to form an online community of inquiry as they respond to a difficult reading assignment. Notice the way in which the teacher uses an excerpt from the reading to focus the students' attention, followed by questions that are meant to stimulate open-ended inquiry.

Your passage from Plato's *Republic* comes at the conclusion of his famous "allegory of the cave." To refresh your memories, both now and in the future, here is the passage:

"This entire allegory, I said, you may now append, dear Glaucon, to the previous argument; the prisonhouse is the world of sight, the light of the fire is the sun, and you will not misapprehend me if you interpret the journey upward to be the ascent of the soul into the intellectual world according to my poor belief, which, at your desire, I have expressed—whether rightly or wrongly, God knows. But, whether true or false, my opinion is that in the world of knowledge the idea of good appears last of all, and is seen only with an effort; and, when seen, is also inferred to be the universal author of all things beautiful and right, parent of light

> and of the lord of light in this visible world, and the
> immediate source of reason and truth in the intellectual; and
> that this is the power upon which he who would act rationally
> either in public or private life must have his eye fixed."
> (Plato 1996)
>
> Now then, let's begin with your questions. What questions do
> you have about this passage? What don't you understand, but
> would like to clarify in your own mind? What would you like
> to discuss?

While this approach works well with students who enjoy asking their own questions, there are occasions when the teacher may wish to be more directive, particularly with a group that loses focus or interprets the intellectual freedom of open-ended questions as an invitation to turn a serious discussion into an undisciplined chat session. The following prompt, therefore, was designed to focus students' attention upon concerns that the teacher wished to discuss about a film adaptation. In this instance, the teacher wanted to make certain that students had "read" the film carefully, before shifting to a more open-ended discussion of thematic concerns. By setting a time limit, meanwhile, the teacher hoped to focus the discussion on the text, limiting digressions that could subvert the exercise.

> Ray Bradbury's novel, *Fahrenheit 451*, depicts a utopian
> society that some might consider dystopian. Before making
> such judgments, however, it's important to establish the
> "facts" upon which an argument is founded and explore their
> causes. As a group, therefore, I'd like you to discuss the
> following with respect to the film adaptation of this novel.
> You may address these questions chronologically or simulta-
> neously, but we'll limit this Interchange session to 15
> minutes.
> 1. What were the most striking rules and customs in this
> utopian society?
> 2. What caused this society to create such rules and customs?
> 3. What parallels, if any, would you draw between this soci-
> ety and yours?
> 4. What is the implicit "recommendation argument" of this
> film?

Although important, setting a good example and establishing high standards for online discourse may not be enough. Prompts like these give direction to students, but things can quickly run amok if the teacher fails to moderate the discourse that evolves in either synchronous or asynchronous online forums. This raises a serious concern—one that requires vigilance and, occasionally, intervention on the part of the teacher.

Case Study: Paul M.

What does a teacher do when a student resists instruction, ignores prompts, and generally behaves as if a synchronous, classroom discussion is just another anonymous chat room where anarchy is not only tolerated but encouraged? The same thing that teachers have always done in response to inappropriate behavior: Confront it. In some cases, a difficult individual may need help that the teacher cannot give, but before jumping to conclusions it is a good idea to talk with the student. More often than not, students are not fully aware of the discursive habits they have acquired through recreational chat sessions. They have grown so accustomed to treating people in disrespectful ways that they do not see any problem with bringing that behavior into an online synchronous discussion in the classroom.

Take, for example, the case of Paul M., the student in the earlier Interchange session who thought it appropriate to discuss the outcome of the Super Bowl rather than the designated topic. When questioned about this, Paul M. simply stated, "That's just my style." When asked how he had acquired it, Paul M. informed his teacher that he had spent a lot of time in chat rooms, where it was acceptable to "flame" others and talk about "whatever comes up." Perhaps most telling, however, was an incident that took place just a short time after this Interchange, during an asynchronous conversation in the Web-based discussion forum the teacher created for the class. The following prompt triggered this incident:

> How has your study of rhetoric, both reading and writing arguments, affected the way you "see" the world? Have you detected any change in the way you watch movies, read the newspaper, participate in conversations, etc.? Do you find

> yourself filtering the world through new terms such as ethos, pathos, and logos? What does this say about the relationship between your learning and your perception of the world around you?

A short time later, Chris O., a student who rarely spoke in class, posted the following response in the discussion forum:

> After reading and learning about rhetoric, I find myself looking for ethos, logos, and pathos when I watch TV or read the paper. I try to understand what the author or the company is trying to do with their ad or article. I guess this means that I am applying what I have learned to everyday life.

The next response to this *thread* (as it is called in online discussions) came from Paul M., who chose to remark upon his classmate's comments before addressing his instructor's questions. Pay special attention to the voice of this message, the discourse style of its author, and its attitude toward others:

> Puckered up enough chris? The way i see things has not been changed at all. i have always seen an advertisement and thought, what are the really tring to say. like that folders, good till the last droop sign on the freeway to houston, i mean that could really screw things up for them, or at least that is what i thought at first, then while my friend and i drove there we sat there and tried to figure out who the sign was for for like 30 min.s, and we did and the sign sticks in my head today, so i guess they did a good job, but i wonder who they are advertising to though. i mean it is not someone who is on there way to work that will sit there and try to figure out what they are tring to say, no it is two board teens on there way to houston that does that, so i guess we are there audience!!!!! TADA, i got lots to say!!!!

When asked about this exchange, Paul M. shrugged nonchalantly and said, "It's no big deal, we do that all the time on the AOL chat room." When asked how he thought Chris O. might feel about this, particularly since Chris O. was a reticent member of the class and not familiar with chat rooms, Paul M. shrugged again, and replied, "It's nothing personal, just words." Clearly, Paul M. had gained the technical skills necessary to participate in online discussions. What he lacked, however, was an understanding of civil literacy and a mature appreciation of discourse literacy. He did not understand his teacher's irritation, nor did he see any reason to apologize to his classmate. What he needed, obviously, was to understand that words are actions and that behind those actions are human beings with human emotions. Although Chris O. never complained, the teacher would have been remiss had he not addressed this incident with Paul M. Although this case may be a bit more extreme than most, there is nothing singular about Paul M.'s extensive experience with uncivil discourse and insensitivity to others. Many students lack discourse literacy, which makes it difficult for them to create or sustain civil conversations online. Once again, teachers cannot flee from this reality, nor should they dismiss the activity or suspend students like Paul M. indefinitely. Rather, they need to approach these occurrences as learning opportunities, raising student sensitivity to discursive practices and their impact on a community of inquiry.

Paul M. never fully reformed, but he did learn to temper his language as the semester progressed. Later Interchange sessions, as well as discussion forum postings, revealed more self-consciousness and respect for his audience. Nonetheless, his earlier contributions had already set an unfortunate precedent, establishing an online persona that would occasionally provoke hostile reactions when Paul M. simply made an appearance in future exchanges. Ironically, Paul M. would point to classmates who indulged in reckless or offensive outbursts against him. Again, the teacher felt obligated to step in at such times and remind students of the "greater expectations" required in order for this activity to serve a useful, educational purpose. However, once the Pandora's box of uncivil discourse has been opened by a member of the online community, it can be difficult to close—particularly when the rest of the group wishes to slam the lid of that box upon the culprit's head!

Establish the Rules, Play by the Rules

So, what should be done about this? Wringing one's hands or pulling the plug on networked computer technology will accomplish very little. Those are evasive maneuvers, not educational ones. A more appropriate response would establish the rules for discourse locally before turning students loose in telecollaborative projects that involve a wider community. As mentioned previously, printing out a transcript from a synchronous discussion and performing it aloud helps remind students to take responsibility for their words and actions online. From there, the golden rule applies. Whether one is conducting synchronous conversations within a networked classroom or asynchronous conversations on an international level, "Write unto others as you would have them write unto you."

Younger age groups may need more specific guidelines than this, so it is worthwhile to spend a few sessions analyzing discursive practices with them. In general, students are more likely to follow the rules if they understand why they exist, which requires some sense of ownership. Thus, it is mutually beneficial for the teacher to include the students in the rule-making process. One might begin by listing the "turn-ons" and "turn-offs" of online discourse; letting small groups discuss what they find enabling rather than disabling; and defining the steps they might take as a group to limit harmful interactions and hold one another accountable. By starting to establish healthy discursive habits locally, teachers fare better if and when they decide to extend the classroom to a more global conversation. Working through these issues with a group they see in face-to-face sessions helps teachers understand why online discourse sometimes deteriorates into flame wars and monologues rather than developing into civil dialogues.

There are also lessons to be learned about keeping online discussion groups small, writing good prompts for synchronous sessions, and granting students the latitude to "play" with language and ideas. As always, there is no substitute for experience when it comes to learning these lessons, although pedagogical experiments such as the following may help teachers learn more rapidly.

DISCOURSE LITERACY CHALLENGE #3

Role-Playing Online

New possibilities introduce new responsibilities and problems. How, for instance, does the teacher prevent students from simply "typing" instead of thinking, reflecting, and writing? If one is not careful, synchronous discussions may become little more than a typing competition, a new discourse in which the privileged ones are the students who type the fastest. As a corrective to this situation, one teacher deliberately slowed the pace of the exchange. Students were given a prompt and asked to compose an opening statement as a separate document, save it on a diskette, and then post it in the forum after a brief period, rather than plunging directly into the fury of a synchronous discussion. At that point, they were required to read all of their classmates' opening statements before typing a response.

What to Do

1. Place in a hat the names of important individuals that students have encountered during a study unit. These could be political figures from the past or present, famous scientists, mathematicians, artists, or authors.

2. Ask each student to draw one name from the hat and review their readings and class notes about the individual whose name they drew.

3. Instruct each student to adopt that individual's name and viewpoint for a synchronous or asynchronous discussion. Tell students to keep their "identities" secret.

4. Challenge the students to see how closely they can simulate their character's discourse style and point of view.

Case Study: Online Role-Playing

In the following example, students were asked to discuss whether they believed the Internet would lead society to the bliss of *cybertopia* or the discomforts of *cyberbia*. Students adopted the identity of authors studied throughout the semester, which compelled closer examination of respective works and their creators. To provide guidelines and inspire thoughtful discussion, the teacher adopted the role of Plato and offered the following prompt.

> Plato: As you know, our group has studied "The Rhetoric of Utopia" for the past three months, investigating the historical roots of utopian rhetoric as well as modern examples of

utopian/dystopian visions. Today, we'd like to hear your views on some controversial issues that speak to the future. You hold a prominent place in current debates over the role of media in society. While many people have noted that ours is an increasingly "mediated" world—that is, a place in which experience and perception are shaped by print and electronic media—there's far less agreement about whether this is good or bad. Where do you stand in terms of this debate, and what would you suggest is necessary to make our "mediated" society more satisfying?

We'd also like to know what you think of the prospects for online communities. Imagine, if you will, a society in which all the citizens are online, using e-mail and the Internet on a daily basis. What kind of society do you envision? Is it a brave new world that we might call "cybertopia" or a nightmarish vision called "cyberbia?" What proposal(s) would you offer to help us create the former rather than the latter?

Please take a few minutes to compose your thoughts, then post them in your group's Interchange session and wait for your colleagues to post their messages. After you've had a chance to read and reflect upon their visions, please respond to their ideas in dialectical fashion.

Student Dialogue

Students were given approximately five minutes to compose their initial thoughts. As a result, their first posting offered a rather static declamation, which would prove critical to subsequent exchanges. By requiring participants to read their colleagues' opening statements before engaging in the synchronous exchange, the teacher hoped to engender a more thoughtful discourse, encouraging critical inquiry and the exploration of ideas. The following excerpt features the opening statements from one discussion group, which involved seven role-playing students. The text appears exactly as the students created it.

Kevin Kelly: I feel that we should all view the internet as a wonderful phenomenon which brings the world together into one

76

big "family." What would make our "mediated" society more satisfying would be to see everyone participating. We should work as a group in order to progress to the next level of technology. If everyone were online everyday, individuals who thought that they were nothing before could now be someone, helping everyone else in the community achieve similar goals. I believe that this would be a "cybertopia," but in order for this to occur, people would have to learn to use the internet responsibly.

George Orwell: The image of a society whose perception of reality is the product of a print or electronic-based medium is a frightening one. How is it possible to know who or what is ultimately controlling these information sources? We are told that the organizations which have their names at the top of the page or screen are responsible for all content, but there is no way to be absolutely sure. Human beings need to interact with human beings in order to create a truly meaningful reality. Interaction with information alone and belief or action based on the same makes us slaves to those who disseminate the information. If we do not educate ourselves about the dangers of reliance on media, we are damned. As far as the Internet goes, the result of blind allegiance would be "cyberbia" indeed.

Neil Postman: Our perception is greatly influenced by print and electronic media, but this may be detrimental rather than beneficial. The reason that a "mediated" world may have harmful effects is because we, as consumers and educators of others, have not learned how to use this technology and its implications. We must be careful of the Huxleyan world. People do not take the time out to ask where the information is coming from and what the information is exactly. The best solution I can propose lies within education. We are not going to stop watching television and using the internet so we must learn how to use them. It is the job of the schools to educate our children about this, but that is much harder than it sounds. Schools have never been asked to do this before and the educators themselves may not be prepared to handle such a task.

Sven Birkerts: Considering a large part of our population is run through this vast computer system, I think we are already dealing with the inter net as a daily part of out lives. Our problem lies with the question of why we are using the computer daily. Is it because we are expected to do five tasks at one time? Since time is our problem, we have lost the desire to question where we are and why are we on the computer.

Aldous Huxley: A world in which experience and perception are shaped by print and electronic media will only bring about false happiness and the demise of deeper philosophical thought. As I wrote in my book, Brave New World, the greater the dependence on technological devices to provide pleasure, the shallower people became. In order to preserve this new forum, and prevent it from becoming this "cyberbia," I would propose that an educational program to teach people how to integrate the internet into their lives, and not have it take over their lives.

Howard Rheingold: I am just afraid that the entire world will become so caught up in the fun part of this technology, that they will not question why it has been created. As a questionless society we are succumbing to great pleasure, not realizing that there must be consequences.

By now, six of the seven members of the group had posted their opening statements. The seventh member had been excused for a short period at the start of the session. At this point, the teacher asked the rest of the group to read each other's opening statements and compose replies directed to one of their colleagues. The seventh class member, who was playing the role of Kurt Vonnegut, would post an opening statement and join the discussion in progress after returning.

Kevin Kelly: Huxley, Don't you think that we can use the internet as a gathering place, to exchange ideas and maybe to implement them? Once we are connected, we are like a bee hive, working together for a common purpose.

George Orwell: Aldous - I agree with your proposal, but an equally important proposal to go along with teaching people how to integrate the internet into their lives would have to be teaching them what the internet is. Most people are oblivious to the source of information, often with disastrous results.

Howard Rheingold: Orwell, not to mention that a lot of the information is often bogus and unreliable.

Aldous Huxley: Kelly, what do you think would happen to individual personas once we all became assimilated into this new "family"? And is achieveing that next level of society really going to better society? I believe that grouping these people into a collective will only stifle creative thought. People will not be able to find inspiration in nature, or satisfaction in a one-on-one conversation. And increased technology could lead to the medicalization of society and the development of God complexes amongst the scientists.

Kurt Vonnegut: Electronic media has the possibility of controlling your mind. Machines and computers do not enhance intelligence. The Internet does not provide a medium which encourages learning, communication or creativity. The Web may approach "cyberbia." Unless we begin to understand what it is and what its purpose is, it will produce the same quality of entertainment as TV. We can ignore it, allowing it to take its course, trusting that future generations will use it more productively than we have. Or we can understand what drives the Internet and TV (corporations, money), and then comprehend what kind of medium this is and what we should use it for. However, it may not be entirely bad. Just as the arrival of paperback books provided a cheap way for unknown authors to be published, so can the Internet provide a place for a community of artists who are able to show their writing, films, paintings and music.

George Orwell: Kurt - I agree with everything you say. The Internet does have potential, but only if its users know what runs it.

Kurt Vonnegut: Kelly, you mention that those who have no identity can now have one. However, do you think this is a true identity, or one which they create and wear as a disguise?

Neil Postman: Orwell, that is precisely what I was talking about. People are blindly following what the internet is offering, without questioning their sources. Even after obtaining some sort of information, the majority of people using this technology do not know how to use the info they have just gotten.

Kevin Kelly: Aldous, People woud still be able to find inspiration in nature, but they will have a new way of sharing it with the rest of the world.

Howard Rheingold: I cannot deny that the internet has brought the entire world one step closer to the brotherhood we are always advocating. There are educational websites and places to discuss current laws and proposals on the internet. Vonneget, I believe that yes we are embracing this much too quickly and with not enough doubt.

Sven Birkerts: Kelly, Think about the term "bee hive". Do we really want to be workers doing our jobs without question. We don't know why we are doing, all we know is it is our place in this technological society.

Plato: Vonnegut, Do you think that all this technology is leading us toward something like the situation you described in your short story, "Harrison Bergeron"?

Kurt Vonnegut: Huxley, I agree that we will become assimilated into this one computer-generated world. We cannot remain individuals while we are personified as names on a screen.

George Orwell: Postman - Not only do they not know how to use it, but they don't know how it (or those that broadcast it) might be using/controlling them.

Kurt Vonnegut: Plato, Yes, I see this technology as having the possibility of controlling our minds instead of us controlling technology. It could give us no identity by making us all equals, equals in that you and I are no different from anyone else.

Neil Postman: Kurt, while the internet can be a place for artists to show their talents, it can also be place where people can publish anything, and therefor deceive the public.

Aldous Huxley: Kelly, why can't we GATHER in person? why must we begin using a false forum? the internet is a false forum b/c we "connect" to other computers, other two-dimensional images and "personas"- not real human beings. All deep meaning can be lost when using a cold, lifeless machine to bring us to other people via an imaginary "highway". Ideas may be exchanged, but we never know where the ideas come from- like they appear from thin air. And once "connected", like a "bee hive", won't we all turn into the working drones, void of individual thought and complying to everything the queen says? Is the bee hive analogy truly a utopian concept? doesn't it just scream hierarchy, loss of individual freedoms?

Howard Rheingold: I agree with all of you. But we must have some faith in the human race. In order to believe in utopias we must believe that there are people who can create them.

Kevin Kelly: Kurt, If people want to make up their own identities, that is possible, but if people are true to themselves and want others to see them as who they are, why would they use disguises?

Sven Birkerts: We could still question why we would have to do things. The computers would not necessarily be controlling us.

Kurt Vonnegut: Orwell and Postman: I wonder how we should use the Internet once we understand that it is controlled by money. Do you think it should be entertainment only?

The Internet is at essence just a tool; it does what its users tell it to do. What I worry about is the desires of its users - how might THEY want to control our minds.

Neil Postman: Orwell, true true. That furthers the point that only education can help the situation. Since this technology has already been introduced and so widely accepted, we cannot take it away. Our only choice is to go forth with more knowledge about how to use it wisely.

Kurt Vonnegut: Birkerts: I hope that people would question why, but I fear that it will become another television, only more frightening, as it has the capability of replacing real life: in virtual reality and video games.

Sven Birkerts: Do you think the majority of the people using the internet and watching 30- 40 hours of television a week step back and ask why they are so addicted to this screen?

Kevin Kelly: Aldous, Yes, we could GATHER in person, but that group would be so limited. Using the internet, we can expand that group endlessly.

Howard Rheingold: Nothing can replace real life. There is no exchange for human interaction. However, if introverted, shy people are able to gain confidence because of their voiced opinions on the internet, then they will become more likely to go out in public and share their views.

Kevin Kelly: Birkerts, I don't think people even realize that they are addicted to the screen.

Kurt Vonnegut: Kelly: People can use disguises if they are incapable of dealing in social situations. They may see the Internet as a way to "become someone else." Someone who is not incapable of functioning in a social setting. Then, they have ignored the real problem, which is, why can they not act this way in one-to-one conversation?

Sven Birkerts: Vonnegut: How do you propose we look at and question the mind set of addapting humans?

Aldous Huxley: Rheingold, should we really have faith? think about the term FAITH: absolute, blind trust; should we have faith in a group of beings that inherently do bad things to one another?

Neil Postman: Kurt, I think entertainment only would not be beneficial to us. There are great resources provided by the interent. We can find things of value so long as we can determine where the information comes from, that is that it's legitimate.

Howard Rheingold: Huxley, humans are animals, just as dogs and lions are. Therefore, in order to survive only the fittest go on to live and reproduce. Blind trust is what keeps some people living on a daily basis.

Kurt Vonnegut: Rheingold: Yes, that's possible, but I also see that these same people could become trapped by the computer, unable to go out in their daily lives and reenact the characters they've made on the computer. They become so wrapped up in what's going on with their chat room friends, that they ignore the world outside.

Plato: Postman, good point! How do we make sure that dialectical discourse—something that's on your mind a good deal—is alive and well in cyberspace? How do we prevent it from becoming just another version of television, where people accept information passively instead of interrogating it? Rheingold, would you care to comment as well?

This brief excerpt from one small group's synchronous online discussion reveals a good deal about the potential for this type of learning activity. Clearly, the creation of a thoughtful prompt, allowance for student reflection and composition, and a slow, deliberate start helped generate a rich, intellectual discussion. It should be noted, however, that the teacher did not stumble on such a strategy without a significant number of trials (and even more errors). With experimentation and patience, however, one learns to use synchronous online discussions to stimulate open-ended inquiry and alter the classroom dynamics. Consider, for example, how often every student contributes half a dozen statements during a conventional class discussion. How often do face-to-face discussions enable this kind of decentralized discourse without losing their focus? Of course, the quantity of student participation does not guarantee quality. Nor does it mean that every use of synchronous online discussions will be more satisfying than face-to-face ones. Nonetheless, this excerpt demonstrates what can be accomplished when the teacher establishes high expectations and arranges the sessions to help students meet them.

Student Reflections

What do students think of this type of learning activity? Reactions vary, but one of the unanticipated benefits of holding class discussions in a new medium is that it calls attention to the pedagogical strategies that the teacher employs. It is often beneficial for both the students and teacher to write a reflection at the conclusion of such an exercise. In the following examples, students voice both approval and frustration after participating in a synchronous, role-playing discussion online. Consequently, their insights help the teacher consider the influence of online writing activities on individual students and the group as a whole, inspiring reflections on this new learning environment and ideas for future adjustments or innovations.

The Importance of Being Anonymous

> This interchange was very interesting and stimulating. I'm not convinced that the knowledge gained was any better than in previous interchanges, but I know that ours became pretty heated. The frank discussion on the basis of anonymity was amazing, though. However, I'm not sure that everyone in our group was representing their author's views instead of their personal ones. In our group, the person playing Atwood said that she was a "mentor". This is a small detail to know about a person, and I think I remember someone in our class saying that she was a mentor, so this was a problem. This activity would have been much worse in a face-to-face situation. We know each other now too well to get riled up about these things without anonymity. Also, it was quite difficult to know how authors like ours would respond to the internet, I guess that was part of the brain work involved with this assignment. —Brian E.

The Advantages of Small Groups

> Today's interchange session was great. I really enjoyed the role playing. I think it helped us understand what the authors were trying to say, and it definitely brought up issues that I would have otherwise missed. The past interchange sessions were good, but I liked this one better for several reasons. The other ones seemed too large. I felt like I was saying plenty, but I never felt like I could keep up with the different strands of conversation. This time also, I felt like it made people prepare better. It kind of made us as a group really pay attention to what we were saying since it was as though we were a representation of that person.
>
> —Ericka J.

The Significance of Identity

> I think that this interchange was very different. Although it allowed people to put up another barrier to their identity, it allowed them to identify themselves through their openness. This environment is good because you have to adopt someone else's view that might not be your own. This helps to make what you believe stronger or change because you consider another viewpoint. I don't think that this would have worked as well in a face-to-face discussion because people would have felt it silly. On the Internet they can hide there faces. —Manish C.

Separating Messages From the Messenger

> This interchange was different in that it allowed us to understand how others interpret the readings that we have been doing. To argue well one needed to actually think in the way their author would. This required a good grasp of their topic and an understanding of the point the author was trying to make. The interchange was also interesting because it put many famous viewpoints together in a forum that would not be possible otherwise. These authors would never have the chance to argue their point with the others. I think it is better than a face to face interaction because it allows anonymity. We didn't know whom the others were when taking on their persona. This allowed us to better listen to the arguments objectively. —Mike S.

The Constraints of Assumed Identity

> I did not like this interchange. I did not like the idea of speaking someone else's opinions that were not necessarily the same as mine. I think it lead to a discussion that was

not very real, and I feel like we didn't get much accomplished. This activity, however, would have been less effective in a face to face situation. It is hard to talk and
think about something at the same time, which one can do in
an interchange. —Nick W.

Suggestions for Improvement

The interchange worked better this time than in times past.
People seemed more prepared to discuss and the role playing
made them think about what they were going to say. The dialogue slowed down a little. On the other hand, the role-
playing limited us to a certain extent. We had to conform to
the ideas of a person that limited our range of argument. A
looser definition of the roles may help. Each person could be
a supporter of their author and not necessarily the author
himself. In that way the basic idea of the authors could
boost our thinking but not limit us to a narrow opinion which
is harder to develop beyond the author's original text. With
strict role playing a face-to-face discourse would have
ruined the role-playing. I think looser role-playing could be
done effectively if in a different manner in each form of
discussion. —Kevin W.

Personal Literacy

Discourse literacy—the ability to read, understand, and abide by norms that govern the discursive practices of a particular social group—is obviously a fundamental skill for students in both online and offline discussions. In many ways, it is the beginning of a student's initiation to the world and to the self. Although it is liberating to play roles and emulate another writer's style, point of view, or ideology, at some point students must come back to themselves. Otherwise, teachers run the risk of pandering to students, providing only the "edutainment" that critics fear. Thus, role-playing serves a useful purpose, but its educational value suffers if it becomes an end in itself. At some point, students must graduate from discourse literacy to investigations of themselves and their own views, developing the skills necessary for *personal literacy* in cyberspace.

Personal Literacy: Discovering Oneself Online

When people adopt an online persona they cross a boundary into highly charged territory .

(Turkle 1997, 260)

Although many students enjoy using pseudonyms in online activities, they should beware the temptation of incessant role-playing, which distances them from their own thoughts, feelings, and identity. The reason for this is that one of the most important questions for adolescents remains a nontechnical one: Who am I? Defining the self, and understanding the forces that shape it, is a lifetime skill that requires *personal literacy* (see Figure 4.1).

As with discourse literacy, this did not begin with the advent of cyberspace. Nonetheless, online interactions raise new questions and concerns about individual identity. Students must learn how to create an online persona through the words, expressions, and ideas they put forth; this also

---

Personal Literacy

Personal literacy is the ability to undergo a personal initiation to the self, recognize how others read and perceive that self through social interactions, and understand the social forces that shape an individual's identity.

Figure 4.1

requires sensitivity to the way in which others "read" an individual online, as well as an open-minded exploration of the self. This is no simple feat, of course, particularly for adolescents who are more comfortable playing roles and imitating the discursive styles or viewpoints of others. As Sherry Turkle, an MIT professor of clinical psychology, observed in *Life on the Screen*, there is a seriousness lurking behind our playful experiments with online persona, one which students may not fully grasp, but which educators cannot neglect:

> Some are tempted to think of life in cyberspace as insignificant, as escape or meaningless diversion. It is not. Our experiences there are serious play. We belittle them at our risk. We must understand the dynamics of virtual experience both to foresee who might be in danger and to put these experiences to best use. Without a deep understanding of the many selves that we express in the virtual we cannot use our experiences there to enrich the real. If we cultivate our awareness of what stands behind our screen personae, we are more likely to succeed in using virtual experience for personal transformation. (Turkle 1997, 269)

Initiation Stories

In literature, such transformations are often spoken of as "initiation stories," which focus primarily on two types of situations: initiation to the world and self. Of the two, the latter is far more difficult, particularly for people who are afraid to explore their personal histories, beliefs, and identities. In many ways, this describes adolescents fascinated by images flashing across their computer screens. Educators must help them use the computer to acquire personal literacy, discovering who they are and how others "read" them online. In the following excerpt from the start of a synchronous online discussion, notice how the teacher's prompt catches several students by surprise. They struggle with the idea of a personal voice, discussed in the previous chapter, as well as the question of self-definition.

> **Teacher:** In the initial phase of a writing assignment we must discover what we think, working in an "exploratory" fashion. Later, we express those thoughts in "demonstrative" fashion,

stating an argument and supporting it. Throughout, the essay itself is a means to an end: greater knowledge and understanding of the world and self. I'd like you to reflect for a moment upon the Definitional Arguments that you just completed. What did you learn about yourself, your topic and other matters during the "exploratory" phase of this project - from topic proposals to groupwork, research to rough drafts? What did you learn during the "demonstrative" phase - while refining your thesis and criteria, locating secondary sources, and revising the final draft of this essay? HOW did you learn these things? Ultimately, how did your work on a definitional argument help define you?

Howard S.: ... .

Adam J.: I learned to keep my topic simple

Nick F.: Before I started my paper I only had a basic knowledge of my topic. After writing and revising the paper I had gone so far as to form a strong opinion about my topic. I also learned a great deal about the nature of education and society

G.J.: I learned a great deal about my topic. I went into the paper not knowing much about the subject, but finished feeling that I could describe it to someone else.

Adam J.: if it is not a specific thesis there are too many holes to plug in the essay

Teacher: Nick, what was your topic?

Howard S.: I learned that I let the media form my opinion for me on certain issues .I sometimes create my opinion from the biased way they cover a story. After doing the research for my def argument, I was able to find the whole truth insted of the minute bit of truth told by the news the first time I heard about my topic

Jennifer G.: I learned how to better express my views

Chris O.: I learned through the topic proposal stage that not all arguments are as easy as they first appear. Defining a language is a lot harder than it seems. I changed my topic to something much simpler which I already knew about.

Nick F.: "Meritocracy in Modern America?" was the title to my paper, teach. I discussed the "true" nature of our society and why the US is really not a meritocracy.

Brian K.: I found that I wasn't really sure how I felt about my issue, capital punishment, and that my opinion changed numerous times. I found that there are a lot of positives as well as a lot of negatives relating to my issue.

Adam J.: i learned to question the credibility of sources from class... it makes all the difference in presenting a persuasive argument

Teacher: Brian and Howard: I'd be interested to know how you finally found your own "voice" and argument in this essay.

Brian K.: What exactly is meritocracy?

Chris O: Howard, yes the left-wing media has a certain way of portraying issues that make it seem simple to understand but when you research the topic you find out that it is different than they portray.

G.J: Like we said just a minute ago in class, I think everyone goes into a paper with some type of pre-conceived idea. It's only after you research that you can see that you most likely missed a lot of important ideas concerning the topic.

Nick F.: Meritocracy is a system by which you are promoted or given credit to based on merit. The military or higher education are examples of this.

Howard S.: I found my own "voice" from my research

G.J.: What do you mean by "voice"? I couldn't tell you right now what my voice truly is . . .

This excerpt from a synchronous, online classroom discussion reveals a good deal about students' perceptions of themselves and the ways in which those selves are defined. A close reading reveals, among other things, far more comfort talking about the subject of their study and far more knowledge of that subject than of themselves. Although they may volunteer information about their research and interests, most adolescents prove far less generous with insights about their study's impact upon themselves. This presents a delicate conundrum for teachers, who must respect a student's right to privacy, which may explain a student's decision not to divulge personal information, while simultaneously encouraging the exploration and reflection that lead to self-knowledge.

Fostering Personal Literacy

How do teachers help students acquire personal literacy, developing the ability to read and interpret their words, beliefs, and selves? Although this sort of activity makes some educators uncomfortable, it remains imperative for an online community that wishes to establish civil literacy and hold students responsible for their discursive habits. In effect, teachers must help students examine themselves through critical literacy, an ability to make thoughtful judgments, which derives its meaning from the ancient Greek term *kritikos*. Unfortunately, its modern descendant in mainstream culture, the word *critical*, usually suggests something negative or unflattering. As a corrective, educators must encourage students to think critically, making informed judgments of their own ideas—their origins and expressions—so that they develop personal literacy skills. Without the ability to subject themselves to a critical reading, arriving at a better understanding of why they think what they think and do what they do, students are condemned to an unexamined life, which Socrates long ago said was not worth living.

One of the best ways to develop a more critical, personal literacy is by asking questions. Not just any question will do, however. Students must discover or invent a thoughtful, open-ended "Why" question that challenges them, because analysis begins with the question "Why?" This notion puzzles students initially, perhaps because so much of their schooling—including their use of computers and the Internet—has encouraged them to ask only "What?" When asking "What do I need to do to make this software application work?" the questioner invites close-ended inquiry that perpetuates an impoverished, technical definition of computer literacy. However, one opens the inquiry by asking "Why do I need to make this software application work?" allowing for authentic learning to take place. By simply demonstrating the distinction between "what questions" and "why questions," a good teacher opens the door to analysis rather than summary, an investigation of cause rather than a recitation of symptoms.

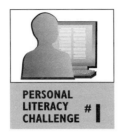

**PERSONAL
LITERACY # ▌
CHALLENGE**

The Why List

After students understand the distinction between summary and analysis, they are ready to engage in an activity that will awaken their critical thinking and personal literacy skills: The Why List.

What to Do

1. To begin, ask students to think of a "Why" question that they cannot answer. They should try to make it something substantial, something that they really would like to answer because it will help them discover what they think and why they think it. Quite often, a social phenomenon or local problem works well for this. For example: "Why do people enjoy violent computer games?" Each student writes three or four "Why questions" that could serve as a starting point. After they have their questions, ask the students to choose one to investigate more thoroughly. This should be one for which they do not have an answer but would like to figure out.

2. Tell students to log on, open a file, and write their own "Why List."

3. Have them type the "Why" question for which they do not have an answer (make sure that it is neither trivial nor absurd. For example, "Why do people enjoy violent computer games?").

4. Ask them to attempt an answer to that question. They are to begin with the word *because* and write a one-phrase response ("Because violent computer games provide an escape from reality").

5. Have them ask the "Why" question that their "Because" answer prompts ("Why do violent computer games provide an escape from reality?").

6. Ask them to answer this new question, beginning with the word *because*, and write a one-phrase response ("Because reality is monotonous and these games are not.").

7. Then, have them ask the "Why" question that their new answer prompts ("Why is reality monotonous, but not computer games?").

8. Have students continue in this fashion until they have written ten "Why" questions and ten "Because" responses.

9. When students have finished, have them read through their list and see where it took them. Then, they should write a brief analysis of the list itself. Did the Why List help them answer the initial question, take them further away from it, or simply cause them to spin in circles? Do they see any causal relationships now that they could not see before?

10. When everyone has finished, ask for volunteers to share their Why List.

Expanding the Challenge

As a class, select Why Lists for further examination as a collaborative exercise. Divide the class into pairs and have the pairings conduct another Why List exercise via synchronous conversation, with one person asking the Why questions and the other responding. When they find the exercise is not taking them any further, ask them to discuss what happened and prepare a brief presentation for the class.

> **Teacher's Tip**
>
> This exercise works especially well in a networked computer lab where students and teachers can review individual files. With practice, this helps students discover the evolution of their thoughts. They may write their lists on word processors and save the file on diskette before posting it to a class discussion forum or mailing list.

Why Ask Why: Increasing Student Awareness

Asking students to generate their own questions rather than respond to those of a teacher or standardized exam should seem liberating. However, the open-ended inquiry of The Why List may intimidate some students, particularly those who are uncomfortable with ambiguity. In such cases, it helps to present Personal Literacy Challenge #1 as individual brainstorming triggered by the technology of questions. Indeed, it requires a good deal of knowledge and skill to invent a good question. Students are not compelled to reach conclusions and should feel no pressure to arrive at any. However, they need guidance as well as reassurance that what they are doing is "right." If allowed to ask questions without the pressure of a grade or a final destination hanging over them, they may discover that "why?" leads on and on, prompting an infinite succession of inquiries, insights, and associations. It is worth asking them where, on examination of The Why List, they would have gotten had they begun by asking "what?" instead of "why?" With time, they come to realize "what questions" lead them to the cul-de-sac of static answers rather than the open road of dynamic, arguable ones.

A few excerpts from student process journals will illustrate The Why List's contributions to a writing process. In chapter 8, I will take a closer look at the way process journals assist students as they compose and develop the skills necessary for evaluative literacy. The present purpose, however, is to examine the way in which The Why List helps students discover ideas, examine their genesis, and acquire the awareness necessary for personal literacy. Certainly, The Why List and student reflections on the exercise could be handwritten and exchanged in a traditional manner. However, networked computers enable exchanges as well as innovations between students and teachers that a conventional approach could not support. For that reason, the following why lists were composed with a word processing program and saved in online folders where students kept their process journals.

Generally speaking, students find The Why List usually takes them in one of two directions, either circling their topic or moving away from it as the inquiry progresses. Let us begin by looking at the latter, which illustrates the impact of The Why List upon one student's composition process.

Esteban's Why List

The primary appeal of this exercise is its potential for intellectual and personal discovery. If properly engaged, students will go beyond unexamined assumptions. Like a rower paddling with both oars in the water—in this case both hemispheres of the brain—students embark upon an intellectual journey that begins on a familiar riverbank, but explores unfamiliar waters. The following Why List illustrates this type of journey, undertaken by a student named Esteban as part of a literature class. In the first semester, his class had studied a William Wordsworth poem that claims "The child is father of the man." The following semester, he discovered echoes of the idea in a West African novel. Rather than accept this platitude, however, Esteban chose to investigate it in the following manner:

Q. Why is the Child supposedly Father of the man?

A. Because the habits and experiences of childhood shape adults.

Q. Why can't the adult overcome those habits and experiences?

A. Because we are all creatures of habit and it takes tremendous will power to overcome those that are ingrained.

Q. Why don't we have the will power to overcome these?

A. Because we are weak.

Q. Why are we so weak when confronting our habits?

A. Because we are comfortable in our habits, even if they are bad habits.

Q. Why are bad habits "comfortable?"

A. Because they are OUR habits.

Q. Why can't we break OUR habits?

A. Because we don't want to break them.

Q. Don't "want" to or "can't?"

A. Don't want to.

Q. If we wanted to break them could we?

A. Yes, though it'd be difficult.

Q. Why would it be difficult?

A. Because it threatens us and it could change us.

Q. Why is change threatening?

A. Because it could bring the unknown.

Q. So we prefer the known "evil" rather than the unknown potential evil?

A. Yes.

Q. So that's why the Child's the Father of the Man?

Why Ask Why: Inviting Response

Following this exercise, it is important that students take a moment to see where it led them and ponder what it revealed. It is often helpful to have a classmate read and respond to the list. For example, ask students to read a classmate's Why List and respond to it by indicating what interests them and why. They can circle the most interesting question and answer on the list (perhaps the ones they would choose to launch an essay if it were their list). For example, in response to Esteban's list, a reader might select the following pair:

Q. Why is the Child supposedly Father of the man?
A. Because we are comfortable in our habits, even if they are bad habits.

This helps the author of The Why List in a number of ways. For one thing, the author sees which questions and answers others value. This furthers the investigation of ideas and encourages the search for an elusive thesis statement and for more satisfying insights. For another, the juxtaposition of a formerly separated question and answer may reveal a causal relationship that the author had not noticed. Following discussion with their peer reviewer, the author of The Why List could be instructed to use either the question that the reviewer selected or another one that the author wishes to explore. That question is used to generate yet another answer, which may provide the kernel of a thesis. The author then refines that statement until it articulates a clear and cogent argument.

In this instance, the essay that evolved from Esteban's Why List, although somewhat flawed, was one of the liveliest and most insightful in the class. What is pleasing for the reader of such an essay is to see how active the writer's mind is while wrestling with the text. Such essays seem to evolve, exploring issues rather than taking them for granted, questioning ideas rather than merely reciting platitudes announced in the first paragraph. When asked what was most helpful in arriving at his thesis, Esteban was quick to cite The Why List. Although there was obviously far more work to be done, the intellectual journey that began by questioning a cliché allowed him to apply new insights to a text written in a different century and continent. Whereas the "why questions" led to the analysis of character and setting, "what questions" would have looked at only the habits of an individual, the symptoms of a behavior rather than its causes. Esteban enjoyed playing with why questions on the computer because he could continually change directions, erasing a response or considering other possible answers with a keystroke. Consequently, his thesis paragraph revealed a sophisticated analysis, synthesizing literature to arrive at a unique argument:

> "The Child is Father of the Man" wrote William Wordsworth. Indeed, his opinion is reinforced by the character of Ousmane in Mariama Ba's novel, *Scarlet Song*. The Child who would become Ousmane, husband of Mireille, develops habits which will later enslave that man. His habits and reluctance to shed them are essentially responsible for his slavery. Ultimately, one learns from Ousmane that if we do not shed habit, risking change and personal turmoil, we are destined to remain forever controlled by the child within us.

April's Why List

Although it is rewarding to see students put both oars in the water, on some occasions they find their boat spinning in circles because of their obsession with the topic. To extend the metaphor, hanging on to the original question and topic instead of making an intellectual departure is like paddling with one oar in the water and the other in the boat. The following presents a student who was spinning in circles, desperately clinging to the original topic by asking only variations of her original question. After consultation with her teacher, however, she decided to let go and see where the questions would take her. It is worth noting, too, that where Esteban was concerned with the composition of an essay, this student employed The Why List to examine a complicated text. Notice the evolution of her inquiry and the subsequent amusement in her reflection at where this has led her:

> Q. Why weren't the men's actions controlled in *The Handmaids Tale*?
>
> A. Because it was the woman's responsibility.
>
> Q. Why is it the woman's responsibility?

A. B/c we were the birthing gender.

Q. Why does that matter?

A. B/c men say so.

Q. Why does it matter that the men say that?

A. B/c they are the ones in power.

Q. Why are they in power?

A. B/c women were taught to be submissive

Q. Why were women taught to be submissive?

A. B/c we are the weaker sex

Q. Why are we the weaker sex?

A. B/c we are not as physically able as men.

Q. Why does that play a role in power?

A. B/c in order to win we have to be strong.

Q. Why do we have to be strong physically?

A. B/c war needs us to be.

Q. Why do we worry about war?

A. B/c rebellion is constantly around us.

Although this particular list may not accomplish as much as Esteban's, it is an important part of April's thought process. Before she begins to write an essay defending her position, she needs to discover what that position is and why she holds it. The Why List may help her identify assumptions, notice subconscious patterns and connections, and, ultimately, discover questions that inspire further inquiry and deeper understanding of her views. April's reflection takes her beyond superficial concerns and shows her marveling at the distance she has traveled, noting a curious parallel that could plant the seed for her essay:

> A brief analysis would lead me to think that I totally went
> off the subject. I was evaluating the men's actions and their
> lack of supervision and I ended up with worrying about war. I
> guess if you think about it the men's actions weren't con-
> trolled because they were at war. And in order to win the war
> their minds have to be free of "inconsequential things" like
> sexual promiscuity and pregnancy. It's funny how I ended with
> war and I wasn't even thinking about it. The movie's setting
> was during a war.

Kara's Why List

April has clearly launched an intellectual journey by liberating herself from the constraints of the initial topic and question. However, not every student writer finds this situation comfortable. In the following example, Kara takes a similar journey. Indeed, The Why List has once again taken on a life of its own, but as the reflection indicates, Kara does not know what to make of this. Is it cause for celebration or consternation?

> Q. Why is modern society transfixed by television?
>
> A. B/c they like the shows.
>
> Q. Why do they like the shows?
>
> A. B/c they're interesting.
>
> Q. Why are these shows interesting?
>
> A. B/c they are about human life.
>
> Q. Why do people want to watch shows about human life?
>
> A. B/c it inspires them.
>
> Q. Why does it inspire them?
>
> A. B/c they think their own lives are boring or lacking
>   excitement.
>
> Q. Why do they think their lives are boring?

A. B/c they aren't doing the things on the shows

Q. Why aren't they doing the things on the shows?

A. B/c they don't have enough time for them.

Q. Why don't they have enough time?

A. B/c they work long hours.

Q. Why are they working long hours?

A. B/c they want to earn money.

Q. Why do they want money?

A. B/c they want to buy stuff.

Q. Why do they want stuff?

A. B/c society says stuff is good.

Kara's Reflection

I don't think my why list went in the direction I wanted it to go—it led to consumerism when I thought it would have led to the dumbing down of society, or something along that line. But I guess if I had answered something differently, it would have gone in that direction-or a totally different direction.

What should the teacher do in cases where students are spinning in circles or uncertain about the direction in which their thinking has taken them? Teachers must tread carefully, offering guidance and encouragement without doing all the work for a student. This requires a delicate balancing act: on the one hand nurturing, so the student does not lose faith in the enterprise, yet on the other, demanding intellectual courage. Without striking such a balance, the student could falter and give up hope of discovery. With an excess of attention, however, teachers may interfere with the journey, their desire to help paradoxically hindering the development of the critical thinking skills necessary for students to acquire personal literacy. This is where networked computers prove an ally, however, providing opportunities for students to collaborate in synchronous discussions during class or asynchronous discussions afterwards. As a result, students can continue The Why List in an online writing environment, maintaining focus and energy in an online writing environment in a manner that would be difficult and tedious offline.

Case Study: The Why List Online

Although one could, of course, have students write The Why List without computers, computer technology helps facilitate not only this exercise but variations and discussions of it. Beyond this lie opportunities for collaboration, including the synchronous discussions introduced in chapter 3.

In the following example, the teacher arranged a group discussion of Why Lists to inspire open-ended inquiry and introduce students to a new writing environment. Indeed, this transcript is drawn from one group's initiation to synchronous, online discussion. In it, the teacher encourages a movement from broad, general questions that reveal superficial thought toward more specific ones that demand closer examination. Because this was their initiation to a new medium many of the students found this exercise particularly challenging, but notice how much they accomplish through this telecollaborative effort. Their discussion helps them sort through questions as an online community of inquiry, discovering causal relationships that they had not previously considered. It is these relationships that the teacher hopes will become more apparent, taking the students to a new level of comprehension, a place where they learn something about the world and themselves.

Before proceeding to the transcript, it is worth noting that it presents the most difficult synchronous discussion presented thus far. Given the nature of this communication medium, which allows students to simultaneously type responses and post them to the shared writing space of the synchronized bulletin board, many of the threads seem to cross one another. In other words, one speaker may make a statement that is not addressed until several other speakers have also posted, due to the simultaneity of the composition and serendipity of their posting. This presents challenges for the reader of this text, because it is sometimes difficult to follow a particular thread of the conversation, but this challenge mirrors the one that the participants confronted. Furthermore, because of the limitations of the computer screen, it can be difficult to keep up with messages as they scroll down the screen, pushing their predecessors out of sight above them. To approximate the experience, imagine that, after twenty lines of text, each subsequent line, which appears at the bottom of the screen, displaces the one at the top. This means students must read quickly, type brief responses, and concentrate on particular threads as they evolve.

Teacher: I thought we'd use this inaugural Interchange session to discuss the "Why Lists" that you just created in class. Here are a few questions that we can begin with: What was your initial question and where did your "Why List" take you as you proceeded? What, if anything, did the "Why List" help you see in terms of causal relationships that you couldn't see before? Did you find yourself moving further away from your initial question or simply spinning in circles around it? What might you do next to pursue this investigation? OK, so what question would you like to begin with?

Nick W: Why do businesses like to take advantage of customers?

Darlene D: I asked: Why MLK Blvd has deeper holes than the Grand Canyon?

Brad N.: I started with the question, "Why is it so hot?"

Brian E: I asked "Why are we protecting the Barton Springs Salamander?"

Kelsey M: Why do people like to gossip?

Ericka J: That's a great question Darlene, my car thinks so too!

Nick W: Because our tax money is being wasted.

Andrea T: I asked why do so many underage kids abuse drugs and alcohol?

B.J: Why are college students now taking so much longer to graduate?

Zach V: The why list helped me realize how many factors their can be in a simple question

Darlene D.: Nick, What was your last answer to why businesses take advantages of customers?

Nick W.: Kids abuse alcohol because they were not raised right.

Teacher: Was the initial question the most interesting one that you asked?

Tina D.: My first question was why some people risk their lives by participating in activities such as high-speed roller coasters or bungee jumping.

Mike S.: What businesses do you think take advantage?

Brad N.: I think kids abuse alcohol because they want to get "away"

Kelsey M.: Andrea, Because it gives them a false sense of being grown-up... gives them freedom

Andrea T.: I thought that kids abuse alcohol because they have low self-esteem.

Nick W.: Every business takes advantage in some way.

Teacher: ...or, did you discover a more insightful question further down the list?

Manish C.: Why is the personal life of a political person such a big deal?

Brad N.: Advertisers take advantage!!!

Darlene D.: Nick, that's pretty funny, how did you get to that?

Ericka J.: Yeah, I think the businesses aimed at youth exploit the most though.

Nick W.: Because the American public is infatuated with SEX.

Kelsey M.: I ended up linking gossiping to personal security....

Andrea T.: Tina: what did you put as your first answer?

Mike S.: I think "taking advantage" is what they feel they need to do to get ahead.

Teacher: Nick, to whom are you speaking about Sex?

Kelsey M.: Nick: why does sex sell?

Zach V.: There were more insightful questions, like why do people want entertainment instead of knowledge

Matt S.: Andrea, perhaps because it is semi-taboo in our culture. At the same time that authority figures tell them of the terrible evils of drugs and alcohol, their peers likely appear to just be having a good time with it. So, youth just feel misinformed perhaps and want to experiment, at least initially.

Neal R.: My initial question was "why does it take an average of more that five years to graduate from UT?" The question took me to questions about funding the university. This was quite far away from the initial question. I figured it would not go very far. Next I might look at students choices that might cause them to stay at UT longer than necessary.

Matt S.: Knowledge takes work.

Nick W.: I'm talking to the person who asked about a politician's personal life.

Tina D.: I found that my question went from being a light-hearted curious one into a deeper self-examining one, if that makes any sense.

Brad N.: Anyways, I started with Why is it so hot, and ended up with something like Why are there so many people studying research in medicine?

Lisa C.: People like to gossip negatively because they want to make themselves look good.

Zach V.: whats so bad about work?

Darlene D.: Lisa, What's so bad about making yourself want to look good?

Brad N.: People gossip because they feel bad about themselves some how.

Matt S.: My question strayed a lot. It started with the relation of rational to intuitive aspects in education and ended up with why people fear death.

Kelsey M.: lisa... that was my first answer....

Mike S.: Work takes work

Andrea T.: I finally came up with that the reason kids abuse alcohol is because they have low self esteem which comes from an unending cycle of bad parenting.

Kelsey M.: why does sex sell?

Ericka J.: I found that as I got deeper into asking more questions, I really had no answers...they were random guesses.

Manish C.: I saw that in the end we had to choose that person to make decisions for us and we want him to be more repersentative of who our ideal person is.

Matt S.: Kelsey: Because it is interesting and primal?

Teacher: Tina — how, specifically, did that happen? Were you conscious of it at the time or did it just seem to evolve beyond your control?

Tina D.: Neal, personally I think it's important to take breaks during one's academic career. Having a little bit of fun complements the hard work that goes with college life.

Nick W.: Sex sells because people are bored.

B.J.: My questions became absurd quickly as I asked questions about the workplace and the possibility that if people aren't required to take more classes then we might as well have robots take over our day to day jobs.

Matt S.: Brian: Ditto. My experimentation was exactly that. What I'd been told via normal courses of education didn't add up to what I was seeing around me.

Neal R.: Tina: if you were at a private college and had to pay a lot higher tuition, would you have the same opinion?

Lisa C.: Sex sells because it is a prohibited form of expression-we jump on anything that's taboo, that deviates from the day to day cultural norm of existence.

Manish C.: I found me self moving to another question.

Matt S.: Tired of not having meaning in their lives? Or at least, not what they percieve as meaning?

Teacher: If we think of the "Why List" as a process, not a product, then what does it tell us about the process of discovering causal relationships?

> **Nick W.:** Maybe we all need to release some tension in some way.
>
> **Tina D.:** Mr. B: I was conscious of it at the time. It seemed to occur about the 2nd or 3rd question. People looking for thrills, people bored with life, people not happy with decisions in their lives . . .
>
> **Brad N.:** I think my questions went too far from my subject
>
> **Manish C.:** Ask a new why question with my initial question in mind.
>
> **Zach V.:** That causal relationships are complex

As one can see from this brief excerpt (if printed in its entirety, this ten-minute session would continue for another fifteen pages), for the most part these students began with superficial questions and knee-jerk reactions. Like many adolescents, they were more inclined to offer superficial answers than ask questions that would further their inquiry. Some of the questions may not yield thoughtful insights, for they lead to close-ended answers ("Why is it so hot?"). However, one can already see that the collaborative questioning helps individual students dig beneath the surface questions to discover a more challenging line of inquiry. The chances are good that these students will stumble upon personal epiphanies, ones that begin with an initiation to the world but may lead to startling self-revelations. Notice, for instance, Zach V.'s discovery: "The why list helped me realize how many factors their can be in a simple question." Nevertheless, a flawed question riddled with assumptions gives way to a flawed answer and still more flawed questions. At some point, students need to step back from their Why List and consider alternative answers for a particular question, each of which could inspire a different answer.

PERSONAL LITERACY CHALLENGE #2

The Hypertext Why List

In this challenge, synchronous discussions not only help students develop greater discourse literacy, but also encourage them to explore the ideas generated in their Why List to arrive at a more satisfying personal literacy.

By doing so, students are compelled to question assumptions and dive beneath the surface of their initial questions and answers.

What to Do

1. With the aid of a liquid crystal display (LCD) panel, have students present their Why Lists to the entire class.

2. As students present their lists, encourage discussion of each list's evolution and pause to consider alternative questions or answers. Students can quickly demonstrate the thought process involved in the early stages of an inquiry.

3. Following the presentations, arrange the class in small groups to create "Hypertext Why Lists." This can be done on paper, within a text file, or as a hypertext document (depending upon the teacher's comfort level with technology).

4. Each group must generate questions that could potentially invite several responses. Encourage students to write down all the possible answers for each question, then all the possible questions they can think of in response to an answer. Soon, their paper, text file, or hypertext document will be filled with questions and answers that indicate the exponential growth of questions. Figure 4.2 offers an illustration by starting with a question raised earlier in this chapter.

Figure 4.2

Beyond Personal Inquiry: Community Literacy

The sequence of challenges in this chapter demonstrates how classroom teachers can use networked computers to help students develop personal literacy skills. The students' composition of The Why List initiated a personal exploration, helping them delve beneath the surface of their assumptions. However, in some instances they found themselves unable to go beyond certain preconceived notions, their thoughts limited by what they had already embraced as true without understanding why. At that point, they needed to test their ideas within a community, which is what the synchronous, online discussion enabled. Although this encourages a further extension of their ideas and a deeper intellectual odyssey, it may still allow them to neglect certain "blind spots" in their thinking. What if, for instance, their initial question betrays a stubborn assumption, one they cannot perceive because they are too immersed within a culture that accepts the belief ("Why are televisions such a good medium for broadcasting information?"). Worse still, their responses to these assumptions may draw on prejudices that they seldom question because their social milieu does not encourage them to consider alternative viewpoints ("Q: Why is country music so stupid? A. Because only stupid people listen to it."). By employing The Why List in various forms and through various media, teachers can help students move beyond their assumptions to acquire a more satisfying personal literacy.

Indeed, questions are an important technology employed within every class. Too often, however, it is the teacher who generates the questions. By assigning that responsibility to students, however, teachers enable them to acquire more control and ownership of their education. The Why List and the exercises it inspires help students realize the significance of questions, including the way in which particular questions dictate certain answers. This, in turn, teaches them the importance of refining their questioning skills. Ultimately, they cannot ignore the assumptions that their questions and answers rest upon. If the teacher explores those assumptions with students as part of an online exercise, it helps them develop a greater awareness of who they are, the ideas that shaped them, and the history of those ideas. Clearly, this is an essential part of the self-discovery required for personal literacy. Also, it serves students well when they enter a community of inquiry where they need to "read" others as well as themselves.

That thought leads to the focus of the next chapter, which asks students to turn attention away from themselves and look outward, acquiring the skills necessary for community literacy.

Community Literacy: Composing Ourselves in a Virtual Community

A recurring vision swirls in the shared mind of the Net, a vision that nearly every member glimpses, if only momentarily: of wiring human and artificial minds into one planetary soul.

(Kelly 1996, 77)

How does one find a niche within a community, contributing to its development while respecting its ethos? How does one learn to "read" a community from afar? The answer to both questions has more to do with personal maturity and initiation—to both the world and the self—than it does with technology. However, by using networked technology teachers can help students build upon the personal literacy skills discussed in chapter 4, while finding a meaningful place and purpose within an online community (see Figure 5.1).

Prior to the creation of the World Wide Web, champions of virtual community sometimes made it sound as though all one needed to become a

---

Community Literacy

Community literacy is the ability to engage with "the other," developing mutually beneficial relationships through collaborative endeavors intended to transform an indifferent society into a supportive community.

Figure 5.1

member of one was a computer and modem. However, this is akin to saying that all one needs to become a member of a physical community is a street address. In both cases, genuine participation demands far more. Howard Rheingold, an early advocate of virtual community, has observed modern distinctions between *community* and *society* while conceding that these terms may not adequately describe what occurs in cyberspace.

> When we say *society*, we usually mean citizens of cities in entities known as nations. One takes those categories for granted. But the mass-psychological transition that people made to thinking of ourselves as part of modern society and nation-states is historically recent. Could people make the transition from the close collective social groups, the villages and small towns of premodern and precapitalist Europe, to a new form of social solidarity known as society that transcended and encompassed all previous kinds of human association? Emile Durkheim, one of the founders of sociology, called the premodern kind of social group *gemeinschaft*, which is closer to the English word community, and the new kind of social group *gesellschaft*, which can be translated roughly as society. All the questions about community in cyberspace point to a similar kind of transition that might be taking place now, for which we have no technical names. (Rheingold 1993, 63–64)

While we may lack terms to describe some of the online transitions and social groups, we clearly attach different meanings and connotations to *society* and *community*. "Society" is the less personal, modern derivative of the romantic "community." While a public society requires little more than physical existence and common law, a community defines itself through a shared sense of purpose and agreements that hold individuals accountable without necessarily regulating their every action. Societies speak of laws and contracts, but communities rely more upon the implicit trust of covenants and individual commitment to the well-being of the group. Consider, for example, how a school community depends on an understanding of the unspoken rules. By the time students reach high school, they have been conditioned to raise their hands when they wish to speak. How did this come about? Where is this rule written? Perhaps it was written on the chalkboard or poster paper in an elementary school classroom, but by the time students reach high school it is simply understood that this is the way to signal their desire to speak without interrupting someone else. It is a tried-and-true convention that supports turn-taking and civil discourse practices that signal respect for others and a commitment to the well-being of the classroom community.

So what are the rules for discourse in an online community of learners? How do participants facilitate discussions to make sure that turn-taking occurs, that outspoken students pause to let others speak and reciprocate? How do they develop a sense of community rather than become an indifferent society? This is not merely a matter of semantics. Rather, it speaks to the fundamental concept of "sharing" something with others, which is implicit in the ideas of "co-mmunication" and "co-llaboration" within a "co-mmunity." Yet, what if there is no shared sense of purpose, no reciprocal correspondence, and no collaborative effort? Can one honestly apply the term *community* in such instances? Or would it not be more accurate to think of this as a social group whose members, like suburban households sharing the same zip code, possess a common trait but not a common purpose or commitment to one another?

In essence, this describes the difference between genuine, reciprocal relationships and dysfunctional ones. Despite the hype that claims the Internet will fulfill the promise of a "global village," reciprocity remains a critical issue in telecollaborative learning activities. Quite often, students become so preoccupied with what they want to say—which manifests itself in an obsession with *their* postings, *their* Web pages, and *their* life— that they forget to think about the concerns of their community. Consequently, they fail to engage with "the other," forfeiting opportunities to develop the mutually beneficial relationships that transform an indifferent society into a supportive community.

How do educators avoid such a sad state of affairs? The next challenge will help students think about their role within an online community. It places turn-taking in the foreground, emphasizing not only the participants' need to listen to others, but also building upon their ideas in a truly collaborative manner. Hopefully, it will initiate them to the idea of community literacy and the skills required to achieve it.

COMMUNITY LITERACY CHALLENGE # 1

The Sequential Story

The Media Literacy Challenge at the end of chapter 1 offered an exercise designed to help students think about the impact of writing technology upon their writing process. The writing activity at the core of that exercise, which divided the class into small groups, was a "sequential story." Let's return to that exercise now to help develop an online community, engaging students in a telecollaborative writing exercise. Rather than employ a variety of media to compose this story, however, they will conduct all of it through electronic mail.

What to Do

1. Create groups of two to three students.

2. Ask each group to designate a group e-mail address.

3. Create and share with students a "sequence" so that each group knows to whom they should send the narrative when they have finished adding their paragraph.

4. Share the following instructions:
   You have been selected to participate in a unique experience that will blend collaborative work, electronic mail, the Internet, and our collective creativity.

Welcome to The Sequential Story!

Here's how it works. Each group will have an opportunity to write one paragraph of a collaborative story about a person in a place with a problem. Your teacher will compose the opening paragraph, which describes the person, place, and problem. When you receive The Sequential Story, read what others have already written. Then, compose a paragraph that continues the narrative and add it to the bottom of the story. "Forward" your revised version of the story in an e-mail message to the next group on the list, and a send a copy ("cc") to your teacher. To avoid confusion, please DO NOT send a "cc" to anyone else. Here is the "sequence" we'll use:

The Teacher:
1. Group 1:
2. Group 2:
3. Group 3:
4. Group 4:
5. Group 5:

Teacher's Tip

Depending upon the size of the class and ratio of students to computers, divide the group into pairs or trios. Even if there is a 1:1 ratio of students to computers do this to encourage a collaborative effort. If space allows, trios often work well, allowing one student to sit at the keyboard with partners flanked on either side. For a smaller class, pairs will work, but the more groups there are the more chances something will go awry.

6. Group 6:
7. Group 7:
8. Group 8:
9. Group 9:
10. Group 10:
11. The Teacher: Ultimately, the story will return to your teacher, who has an opportunity to bring the story to a close.

Here's what each group should contribute:

As we've seen before, stories are usually about a person in a place with a problem. This story is no exception. Describe what happens to the main character when he or she visits your school (or town, neighborhood, home). One special request: Please conclude your paragraph with a QUESTION that our character may ask the next group on the list. When you send the story on, make certain you type in the correct e-mail address in order to keep the process going.

Case Study: A Telecollaborative Sequential Story

There are many ways to build an online community, but a telecollaborative, sequential story proves to be a good starting point. During a World Links for Development (WorLD) seminar, a group of teachers in Uganda used this exercise to compose the story featured in this case study, "Marabou Michael's Quest." Since the teachers were learning about telecollaboration at a time when their schools lacked Internet connectivity, they created a scenario that closely paralleled their own. The "person in a place with a problem" was Marabou Michael, a teacher who wanted to create an e-mail project for his students but lacked access to the Internet and experience with electronic mail and telecollaborative learning. The respective groups, comprised of teachers from ten different schools in Uganda, were encouraged to offer a brief "dialogue" Michael might have with one of the teachers involved in the training session or a school administrator who was working on the creation of the school's network.

As experienced teachers know, it's essential that they modify exercises like this to meet the needs of their students and curriculum. While this scenario might not apply to many cases, it illustrates how online activities can help establish and support collaborative work and a community of learners. The transcript below is the result of a week's effort, in which the sequential story was passed from the workshop leader to the respective groups. As indicated in the instructions, each group added a paragraph to the narrative before passing it along via electronic mail. While they did meet in face-to-face sessions throughout the week, this exercise could have been conducted entirely at a distance. What mattered most, though, was helping the participants gain an understanding of how members of an online community can help one another, working together to construct something in just one week that they would have needed much longer to accomplish alone.

Marabou Michael's Quest

Teacher: It was another rainy afternoon in Jinja. Marabou Michael was restless. He had just finished reading an article in *The New Vision* that made him anxious. "Innovative Teachers Create Email Projects" read the headline. The article described extraordinary projects that these teachers conducted through electronic mail and the Internet to teach their students in Uganda. Marabou Michael, who taught history and geography at Lugazi High School in Jinja, wondered how he might begin to do such things. He had heard from a friend of his that teachers at Mukono Bishop's College had participated in a recent training program. Perhaps they could help him? Yes, perhaps. So he decided to take a journey to ask the teachers at Mukono Bishop's College this question: "What technology would he need in order to participate in such projects?"

Bishop's: At Bishop's Senior School, the teacher, Mr. Kigozi who is in charge of the computer lab advises Michael that he will need the following items: a computer; telephone line; modem; and a room. He is then advised to proceed to Mwiri for more assistance. At Mwiri he asks this question: "How can I integrate this into the school curriculum?"

Mwiri: At Busoga College Mwiri, the deputy headteacher (Daudi M.) and the two teachers who had earlier on attended a WorLD workshop (Henry M. and Charles K.), advised as follows: the computer had to be a multimedia computer; the telephone line had to be reliable; and they needed a steady and stable power supply. On the question of the curriculum, they did not have all the necessary information and advised that Iganga SS could help out if he asked them: "Which class should I introduce this to? My Western Africa history course or my A-level Land Forms course?"

Iganga: We are planning to run a project on ecology with an A-level class. It is appropriate for us because it requires research and exchange of information with other schools. It does not require any complicated diagrams. As for your case we would advise you to start with African History because it does not require complicated diagrams. For more information we advise you to contact Bukoyo S.S. and ask them: "Which subject do you think is most appropriate?"

Teacher: Apparently, nobody was home at Bukoyo, so Marabou Michael went to Ntare to see if they could answer this question.

Ntare: We think that the most appropriate subject to start with is History. This is because it involves alot of arguments. If different schools are given questions on different topics, the results would be amazing. However, we are sending you to Bweranyange to ask the following: "How long would you give the different schools to send their feedback? How frequently will they exchange email?"

Bweranyange: We would advise one week for a school to get well researched information. Does Kibuli find this idea practical and beneficial?

Kibuli: On arrival at Kibuli, Michael met Richard who had attended the World Links workshop. He agreed with Bweranyange that one week was actually enough time for research, provided you have partners who are active. Michael was then advised to contact Makerere College to ask: "How should he prepare both teachers and students for the project?"

Makarere: At Makerere College School, Michael had a discussion with the three teachers that attended a WorLD Links Training Workshop. Mr. Darnis K., the coordinator, Mr. Peter D., the Assistant Coordinator, and Mrs Joy M., the Headmistress, advised him to link up with either St. James SS in Jinja or Namilyango College in Mukono that have the Internet

connection to help him train the Resource Teachers. For the training of the students, he was advised to contact Bombo SS. "How should he prepare students for the project? What age group should he begin with?"

Bombo: We in Bombo are not very familiar with such projects. We have just had the training in Internet connection but we are equally interested and we have made a start. We would like to advise you to start with the age group between 14 and 16 that is senior 2 to senior 4 students. This is because they would have been in school long enough. However, Kitante may be able to give you more advice. Ask them this: "How supportive is your headmaster of such projects? What must I do to get support from my headmaster?"

Kitante: Mr.K. the deputy headteacher in charge of computer studies informed Mr Marabou that the headteacher at Kitante Hill School has been very supportive of such projects. It may, however, require some funding from the parents. To get support from him about the advantages of email he advised Michael to contact Mr. Buddy, the Worldlinks trainer, for more information on how the parents could be convinced to assist.

Teacher: As a teacher, Marabou Michael, I'm sure you have learned that the best way to persuade parents to do something is through their children. So my advice to you now is to include your students in this community of inquiry. I'm sure they've got a few questions they'd like to ask. So, why not ask them to help you create, develop and sustain an online community? If you build it with them, Michael, I'm fairly certain that their parents will come.

COMMUNITY LITERACY CHALLENGE #2

Putting E-mail in the Right E-nvelope

As The Sequential Story indicates, even the simplest electronic mail activities can inspire enjoyable, educational collaborations. They can do this, that is, if students demonstrate concern for their community, paying close

attention to the individuals and logistics that shape its discourse and interactions. It's also worth noting that the training workshop that produced the sequential story of Marabou Michael had several advantages that teachers may not enjoy while facilitating a telecollaborative learning activity. For one thing, all the participants gathered each day for face-to-face discussions. This provided opportunities to clarify the instructions through traditional classroom interactions. The workshop also presented a fairly controlled setting, with all participants using the same hardware and software. Things are seldom this tidy in cyberspace, however. In the real world—beyond training workshops—the conditions will vary, and participants will occasionally misinterpret instructions or neglect them altogether.

This raises an obvious, though persistent, problem: What should the teacher do when an online community breaks down? How do correspondents handle the confusion when misdirected private messages go to the wrong person or, worse still, a public audience? The print equivalent of this is the situation in which an adolescent writes two letters, one to a grandmother and the other to a friend. Both letters describe what happened at the school dance on Friday night. Of course, the recollection of these events (and the vocabulary used to describe them) is dictated by audience as much as by individual writing skills. After writing the two letters and feeling satisfied they will please the respective audiences, the writer makes the mistake of placing them in the wrong envelopes. Thus, an 80-year-old grandmother gets to read about what went on behind the gymnasium Friday night and a 16-year-old friend hears about "all the really nice chaperones."

One must learn to cope with such awkward moments in life. To help prepare for them in cyberspace let's return to *The Cyberpilot's License* for another challenge to community literacy, "Putting E-mail in the Right E-nvelope." This exercise asks students to consider their course of action when the accidental distribution of a "private" e-mail message through a listserver broadcasts it to a public audience. This presents unique challenges for an online community, especially if its members have not acquired the kind of sophisticated, community literacy required to cope with the situation. What should the sender or recipient of publicly distributed private messages do? How does one handle the conflation of "public" and "private" messages that blurs former distinctions, revealing private intimacies that embarrass the individual and deliver more (personal) information than the community desired?

What to Do

1. To help think through this matter, have students consider a familiar scenario. Imagine that a bored high school student decides to write a personal e-mail message at the end of a class session and send it to a distant peer that she met through a telecollaborative learning activity their teachers had arranged.

2. Share the following message and scenario with students:

The Message

> Hi! I've like finished all my work for this class so I'm gonna use the rest of the time to send you e-mail. This project's kinda cool but it's a lotta work. I wish we could just send fun messages like this instead of doing all that BORING research. Our teacher gets hysterical if we don't find like the best stuff, ya know? After awhile I'm like, omigod, who cares? I don't know about you but my brain aches after searching through all those Web sites trying to find something on our topic. But that's not what I want to talk about. I wanted to tell you about this really cute guy in our class. He's soooo HOT! And nice, too. I've been like flirting with him for the past week and I think he kinda likes me too. I hope so 'cuz he's sooooo HOT! oops, outta time. I'll tell ya more about him manana. ciao 4 now!

The Scenario

Imagine that instead of sending this message to a private e-mail address, as the author intended, that it was accidentally forwarded to a "listserver" that automatically distributed it to an online community's mailing list. Embarrassing, right? Common, too. So, what's the proper thing to do when you're either the author of such a misdirected message or an unintended recipient? Think about this for a moment. Re-read the message. Then, proceed to the next step: the questions.

3. Ask students to use a notebook (such as their Cyberpilot's Journal) to write out their thoughts for two viewpoints before proceeding to the consequences for the recipient and author of a private e-mail message placed in a public "envelope." Tell them to be honest and to think care-

fully about the problem, trying to imagine the potential consequences for each response before advancing to the discussion of them. After all, they'll soon need to make their own judgments in these matters, so it's a good idea to develop their community literacy skills in anticipation of such awkward moments.

4. Share this viewpoint with students:

Viewpoint for Recipients of the Message

What should you do if you're an accidental recipient of a private message? There are many possibilities, but the following are perhaps the most common. In your notebook, jot down what you think about each of these possible reactions, then choose the one that you prefer and be prepared to explain why.

1. Ignore the message

2. Forward the message to others

3. Send a private message to the sender

4. Send a public message to the listserver (i.e. mailing list)

After they've finished writing and thinking about these options, ask students to take a few minutes to discuss them with their classmates in small groups. When all the groups have finished, ask for a "reporter" to summarize responses from each group. It's best to discuss the responses prior to reading the "consequences for the recipient," since they'll have an opportunity to reach their own conclusions before considering some-one else's viewpoint. What's more, they may find that their conclusions, or those of their classmates, are more satisfying within the context of their school and community. When the group is done discussing their own conclusions, discuss the following consequences with them.

Consequences for the Recipient

What should you do if you're an accidental recipient of a private message? Whether you like it or not, your participation in this community of learners requires that you take responsibility for its care and development. What you've just encountered is a message that conflates computer literacy, civil literacy, discourse literacy, personal literacy, and, now, community literacy. What you do, or don't do, will affect everyone in this online community. So it's wise to give this some careful thought before you react. In fact, more often than not an impulsive reaction to a "public e-mail message" causes more problems than it solves. So let's approach this one with a clear head as we consider some alternative approaches.

Ignore the message In many instances this may be the best course of action, particularly if you don't know the author. Why? Well, there's a good chance the author will hear from several other people who *do* know her. For now, rather than overreact, it might be best to view this as an honest mistake. However, if the same author should repeat this error, consider option 3 or 4.

Forward the message to others Not a good idea! In fact, it's probably the worst possible response. Not only are you subjecting the author to further embarrassment, but you're invading privacy and getting cheap thrills out of it. This doesn't speak highly of your ethics. If the author discovers that you've had fun at her expense, making her a subject of ridicule, you can expect similar treatment down the road. Do you really want to set this precedent? Do you really want to create that kind of online community?

Send a private message to the sender If you know the author, this may be the best course of action. After all, the author may not be aware of the mistake. More than likely, this private message went public because the author responded to a message she received through a mailing list, hastily pressing the "reply" button rather than typing her counterpart's personal e-mail address. It's a good idea to break this news gently. You're dealing with someone's feelings, and the shock of this news will likely upset this person. If you don't know the author very well, you might contact someone who does or preface your message by saying, "I was just wondering, did you mean to send that message to everyone?" A question like that is often the best rhetorical approach you can take, because it helps the author see the error without rubbing her nose in it. It also suggests that you're a responsible member of this online community.

Send a public message to the listserv This is not the best option, but if you reach for it be sure to speak in general terms, perhaps as a reminder that the mailing list is reserved for public messages. Just tread carefully. The author is probably embarrassed by the mistake and doesn't need further humiliation. Unless you're looking for enemies, don't single the author out personally; make this a general statement addressing the full community.

5. Share the second viewpoint with students:

Viewpoint for the Author of the Message

What should you do if you accidentally send a private message to a public mailing list? In your notebook, jot down your thoughts on each of these possible reactions, then choose one that you'd follow and be prepared to explain why.

1. Pretend it didn't happen, and forget about it.

2. Send an apology to the mailing list.

3. Change your name and move to another state.

After students have committed their thoughts to writing, ask if they are prepared to explain why they would choose one of these options. If so, take a few minutes to discuss this in small groups. See if they can reach a consensus, creating guidelines—general agreements or principles, not necessarily laws—for their online community. Afterward, please discuss these "consequences for the author" with the students.

Consequences for the Author

What should you do if you accidentally send a private message of this kind to a public mailing list? Here's one way to think about this: What if it had happened in a "face-to-face" discussion in class or in an even larger meeting? If you made a mistake, saying something you really shouldn't have, what should you do? Pretend you didn't say it? Apologize? Flee from the room? Perhaps it's not so strange to discover that this situation parallels your predicament in this online community. The difference, of course, is that no one can see you blushing. However, this leads to new temptations, ones that can prove harmful to the community as a whole. Let's take a brief look, then, at the alternatives we've sketched out.

Pretend it didn't happen, and forget about it This is definitely not a good idea. Ignoring a problem seldom makes it go away. More than likely there are some confused readers out there right now. They haven't a clue what this message is about or why they received it. Don't you owe them an apology? And even if *you* wish to forget it, don't think for a moment that others will let you. At some point, you're going to have to deal with this. In fact, the moderator of the mailing list will more than likely contact you very shortly to remind you of the distinction between personal and public messages, or perhaps someone else will ask if you meant to send that gem to everyone. Why wait for them to tell you what your conscience has already said? Which brings us to the second option.

Send an apology to the mailing list It takes courage and integrity, but most subscribers will understand, forgive, and respect someone who admits the error of their ways—provided, of course, that this doesn't become a habit! Your apology doesn't need to be more than a sentence ("My apologies for sending the previous message to the mailing list"). However, it establishes you as a responsible member of this online community. Learn from the mistake, and take more care before pressing that "Send" button in the future!

Change your name and move to another state Yes, of course it's tempting, but resist the temptation! We're human, after all. We make mistakes. Logging on with a new user name or dropping out of the discussion tells the rest of the community that you're irresponsible. They'll have far more respect if you swallow your pride, admit you made a mistake, and learn from the experience. And while you're at it, remember this experience when you see a "newbie" commit a similar mistake in the future!

Course Web Sites: A Community Work in Progress

Although it may read like fiction, the episode depicted in the preceding challenge remains a common occurrence in online communities. With each new instance, participants encounter difficult questions that merit attention. How, for example, might one prepare for such events—or at least anticipate them? How does one learn to "read" an online community? What rules and regulations guide these communities? Much of this depends on the purpose of the community and on one's place within it. However, the preceding episode inspires three bits of advice that are worth sharing with students prior to their initiation to an online community:

1. Read the community's mission statement and guidelines for participants.

2. Contact the moderator of the community's mailing list if you cannot locate a mission statement or guidelines. Ask about protocol and the rules and regulations.

3. "Lurk" before you leap! This applies to participation in discussion forums, newsgroups, mailing lists, MUDs, MOOs, chat rooms, and more. Students should familiarize themselves with the discourse practices within the community and wait for an appropriate moment to introduce themselves as a new member, ask a question, or respond to a discussion thread.

The creation of a class Web site, an increasingly common classroom activity, could be used to reinforce this counsel. Web site construction serves a number of purposes, provided educators approach it as a collaborative work in progress rather than an individual undertaking at the culmination of a project or course. Unfortunately, a common misconception leads the novice to think of a class Web site as solely a "product" constructed upon completion of a particular project. This can be especially problematic if students—or teachers—work in isolation, creating "digital walls" that are stitched together by hyperlinks at the project's end. Fortunately, new software applications have made it fairly easy to assemble a basic Web site without having to learn the tags that Webmasters have used to write hypertext markup language (HTML). As a result, it is now realistic for teachers to introduce this as a class project to develop community literacy skills. In fact, if educators think of the class Web site as a collaborative work in progress—and an opportunity to practice what they so often preach about the writing process—they can build the site as both an archive and a medium for communication, the former showcasing course assignments and student work while the latter provides interactive writing spaces.

The particulars of a class Web site are left to the imagination and technical skills of the teacher and students engaged in this activity. Rather than stress the technical aspects, it's important that teachers approach this as an opportunity to develop student literacy skills. Much of what has already been discussed—including media literacy, civil literacy, discourse literacy, personal literacy, and community literacy—will apply to this enterprise. What matters most, however, is making certain that students have a genuine sense of ownership, approaching this not as something they must do to satisfy an assignment, but as a cooperative venture. If students and teachers build it together, collaborating in the design, implementation, and maintenance of the site, they can accomplish far more than they would in isolation. Also, this endeavor requires problem-solving skills and a holistic approach that one could not achieve through disparate exercises.

Ultimately, the Web site as a collaborative work in progress is both a creation and reflection of a particular community of learners. It reinforces the notion of community literacy because each individual must consider his or her contribution to the group effort. Students could work in small groups, developing particular sections, but this still requires an understanding of the overarching purpose of the site—the "argument" that the site as a whole wishes to present. Beyond this, the moment they link from a class Web site to an external site, they connect to another member of the Internet community. This is both exciting and problematic, for it will challenge the teacher and students to stretch their literacy skills. How so? Well, if students lack the critical literacy necessary to distinguish good resources from mediocre ones, imagine how readily they might "link" to random sources without careful scrutiny.

Every link contributes to the ethos of a Web site, but this is difficult to impress upon students who lack the critical literacy necessary to distinguish reliable sources from unreliable ones. Chapter 6 discusses how the pathos of fascinating visual images can overwhelm a student's judgment of the content's logos and the creator's ethos. As a result, they may fail to exercise the critical acumen necessary to make good choices or present a clear, coherent argument through the combination of words and images. For that reason, it's best to begin by stressing the sense of community behind a Web page, focusing upon both its form and function, while enabling individual students to learn how each part relates to the whole.

Case Study: Creating a Community Web Site in the Classroom

How might teachers design a course Web site as both an interactive writing space and an archive of student work? Should one create the Web page architecture in advance or include students in the design process as well as the construction? While there are no precise formulas for this endeavor, it clearly helps to approach it as both a process and a product, empowering students through a shared sense of ownership while demanding community literacy skills that ask them to think about the form and function of their Web site. This transports students beyond the words and graphics to a deeper connection with the people within the community that this page represents.

With older, Web-savvy students, the possibilities are endless. One could divide the labors among small groups responsible for designing sections of the site, which will be cobbled together as the semester evolves. With less experienced students, meanwhile, the teacher may wish to establish a simple framework with both interactive and archival spaces, then invite students to join as collaborators in the construction of the Web site as a work in progress. Such was the case for *The Rhetoric of Utopia* homepage, which was created for an undergraduate, computer-assisted course involving a number of HTML novices. The teacher chose to create the architecture in advance, helping inexperienced students see the shape of the site and the function of its sections so they could focus upon content rather than form throughout the semester. Figure 5.2 depicts the index page of the course Web site as it appeared on the first day of class. Two questions immediately come to mind when looking at such a page. Where do the six hyperlinks on this index page lead? How did the teacher choose these categories?

Figure 5.2   Reprinted with permission of R. W. Burniske. Copyright 1999. All rights reserved.

The links take one to a combination of digital archives and interactive communication spaces, which facilitate student interaction as well as electronic publication. In effect, the teacher wanted to create a course Web site that was a communications tool, an online resource, and a record that helped sustain collective memory by preserving its members' contributions. To fulfill this ambition, the teacher relied heavily upon *Critical Tools*, a suite of online tools that make a course Web site truly interactive. Teachers can learn more about these tools and download the freeware necessary to create similar features by visiting the *Critical Tools* Web site hosted at the Computer Writing and Research Lab of the University of Texas (http://www.cwrl.utexas.edu/~criticaltools). Meanwhile, *The Rhetoric of Utopia's* index page (http://www.cwrl.utexas.edu/~burniske/utopia99/index.html) reveals how such tools may contribute to the collaborative efforts of an online community. A quick visit to the Web site will demonstrate how these tools work in an online environment. For now, here's a brief summary of what the respective sections have to offer.

- "The Homepage." The index page provides a context for this community, including the course title, the name of the teacher, academic term, and institutional affiliation.
- "Logistics." The course description, policy statement, assignments, and syllabi describe the sense of purpose, the teacher's expectations, and individual responsibilities.
- "Cybrary." This interactive library, which allows one to locate and contribute resources related to the rhetoric of utopia, supports a collaborative approach to research.
- "Online Learning Records." These electronic portfolios, used in pursuit of more satisfying evaluations (see chapter 8), empower students by giving them an active voice in the assessment process and making the teacher an ally rather than an adversary.
- "Studentopia." This showcase of student work—which includes process journals, essay drafts, and peer reviews—will allow students to publish their work, taking pride in their individual performance while gaining the opportunity to see collective results.
- "Utopian Forum." An archive of asynchronous, online discussion forums enables communication throughout the semester while simultaneously preserving narrative threads.
- "Interchanges." Along with the forums, this archive of transcripts from synchronous, computer-mediated class discussions captures a record of the community's online exchanges. This provides important insights with respect to the evolution of the community and its

discourse, preserving the collective history embedded within the semester's conversations, which are essential to the community's memory.

Building a Community Web Site

How does one present the Web site as an interrelated "community" of documents, pages, and people? How might one show students what one must otherwise tell them about the relationship between the form and function of a Web site? Try this: "Enact" a Web page.

What to Do

1. Collect the following material for this simulation: index cards, a ball of string, two magic markers (one black and one red), and eight volunteers.

2. Ask one volunteer to stand in the middle of the room. Attach a name tag that reads "index.html" to the student's shirt. Use the black magic marker to indicate this is the name of the page, not a hotlink. Inform students that this represents the homepage for the Web site, for it provides the "index" of other features within this community of documents and pages. Beneath the name tag, attach six more index cards written in red ink, each of which symbolizes hotlinks to other sections of the Web site. For example, using *The Rhetoric of Utopia* Web site would yield the following:

    1. logistics/index.html

    2. cybrary/index.html

    3. olr/index.html

    4. student/index.html

    5. forum/index.html

    6. interchange/index.html

    Take a moment to explain that each of these respective sections in the Web site has its own "index," which is why the links from the homepage first direct the browser to a new folder, where they will locate a separate index for that particular section.

3. Now, repeat this process with volunteers who will represent the respective sections. For example, the first volunteer will wear a name tag with the black inscription "logistics/index.html." Beneath that, there should be six red hotlinks: one to each of the other five sections, plus one to the homepage. To discuss the "architecture" of a Web site, take a moment to indicate that the link to the homepage requires going "up" one level within the site's directory, which would be represented as <.../index.html>.

4. After situating the "logistics/index.html" volunteer on the perimeter of the classroom, run a length of string from this individual to the "index.html" volunteer in the middle of the room. The string represents a hotlink, or hyperlink, from the homepage to the "logistics" section of the Web site. What about the links to the other sections? As the rest of the volunteers take their places around the perimeter of the room, forming a circle around the "index.html" volunteer, each will acquire a link with the homepage, plus a link from all of the volunteers who preceded them. This means that each volunteer should be holding six pieces of string, one to the homepage and one to each of the other five sections. Figure 5.3 depicts a scaled-down version of this, minus the intricate network of strings.

5. To simulate the navigation of this Web site, call for a volunteer to "browse" through the site. If they begin in the center of the room, pressing one of the red index cards attached to the "index.html" volunteer, they can proceed to one of the sections on the perimeter. Once there, they have the option to return to the index page or visit another section of the site. This quickly reveals the importance of information architecture, and the intricacies of building a collaborative Web site. Once students understand this, it will be easier for them to present a coherent set of pages representing a complex "community" of interrelated documents.

The Dynamic Archive and the Archival Dynamic

One of the more interesting side effects from the creation of a course Web site as a collaborative, community process rather than as a product created by a select few is its challenge to the print world's distinction between

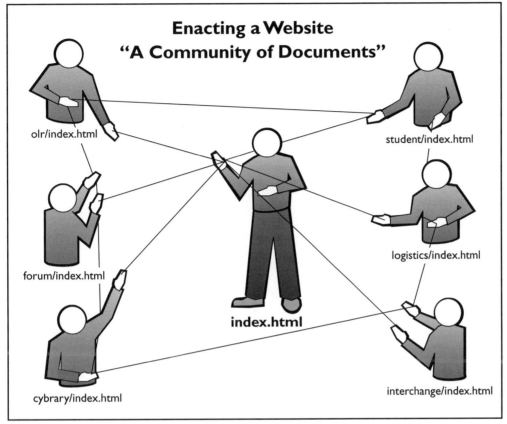

Figure 5.3

dynamic and static elements. This is both a blessing and a curse. The blessing? The possibility of infinite variety. The curse? Is anything stable? Until now, this book has focused mostly on dynamic discourse in e-mail, newsgroups, and discussion forums, yet when educators think of Web sites as "products" rather than "process," they deceive themselves and their students, treating something dynamic as if it were static. The teacher of *The Rhetoric of Utopia* course hoped to challenge this idea, encouraging students to think of the Web site as a virtual meeting place as well as a digital archive. Indeed, only one section ("Logistics") out of six featured on the course Web site did not allow direct student contributions. The screenshot in Figure 5.4 reveals the four principal features of this section.

Despite the Web site's relatively stable character, classroom discussions, scheduling conflicts, and student requests led to numerous changes throughout the semester, revealing the dynamic quality of this seemingly "static" area. Although the teacher retains primary control over the "Logistics" section of the site, he or she may demonstrate responsiveness to

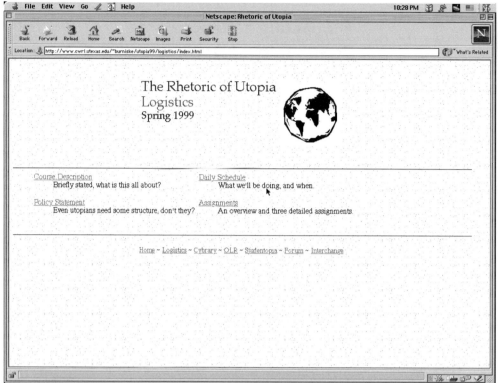

Figure 5.4 Reprinted with permission of R. W. Burniske. Copyright 1999. All rights reserved.

students by changing deadline dates and altering the syllabus throughout the semester. Perhaps the only sections that remained perfectly static—due to institutional regulations—were the "Course Description" and "Policy Statement"; however, the "Daily Schedule" and "Assignments" remained works in progress, enabling the teacher to update sections, create new links, and revise continually.

The tension between static and dynamic qualities also appears in the next section of the Web site, "The Cybrary" (Figure 5.5). In addition to the course texts and recommended readings assembled by the teacher, the "Cybrary" offers two features that turn an archive into an interactive, telecollaborative space. All of the hyperlinks classified as "Utopian References" enable students to recommend an online resource, create a hyperlink to that source, and provide a brief description of it using an "addlink" device. As Figure 5.6 indicates, the teacher can create categories that guide student research while helping to construct a library of online resources that will benefit the entire class, as well as a wider community of scholars, rather than an isolated few. In this instance, the teacher wanted to provide an historical perspective on utopian societies reaching back to ancient civilizations.

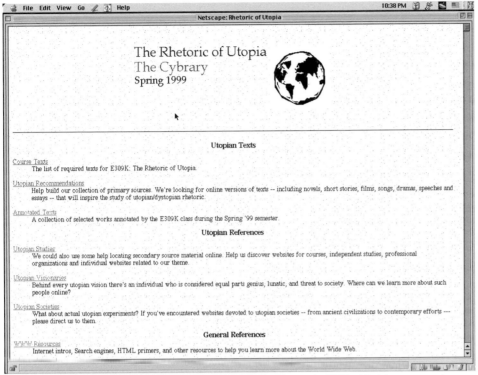

Figure 5.5 Reprinted with permission of R. W. Burniske. Copyright 1999. All rights reserved.

Figure 5.6 Reprinted with permission of R. W. Burniske. Copyright 1999. All rights reserved.

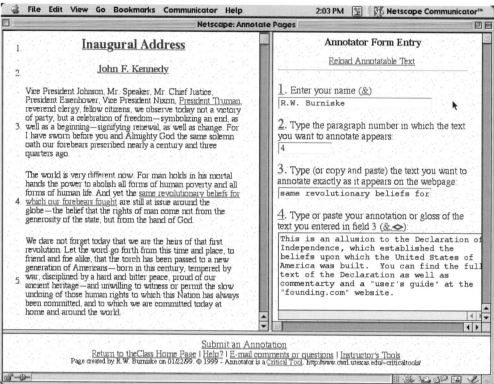

Figure 5.7 Reprinted with permission of R.W. Burniske. Copyright 1999. All rights reserved.

Meanwhile, the "Annotated Texts" link takes one to an interactive "annotator" that allows for the collaborative annotation of a text. With the aid of this device, the teacher can select a text—a poem, speech, or any narrative rich in allusion—and invite students to highlight passages, offer a brief annotation, and provide hyperlinks to online resources. At the start of *The Rhetoric of Utopia* course, for example, the teacher chose John F. Kennedy's celebrated inaugural speech. Working in small groups to encourage collaborative research, students began by drawing one of the speech's allusions from a hat, then proceeded to look for that item using an online search engine. They were instructed to locate several resources but to choose the best one for a recommendation. Finally, they completed the online form pictured in Figure 5.7, providing a brief annotation that described the significance of this allusion and a hyperlink to the online resource that would provide useful background information.

Both the "addlink" and "annotator" features help strengthen the sense of community in a networked classroom. Teachers may wish to initiate this process through in-class exercises, but by extending it to homework assignments, students will learn how telecollaborative efforts can help a

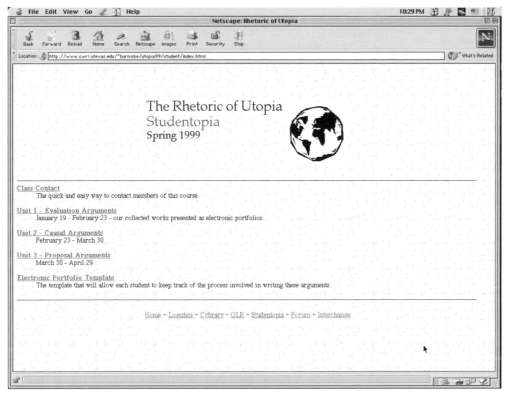

Figure 5.8 Reprinted with permission of R. W. Burniske. Copyright 1999. All rights reserved.

community of learners interpret a text through socially constructed meaning and assist individual members seeking pertinent resources. Such activities are crucial to the development of a community of learners. These activities work best when students see how they fit within the larger context, rather than approaching them as disparate pieces of busywork. As advocates of constructivist principles remind us,

> constructivism cannot make its appearance in the classroom as a set of isolated instructional methods grafted on to otherwise traditional teaching techniques. Rather, it is a culture—a set of beliefs, norms and practices that constitute the fabric of school life. (Windschitl 1999, 752)

The third primary section of *The Rhetoric of Utopia* Web site reserves space for *Online Learning Records,* which chapter 8 examines in its discussion of *evaluative literacy.* This, too, could be dynamic and fluid throughout the semester, or it could be approached as a more static archive. Chapter 8 also describes in more detail the electronic portfolios featured in the "Studentopia" section (Figure 5.8). These portfolios could be arranged so that students upload files through a controlled gateway that

Figure 5.9 Reprinted with permission of R.W. Burniske. Copyright 1999. All rights reserved.

requires an authorized identification and password. Alternatively, the teacher may wish to upload files placed in a class folder. The former empowers students but could make assessment difficult (e.g., when is a "final" draft truly final?); the latter places more of the burden upon the teacher, but does have a greater sense of closure once a project is uploaded. A "Class Contact" feature enables students to provide a "mail-to" form, so that others can send them e-mail directly from the course Web page, as well as a hotlink to their personal Web page, thereby reinforcing the sense of community.

Predictably, the *Utopian Forum* presents the most dynamic area within the Web site, featuring online forums designed to inspire and facilitate discussion. However, one cannot point to this as a purely dynamic area that is all process and no product. After all, once a particular forum is "closed" at the end of a unit of study, it turns into an archive of discussions rather than an active meeting place. Nevertheless, the teacher can add new forums throughout the semester, responding to student requests or sudden inspiration. Thus, the index page listing the forums (Figure 5. 9), as well as the forums themselves, maintain a dynamic quality, reflecting the per-

Figure 5.10 Reprinted with permission of R. W. Burniske. Copyright 1999. All rights reserved.

sonality, interests, and interactions of a classroom community. By semester's end, when the teacher asks students to reflect upon their individual and collective journeys, this dynamic feature will provide a remarkable portrait, a digital "still life" that simultaneously captures the evolution of a community as well as individual strands of their conversation.

Like the discussion forums, the "Interchange" section features text that began as a dynamic interaction but became static the moment transcripts of these sessions appeared on the Web site. As seen before (and as Figure 5.10 confirms), Interchanges can be arranged for either full group or small group discussions. A similar Web site collection might present transcripts from synchronous discussions held in Multiuser Domains (MUDs) or MUD object-oriented spaces (MOOs). Why bother with such transcripts? Why record the online equivalent of a face-to-face class discussion? For one thing, this encourages students to take the synchronous discussions seriously, for they know in advance that their words will appear in the online archive. More important, the records reinforce the idea of the class as an ongoing conversation, affording opportunities for periodic review and reflection. Few things capture the personality of a group like a transcript of its "live" discussions. Here a reader finds the spontaneity, humor, passion, disagreement, agitation, and emotions that define a group of human beings as it tries to shed the skin of an accidental, indifferent society to create an engaged, online community. By semester's end, this collection of synchronous discussions provides an important snapshot of that community's conversations and evolution.

Visual Literacy

While the next chapter focuses upon *visual literacy*, it will draw upon an understanding of community literacy to help one think about Web sites as a process rather than a product. As indicated, Web sites are both the creation and reflection of a community of learners. They may begin as collaborative efforts to synthesize texts, images, and sounds, but they become telecollaborative the moment one contributes to them at a distance or establishes hypertextual links to neighboring Web sites. By understanding the previous types of literacy—media literacy, civil literacy, discourse literacy, personal literacy, and community literacy—students can now apply a healthier critical literacy to their reading of Web sites. Because many authors—and readers—of Web sites pay so much attention to "cool" graphics, chapter 6 will approach these creations through the filter of visual literacy. However, it shall examine these visual effects as an expression of a community's image of itself and its purpose. Thus, community literacy skills, which students acquired and refined in this chapter, must now meet the challenges of *visual literacy*.

Visual Literacy:
Web Sites, Rhetorically Speaking

In no other form of society in history has there been such a concentration of images, such a density of visual messages.

(Berger 1972, 129)

In the beginning, there is the Image.

Before children learn to make words they must rely on physical images to indicate objects of desire. Infants cannot articulate ideas, for they lack the vocabulary to give them expression, but physical images signify a visual world and introduce them to one of the most basic literacies. Nonetheless, one soon wishes to overcome the limitations of a *functional visual literacy*, for the ability to see does not necessarily confer the ability to interpret images. Just as the ability to sound letters and form words provides only the most rudimentary reading skills, so the ability to "see" leaves one short of the *critical visual literacy* one must achieve in order to interpret and understand the visual cues of his or her world (see Figure 6.1).

Visual Literacy

Visual literacy is the ability to read, interpret, and understand what one sees based upon careful examination of the nature and context of the images one encounters.

Figure 6.1

In *Ways of Seeing,* John Berger describes this as a strained relationship between knowledge and vision, one which is at once unresolved and symbiotic:

> It is seeing which establishes our place in the surrounding world; we explain that world with words, but words can never undo the fact that we are surrounded by it. The relation between what we see and what we know is never settled. Each evening we see the sun set. We know that the earth is turning away from it. Yet the knowledge, the explanation, never quite fits the sight. […] The way we see things is affected by what we know or what we believe. (Berger 1972, 7–8)

With the advent of the World Wide Web and "graphical interface browsers" (in other words, software that allows one to see images as well as text), online readers entered a virtual world that presented challenges similar to what Berger describes here. The Web constructs another world of images and text, and first encounters with it may force one to "explain that world with words, but words can never undo the fact that we are surrounded by it." Indeed, as readers broaden their online *bandwidth* (the speed at which information may pass through the network), they invite more complex imagery, incorporating sound and motion pictures to create an elaborate text that presents new challenges to their literacy skills. For many students, "coolness" remains the principal criterion for their evaluation of Web sites, which betrays weak literacy skills. By its nature, this coolness is a superficial concern, one that reveals the intimate relationship "between what we see and what we know" (Berger 1972, 7–8). This concern cries out for development of *visual literacy,* demanding an improved ability to read and interpret what we see on the Web. This, once again, requires critical literacy, acknowledging that one's vision "is affected by what we know or what we believe" (Berger 1972, 8). Without careful examination of their context and deeper understanding of their nature, one may fail to recognize or interpret significant visual cues on the Web, while imagining things that are simply not there.

What Are You Looking At?

How might educators stimulate their students' critical literacy through the development of more astute visual literacy? Once again, this calls for rhetorical analysis. By employing the rhetorical triangle to evaluate Web documents, students can overcome a flawed obsession with "cool" graphics, which often distracts them from flaws within the documents themselves. They might begin with three fundamental questions when they encounter a Web document:

- *Ethos*: What individual, organization, or institution created this document?
- *Logos*: What "argument" does this document make, and is it a logical, coherent one?
- *Pathos*: How does this document attempt to persuade its readers through emotional appeals (visual, aural, or textual)?

The teacher may wish to take a more prescriptive stance, requiring attention to these three essential topics as well as a strict sequence. There's good reason to begin with ethos, testing the credibility of a source before examining the quality of its content (logos). Furthermore, it's wise to investigate logos before turning to the pathos of imagery. As the following case study reveals, this line of inquiry compels attention to matters that might otherwise be forgotten, particularly if the seductions of pathos should overwhelm a student's judgment.

Case Study: The State of the Onion

Mr. Bellamy, the instructor of a rhetoric and composition seminar for undergraduates, had repeatedly admonished his charges to pay close attention to sources they selected from the Internet. All too often, he thought, students would browse the Web looking for something "cool" to put into their essays without considering the source of the information they borrowed. To exacerbate matters, they often failed to provide proper documentation, revealing a scholarly approach that was as casual as it was careless. In the most celebrated instance, one student's citation for a Web site said nothing more than "Internet." Now, as his students prepared for their final essay of the semester, a proposal argument, Mr. Bellamy felt obliged to teach them a lesson in a most unusual manner.

He would pull an April Fools' Day prank.

If successful, it would teach his students the value of visual literacy and the dangers of virtual gullibility. More than anything, he wanted to teach them how to read a Web document with a more critical eye, examining information through the filters of ethos, logos, and pathos. By now, they knew enough about the rhetorical triangle to apply it to written words. They seemed quite capable of analyzing newspaper editorials and short essays that had served as the topic of class discussions. However, something happened when they turned to online sources featuring colorful graphics, animated icons, motion pictures, and sound. To practice what he preached as a composition teacher—"show, don't tell"—Mr. Bellamy wondered how he might demonstrate the consequences of weak visual and textual literacy skills. He wanted to present his students with a document that looked real, even sounded real, but came from an unreliable source or delivered misinformation.

So he went online and used a search engine to locate satirical Web sites. He didn't know where to begin, because he had never before looked for online, satirical publications. He was surprised to find so many but finally settled upon an article in *The Onion*, a weekly publication that specializes in satire (http://www.theonion.com). The article, "America Online to Build Three Million Home Pages for the Homeless," claimed that one of the largest Internet service providers in the United States had announced ambitious plans for a unique social service. Beneath its bold headline (see Figure 6.2), the article featured America Online's (AOL) logo, a picture of Steve Case, the chief executive officer of AOL, and the image of a homeless man pushing a shopping cart full of belongings through snowy streets. Among other things, the article claimed that Mr. Case said "there is room enough for everyone in cyberspace," and that this new program was inspired by the belief that "no American should be without an address."

Mr. Bellamy liked this very much. It was just believable enough to fool gullible readers. The bold headlines, standard journalistic features, and details of the bogus social program established enough ethos to persuade some students that this was an authentic report; the photos of a smiling Steve Case and the man with his shopping cart would capture them through the emotional appeal of pathos; finally, the argument, though clearly flawed, was just persuasive enough to make less critical readers think it a sensible proposal. Would his students see right through this, or would they fall into this satirical web of deceit? Would the seductions of visual imagery overwhelm their ability to critique faulty logic ("Give a person a homepage, and you have given that person dignity")? Would they notice how this satire played with words, combining the ideas of a "home" and

Figure 6.2 Reprinted with permission from The Onion (www.theonion.com). Copyright 1998.

an "address" to create its humor? Mr. Bellamy honestly wasn't sure what would happen, but he decided to give this a try, typing up a brief prompt for an online discussion, one that would help "show" students what he had tried to "tell" them throughout the semester.

On April Fools' Day, Mr. Bellamy greeted his students as he would any other day, then announced that he wanted to hold a synchronous, online discussion to examine a "proposal argument" in preparation for the final essay assignment of the semester. The focus of the discussion would be a proposal he had discovered while reading an online article. He then divided the class of 21 students into three discussion groups, with students numbering off so that the members of the respective groups were not seated beside each other. Students were given five minutes to individually read and study the one-page article on the Internet. They were not allowed to discuss it with their classmates before joining their online groups, which would have approximately ten minutes for their synchronized discussion.

Much to his delight, the groups conducted an extremely animated debate over this proposal. In fact, it was one of the liveliest synchronous, online discussions Mr. Bellamy had ever witnessed. Despite a deliberate prompt, however, the students failed to consider all three points of the rhetorical triangle. To his amazement and alarm, he watched 21 of 22 students fall victim to the prank, engaging in a heated argument over this most foolish proposal. Not until Mr. Bellamy interrupted to ask a question about ethos did 1 student out of 22 pause to consider the source of the information. What follows is an excerpt from the transcript of one of these small group sessions.

April Fools: Homepages for the Homeless

Mr. B: Let's subject the electronic document that you just read to some rhetorical analysis. Here are a few questions to consider:

- Ethos - How does this electronic document establish its "ethos"? Who is its author? Who is responsible for its publication? What type of article is it?

- Logos - What do you think of the "logos" of this document? What are the warrants behind the argument it presents?

- Pathos - Where do you see evidence of "pathos" in this document? How is it used? Ultimately, how effective is this document? Is it persuasive? Why/why not?

Beth: I think there is a problem with the logos in the article.

Ally: I would like to know how many homeless people really want their own website and how many of them would rather have that money put into shelters or public housing.

John: It sounds to me like the guy is trying to build his and the companies ethos. The whole idea seems a bit outrageous, a homepage doesn't eliminate homelessness. I think giving a homeless person a homepage will do nothing to better his life. Once he leaves the computer center he is still be homeless.

Maya: I agree, I don't see how it will help the overall homeless problem in our country.

Beth: The article assumes that a web site is a home.

Linda: logos- By giving the homeless a webpage, the pain of being homeless is cured? That sounds absurd.

Duane: I agree with yall, this idea is pretty lame... he's just trying to make his cmpany sound good, establish his ethos.

Maya: I guess it may give these people something to do and mabye that will ultimately get them motivated to do something, but directly I don't see a correlation

Ally: The whole subject seems really absurd to me. Apparently Mr. Case needed something to make him feel a little better about himself, like he was making some BIG contribution to society. HA HA HA

Duane: I mean what can a homeless person put on his web page?? And how many do u actually think is going to waste their time to go to a shelter and mess with the computers.

Maya: I THINK MR. STve Case, has nothing better to do with all his money than to make it seem as if AOL is helpling world problems

Beth: Homeless people aren't going to have easy access to a computer. The money for the computers should go to basic living needs.

Maya: I agree Duane, I doubt half of those people can read

Maria: Mr. Case needs to worry about feeding these people if he wants to help. A web address is not going to feed them.

Maria: His intentions are very questionable. He just wants to make AOL more marketable.

Duane: yeah I think he should just donate those money to the charity or something, instead of wasting time and money on this idea.

Beth: If they can't read, there is no way that they will be able to understand the internet.

John: I think it will just give them something to do for a good hour a day to take their minds off of their life style.

But ultimately they are going to get bored with it after they have put all they can on the web site.

Ally: I just finished reading this John Grisham novel about homeless people and never realized how overlooked they are by the government and everyone else, so reading about AOL's little contribution to the poorest of the poor really sets me off.

Duane: I agree with John

Mr. B: I agree with many of your points about the issue raised in this piece, but have you considered the source? Who was the author? Where was this published? How would you evaluate its ethos?

Beth: I think AOL wants to improve their image. The article makes it seem like they are doing something that will save all homeless people.

John: That is a big assumption saying that the majority of homeless people can not read, I don't think right now we can really tell how many of them are really illiterate or not.

Maria: Then again, even if Mr. Case's intentions are self-centered, the project might actually result in something positive. The homeless may become motivated, and by creating their own website they can learn a lot. Maybe they'll even find a job or want to find a job.

Maria: I agree with Beth.

Maya: Sorry I'm sounding so cinical, but I really don't see a point in making computers and technology accessible to homeless people who do absolutely nothing....If Steve Case really wants to add to logos, why not provide jobs with all the money he has to help the homeless

Duane: Well his ethos is good, I mean he is the president and the CEO, so many people will think that he's trying to help but really he's trying to gain ethos for AOL.

Maya: true

Maria: Who wrote this article. Onion, Inc. Is this all a joke?

Beth: AOL has had some problems in the past that hurt their ethos. Maybe this is a way to build it back.

Linda: But is there any harm with what he's doing?

Duane: is this how we're suppose to evaluate a web page? Because I'm confused about how we're suppose to do out assignment.

Duane: our

Maria: How accurate is the article? Did Mr. Case really say all this? The site doesn't even say who wrote it.

Ally: The article is a big SATIRE!!!!

Maya: In his quotes, Steve Case is sucking up major pathos, probably because he can't depend on his logic to gain support

Maria: Is Onion, Inc. like the National Inquirer?

Ally: Look at the bottom of it. It's just a made up story to try to get people to think.

Linda: ya, it's pretty absurd, maybe it is a joke.

Maya: What!!!!!!!!!

Ally: Fiction!!

Maya: Roger That Ally

John: I don't think it will motivate them to get a job. I really think it will just side track them and help them put a side for a few minutes the fact that they don't have a job. It will just entertain them so they don't have to deal with not having a job.

Maya: Don't Agree

Ally: Can you believe just how irate we became over something that was not even true?

Maria: What it says doesn't matter. We can't believe everything we read. It's off the Internet. We have to be careful.

Duane: I think this is all just a waste of time, Case has too much time and money on his hand, so he just want to try to establish some ethos for his company.

Student Reflections

What did the students learn from this exercise? Following the synchronous discussions and the revelation that this had been an April Fools' prank, Mr. Bellamy asked each student to read the transcript of the synchronous discussions, which he posted on the class Web site, and then type a brief reflection on what caused them to fall for this foolish prank. In the first of these, Jennifer B. offers one of the most common reactions, lamenting her failure to consider the source and pay attention to the ethos of the Web document.

> I fell for this April Fool's trick because I assumed it was from a legitimate source. Being in a classroom setting, I did not think that the exercise would be fake. I was concentrating more on the assignment than I was on the source. In reading the Interchange that took place after reading the article, I noticed only one person in the classroom said anything about The Onion as the source. Even after it was posted that the document was fake, no one responded. It was as if no one cared and that they were more concerned with the other aspects of the exercise. I fell into the same trap as the rest of the class. It has taught the class and myself to always begin with the legitimacy of the source.

Jennifer B.'s comments reveal a disturbing tendency, which one might describe as the "transferal of ethos" from one source to another. In this instance, Jennifer and her classmates transferred the teacher's ethos, and their expectations for the kind of article their teacher would choose, to the Web document they encountered. Based on informal surveys of students, this seems a common phenomenon. In the following reflection, Brent S. reinforces this notion. He explains his misreading as a consequence of blind faith in the professor and susceptibility to the pathos of the text and images he encountered, which resulted from a preoccupation with the article's appearance.

> Why did I fall for this article? Well, first of all, I guess I believed it because Mr. B. told us to read it. It was

> something he had found and gave to us. That gave it some credibility in my mind. I thought, "Well, Mr. B. gave it to us, it's most likely not a joke." Why would he give us something to discuss if it weren't real? Now I know why he did it, but that is the main reason why I thought it was real. I also believed it because it looked real. It looked like any other article you would find in an on-line newspaper. It had pictures. It just looked authentic. This experience has hopefully taught me to be more critical of the things I read, especially when they are on the Internet.

There is also the matter of the message. Where the first two reactions stress ethos and pathos, Kara W.'s reflection touches the third point on the rhetorical triangle. She notes the way in which preoccupation with an item's logos—and the heated debates it inspires—can blunt one's attention to other points on the triangle.

> I bought into the article simply because I did not check out the source or author. In fact, it seems that the entire group focused on the logos of his argument, and a little on the pathos. But no one gave a single thought on his ethos. We all over looked the fact that there was no author, no credentials, and no justification as to why this guy has any authority to write the article. Strange, seeing as how this class emphasizes all THREE parts of the rhetorical triangle, and we managed to totally ignore one. In the future, we must all be more wary of where the information is coming from.

Obviously, statements like these are cause for hope, suggesting that this student has learned a valuable lesson about the rhetorical analysis of Web sites. As this final reflection indicates, an exercise such as this helps students learn a good deal about visual literacy and their own skills. Kelly, the author of the following reflection, had already created her own Web pages and used the Internet extensively for research, yet she couldn't resist the seductions of this satirical presentation. Rather than attempt to explain or excuse her misreading of the document, she seizes this opportunity to look upon her own mistakes and learn from them. Much to her credit, she draws valuable lessons from the exercise, recognizing her own tendencies and realizing the actions she must take in order to prevent future misreadings.

> It is interesting to see the discussion others had about the subject. It seems I was not the only one who was duped into thinking AOL was actually going to implement this program. It just shows how people are incredibly vulnerable. It is a little bit scary to think that I can be tricked so easily. This was a harmless joke, but if I believe everything I read than I could be giving people false information and perhaps harming myself and others. In the future, I need to look at the source more carefully. If I would have just looked at the address I would have seen that this did not come from AOL. It is important to examine the address. Who is writing it? Why are they writing it? What audience are they writing to? And what message are they trying to portray? These are some of the questions I need to start asking myself instead of immediately divulging into the article.

Seeing Is Believing (and Other Satirical Lessons)

There are many lessons to be learned from this exercise, but perhaps one of the most important echoes John Berger's earlier observation: "The way we see things is affected by what we know or what we believe." These students, who in many ways are fairly typical undergraduates at a public university, fell for this prank because of what their eyes told them they were seeing. Aesthetically, this item looked like something they might find in the online version of a newspaper or magazine. The bold font style, the color photos, and the AOL logo made them believe they were looking at an authentic document. However, the key to this exercise, and one that Mr. Bellamy understood intuitively, is the manner in which the item is presented. Had the teacher prefaced the exercise by saying, "I thought we'd have some fun on April Fools' Day by looking at some satirical Web sites," students would have brought that expectation—that "belief system"—to their reading of the document. However, since the teacher tied the exercise to the students' assignment—a proposal argument—they brought different expectations with them, expectations that influenced what they saw and how they interpreted it. This speaks volumes about the importance of teaching visual literacy skills. Although educators may not think in these terms yet, the exponential growth of the World Wide Web and Internet connectivity in schools compels them to find ways to teach visual literacy. Exercises like Mr. Bellamy's may help students resist the seductions of fancy graphics and overcome the visual cues that excite the passion of pathos and overwhelm judgment of the author's credibility and logos.

Measuring the Sum of a Web Site's Parts

In Mr. Bellamy's case, one can see how the use of computer technology assisted him in teaching his students about visual literacy. Students began by reading an online publication, then conducted an online synchronous discussion before they reviewed the transcripts published on the class Web site. They then wrote a reflection that would appear in their online portfolios. Obviously, this requires a sophisticated level of technology integration, but as schools gain Internet access and teachers devise new ways to employ technology for teaching literacy, learning activities like Mr. Bellamy's could become fairly common. Nevertheless, teachers need a strategy for improving students' critical reading of Web sites, one that calls attention to the seduction of cool graphics, the weakness of poor logic, and the importance of an author's credibility. This is a complex challenge, certainly, for it requires a rhetorical analysis of Web sites that argues for a much more sophisticated visual literacy.

Teacher's Tip

While some teachers may feel conflicted about deceiving students in this manner, since the relationship between student and teacher depends upon trust, failure to provide an exercise of this kind could leave students susceptible to the rhetoric of Web documents. "What am I looking at?" should be the first question one asks about Web documents, which is precisely what this exercise teaches students to do. To replicate this exercise, select a satirical article or parody from an online publication. If one chooses a well-known publication such as *The Onion,* make sure the hyperlink takes the group directly to a document buried deep within the pages of this Web site. This will force students to seek background information rather than having it handed to them on the homepage.

Perhaps the greatest challenge for teachers will be the presentation of this material. They must try not to betray their intentions, revealing the nature of the article. Ask students to read silently, write a response (before group discussion), and then have a synchronous discussion, either online or face-to-face, to discuss the ethos, logos, and pathos of the selected document. Alternatively, break the class into small groups and have each group look at a

Once again, it's important to distinguish parts from the whole. In the previous exercise, students focused on a Web document, which could be an essay, song, movie clip, or any other item presented on a Web page. In order to succeed, Mr. Bellamy's students needed to examine the Web page as a whole, understanding its context and purpose. Instead, they chose to treat it as an isolated page, neglecting its hyperlinks to other online documents within *The Onion's* Web site. If they had taken that step, their analysis of the individual document would have led them to inquiries about the electronic publication in which it appeared as well as its creator's purpose. Clearly, this is a complicated process, placing rather extraordinary demands upon a reader, but unless students make such an effort their visual literacy skills will remain stunted, achieving a functional literacy, but not a critical one.

Teacher's Tip (continued)

different satirical Web document. They could begin individually, writing a critique that would let the teacher assess their visual literacy, then turn to small group discussions that culminate with oral presentations. At that point, the teacher will need to bite a lip and let each group complete their report before informing the class about the nature of the respective documents. It's a tough trick, certainly, but a lesson students will never forget.

Case Study: The Rhetorical Analysis of a Web Site

A graduated approach to visual literacy in cyberspace, beginning with a variety of Web documents and Web pages before undertaking the analysis of Web sites, will help teachers devise exercises appropriate to their students' age and ability. Where might one begin? Perhaps another case study will help. Let's take a look at the *Utopian Visions* Web site (http://www.en.utexas.edu/uv) which was created for a global, educational project. Take a moment to visit the site's homepage and review the background information provided in a section entitled "The Vision" (see Figure 6.3). While reviewing the site, ask the following questions:

- How does this site establish its ethos (credibility)?
- How is the logos (message) delivered, and is it a clear, coherent one?
- How do the graphics and text create pathos (emotional appeal to audience)?

Figure 6.3 Reprinted with permission of R. W. Burniske. Copyright 1999. All rights reserved.

Now then, let's conduct a preliminary investigation that will inform the rhetorical analysis of other Web sites. To start, imagine conducting a similar exercise with more conventional texts. An experienced reader of a printed document knows what to look for when answering such questions. The names of the author and publisher appear right at the front of a book, along with the place and date of publication. However, what if a student forgets to look for that information, as was the case with Mr. Bellamy's students? Or, worse yet, what if that information cannot be located on a Web document or site? In the case of the *Utopian Visions'* Web site, there are links to the author's personal page and a date of revision at the foot of the homepage, while "The Vision" provides the background information necessary to place this document in its proper context. How can one verify this information, making certain that one is not the victim of yet another prank? Look beyond the site itself, investigating the credentials of its creators and their institutional affiliation. If possible, use contact information or a "mail-to" form to correspond with the project coordinator or Web site manager via electronic mail. This provides a rare opportunity to check the veracity and legitimacy of the source.

What of the logos and pathos, though? How might students evaluate these? How important is visual literacy in cases where the document offers minimal graphics? This Web page presents itself like a message board or newsletter, presenting five major project categories with a "newsmaker" layout. "Dialogues" are apparently important, which explains why they are placed at the center of the page. The graphics, meanwhile, seem designed primarily to help the reader identify this as the "UV" Web site. The navigation bar at the left and bottom of the page will help visitors move through the site in a logical fashion.

What other questions should students ask in order to evaluate a Web page like this? Where do they begin? How might they proceed?

For starters, most students need guidelines for the critique of a Web site. To help them think of visual literacy as a critical literacy they must subject the entire document to a rhetorical analysis, adopting a systematic approach rather than a random one. Schrock's *Guide for Educators* (http://discoveryschool.com/schrockguide/eval.html) provides a useful starting point, offering evaluation forms for elementary, middle, and high school students. However, teachers might wish to modify the forms to suit their students and circumstances. For example, the following modifications bring the rhetorical concerns of ethos, logos, and pathos to the forefront. Notice the order in which they are presented. Mr. Bellamy's lesson revealed the importance of stressing the ethos (credibility of the source) of a Web document before taking its logos (logic of the message) too seriously; meanwhile, it's a good idea to place the pathos (emotional appeal to the audience) in the background, since the premature emphasis of this—as the reader has seen—may overwhelm a student's critical thinking, precluding careful analysis of ethos and logos.

VISUAL LITERACY CHALLENGE #1

The Rhetorical Analysis of Web Documents

To model the evaluation process, the teacher may wish to have each student evaluate the same Web document the first time. Subsequent exercises might allow students to look at a Web site of their own choosing.

What to Do

1. Ask students to evaluate a Web document chosen by the teacher.

2. Before distributing the evaluation form, discuss the distinctions between a *Web document,* a *Web page,* and a *Web site.* In Mr. Bellamy's case, he asked his students to evaluate a Web document located on a single Web page within a Web site. However, to do that successfully, students must place the document and page within the context of the site as a whole, which is why evaluation begins with general information and a concentration upon ethos before moving to specifics (see Figure 6.4).

Web Document Evaluation

Name of the Web site you are evaluating: _____

URL of the Web site you are evaluating: http:// _____

Access to the Web site:

Via modem? 4800 — 9600 — 14.4 — 28.8 — 33.6 — 56k

Direct connection? T-1 T-3 Other: _____

Browser: ___ Netscape ___Internet Explorer ____ Other (Name: _____)

Part I. Ethos—Authority

1. Who created the Web site? _____
2. What organization is the person affiliated with?_____
3. Is the author's name and/or e-mail address included? - YES / NO
4. Is there a date of last update? - YES / NO
5. If so, is the date current? - YES / NO
6. Does the domain (i.e., .edu, .com, .gov) of the site influence your evaluation? - YES / NO
7. Are the spelling and grammar correct on the page? - YES / NO
8. Are you positive that the information is accurate and truthful? - YES / NO
9. What can you do to check its accuracy?
10. What kinds of secondary sources would help your evaluation of this site?

Part II. Logos—The Content

1. Is the title of the page indicative of the content? - YES / NO
2. Is the purpose of the page indicated on the homepage or elsewhere? - YES / NO
3. When was the document created and updated? _____

Figure 6.4 Adapted with permission of Kathleen Schrock. (Figure 6.4 continued on next page)

4. Is the information useful and significant? - YES / NO (Why/Why not?)
5. Would it have been easier to get the information somewhere else? - YES / NO
6. Did the information lead you to other sources that were useful? - YES / NO
7. Is the information current? - YES / NO
8. Does up-to-date information matter for your purpose? - YES / NO
9. Does the information appear biased? - YES / NO
10. Does the information contradict something you found somewhere else? - YES / NO
11. Do the pictures supplement the content of the page? - YES / NO
12. Is a bibliography of print or online sources included? - YES / NO

Part III. Pathos—The Visual (and Technical) Aspects of the Web Site

1. Do the visual images help/hurt the page? - YES / NO (Why/Why not?)
2. Does the page take a long time to load? - YES / NO
3. Are there helpful headings and subheadings on the page? - YES / NO
4. Is the format standard and readable with your browser? - YES / NO
5. Is there an image map (clickable graphic w/links) on the page? - YES / NO
6. If you have graphics turned off, is there a text alternate to the images? - YES / NO
7. On supporting pages, is there a link back to the homepage? - YES / NO
8. Are the links clearly visible, explanatory, and easy to navigate? - YES / NO
9. Is there a sound or video clip included? – YES / NO
10. If so, can you be sure that the video and/or sound have not been edited? – YES / NO
11. If you are not sure, should you accept the information as valid? - YES / NO

Part IV. Narrative Summary and Proposed Criteria for Evaluation

Looking at all of the data you have collected and the judgments you have made, discuss the criteria for your evaluation of this Web site. Consider the ethos, logos, and pathos of the site, and support your assessment with specific examples.

Figure 6.4 (Continued)

VISUAL LITERACY CHALLENGE #2

Web Sites and Evaluative Arguments

There are many other questions to ask about the documents, pages, and sites one encounters on the World Wide Web. However, an evaluation form with guiding questions provides a structure for a thorough, rhetorical analysis of these items. After working collaboratively on the evaluation of a common Web site, students should test their skills upon sites of their choosing. The teacher may use this opportunity to discuss different genres, beginning with the idea of an "educational Web site." What, for instance, makes a Web site educational? Is it the information on its pages? How does one define "information" on a Web page? Does one include graphics in that definition? This provides an opportunity for students to write a "Why List" (see chapter 4), investigating ideas to discover their own beliefs, which are more than likely undeveloped. Afterward, the teacher may wish to assign an essay that offers an evaluative argument based upon the students' examination of the Web site's rhetorical elements. This will demand critical thinking, drawing upon a number of literacy skills, including those required for visual literacy. Here are some guidelines for that exercise.

What to Do

1. Ask students to choose a "hypertext" document and evaluate it based upon three criteria (a, b, and c) that they establish. Their evaluative claim should use the following formula:

   > X is (or is not) a good example of Y because it has (or does not have) features A, B, and C.

2. Tell students they can use any of the following suggestions to write their evaluative argument, or choose a topic of their own, provided that the subject of their evaluation is an online hypertext. Indeed, they may wish to evaluate whether:
   - an "educational Web site" is (in)effective as an educational tool.
   - a "government Web page" is (un)successful as a resource for its audience.
   - a "nonprofit organization's Web document" is (in)effective publicity.
   - a "business Web site" is (in)effective as an advertising tool.
   - an "online essay" or "electronic magazine" is an (in)effective publication.

3. Share these writing tips with students:

Remember the value of "controversy" in your arguments. Your evaluation won't succeed if a preoccupation with graphics and special effects leads you to ignore the ethos and logos of the document, producing a thesis that stirs only agreement. BEWARE: Do not mistake style for content! Concentrate on the content of your hypertext document as much as its "design" and graphics.

Be sure your criteria for evaluation are appropriate to your subject, since you will have to establish their validity. For example, you may have to explain why the criteria you would apply to critique an "educational Web site" would be different from those you might apply to a "business Web site." For suggestions on how to do this, visit *Evaluating Web Resources* (http://www2.widener.edu/Wolfgram-Memorial-Library/webeval.htm), an online guide written by researchers at Widener University's Wolfgram Memorial Library.

Be specific. The more you narrow your topic, the easier it will be to develop. It will help to have an audience in mind as well as a purpose. If necessary, create a scenario to help yourself. Imagine you're a consultant for a school, business, or institute that wants feedback on its newly designed Web site. Or, imagine you're a panelist at a conference on the future of publishing, and you've been asked to evaluate a hypertext—an online book, magazine, or essay—to determine the effectiveness of this new medium. Use your imagination, as well as your critical thinking skills, and you'll find this exercise both stimulating and rewarding.

State your topic proposal. Your topic proposal should state your evaluative claim or thesis, explain why you think evaluating your subject is "problematic," and describe the criteria you tentatively plan to use in your evaluation.

Global Literacy

After studying the complexities of visual literacy—learning to see online documents as they are, not as preconceptions tell us they should be—students are better prepared for an even more ambitious literacy. This one speaks to the promise of the Internet, which is an "international network" of computers that enable telecollaborative learning activities. Behind the rhetoric inspired by the notion of a "global village," however, lurks a series of challenges that are not for the faint of heart. In order to meet those challenges, teachers must be prepared to bring all of the previous literacies to bear, challenging students to stretch their limitations beyond municipal, state, regional, and national boundaries. In short, it is time for them to acquire *global literacy*. The only problem? How can teachers teach something that they have not learned themselves? How might educators design and facilitate telecollaborative learning activities that inspire global literacy?

Global Literacy:
Reading, Writing, and Dancing to a Global Beat

True ease in writing comes from art, not chance,
As those move easiest who have learned to dance.

(Pope 1979, 2202)

The advent of the Internet signaled the arrival of a brave new world, one that made it easier to correspond with global neighbors, though not necessarily communicate with them. After all, there's far more to communicating than sending and receiving messages through networked computers. One cannot realize exciting new possibilities without confronting a multitude of challenges and responsibilities. The fundamental shift from a local classroom, in which the teacher has autonomy, to a global classroom, where students and teachers collaborate with distant peers, presents some of the greatest challenges. How many students—or teachers—are prepared for such global discourse, particularly in schools where provincial curricula still prevail? This issue seems to have escaped both the technophiles promising a global village and the educational experts promoting a rather impoverished brand of cultural literacy. Consider, for instance, the following endorsement, distinguished by its omissions as much as its emphasis:

> Educational policy always involves choices between degrees of worthiness.
> The concept of cultural literacy helps us to make such decisions because
> it places a higher value on national than on local information. We want to

make our children competent to communicate with Americans throughout the land. (Hirsch 1987, 25)

It didn't take long for the Internet to challenge such views. How can anyone think of cultural literacy in such nationalistic terms now? Have educators not, in their haste to connect schools to the Internet, opened themselves to a discourse that asks their students and teachers, in effect, to "read and write" the world? Once again, educators must broaden their definitions, doing for cultural literacy what chapter 1 proposed for computer literacy. This means educators must help students acquire the *global literacy* necessary to interpret and respond to the words of distant peers.

Global Literacy

Global literacy is the ability to read, interpret, and contextualize the messages encountered through global, telecollaborative activities and effectively communicate with their distant authors.

Figure 7.1

Yet, how does one get from here to there?

How might educators prepare themselves and their students for such a demanding discourse and literacy? What follows is primarily intended for teachers, offering assistance with the thought process involved in the creation, design, and facilitation of a global, telecollaborative project. Although it differs from earlier discussions, and offers fewer exercises for students, its principal aim is to help teachers think carefully about global, educational projects and the skills students will need to develop if they wish to acquire global literacy.

GLOBAL LITERACY CHALLENGE #1

Dancin' to a Global Beat

Anyone who has ever landed in a foreign place where they couldn't speak the language or read the road signs and menus has learned valuable lessons about human communication and personal limitations. Travelers must stretch those limitations, overcoming the initial disorientation to connect with the place in which they find themselves and the people who live there. In many ways, this captures the spirit of global, telecollaborative learning projects: They are the virtual equivalent of travel that makes one a stranger in a strange land. To help prepare students and teachers, it's helpful to simulate this kind of disorientation prior to the start of a project.

To accomplish that objective, as well as stimulate fruitful discussions that sensitize students to the challenges of global literacy, teachers may wish to arrange an activity that employs the universal language of music.

What to Do

1. Create or purchase a short anthology of "Music of the World," arranging several fifteen-second sound clips from distinct regions and cultures. A two- to three-minute tape is sufficient, since it presents eight different sound clips; a three-minute tape presents twelve.

2. Divide the class into groups of four or five students, and arrange them in circles around the room.

3. Instruct them to improvise a dance—either as a group or individually—to the "song" you are about to play. Don't tell them that the song is a pastiche comprising excerpts from several songs. Just tell them to improvise a dance that responds to the music, encouraging them to "feel the rhythm" of the song. Play the tape, and observe their reactions.

4. Following the performance, ask the groups to discuss why it was so difficult to improvise a dance to this unusual song. Have students make a list of things that made it difficult.

5. Then, engage the full group in a discussion. Why did they feel so awkward trying to shift from the music and rhythm of a Balinese *gamelan* to a South African *a capella* group, Viennese waltz, Andean flutes, Louisiana jazz, and so on?

Here's a partial answer: Each of these snippets presents a different "rhythm" that grows out of a rich cultural heritage and a distinct pace of life. Trying to dance to a compilation of all of them was probably a novel experience, unlike any dance the students had ever tried before. It's likely the whole thing felt rather odd to them. The fact that they didn't really know the "purpose" of this dance, probably made them uneasy to begin with. Then there was the "venue": How often do teachers ask students to dance in a classroom? The music itself was strange, presenting unusual rhythms and sounds, which seemed to change the moment the dancers grew accustomed to them. And what about the dance steps? Did anyone really know the steps, or was everyone simply making them up as they went along?

Despite its unconventional approach, this simulation demonstrates some of the principal challenges of global, telecollaborative learning activities. By taking just half an hour to arrange this simulation and group discussions, the teacher will help students understand the difficulty of trying to collaborate online with people from different cultures. This simulation is also one of the most important lessons to remember when something goes awry in a global, telecollaborative dance.

The Design and Facilitation of a Global Telecollaborative Project

While the preceding exercise offers an amusing diversion, it also carries a serious message: It's often difficult to collaborate with people from different linguistic, cultural, and national backgrounds. To *collaborate* means to "share the labors," and yet how can people do this successfully when they are divided by language, culture, and geographical distances? This is not a question often raised by technophiles who speak of the "Internet revolution" as an educational panacea, but it remains an inescapable issue for educators who engage in this type of learning activity. Does it mean that teachers should wait until they've developed global literacy before undertaking such endeavors? Perhaps, but not necessarily. If teachers wait to develop such skills or wander the globe before collaborating with distant colleagues, they may never get onto this particular dance floor. What they should do, however, is approach global, telecollaborative activities with realistic expectations. They might also extend their dance metaphor, thinking of global literacy as a dance that raises five fundamental questions:

- What is the purpose of the dance?
- What is the dance venue?
- Who will be the dance partners?
- What is the music and rhythm?
- What are the dance steps?

These questions provide a useful starting point for educators who wish to design an original telecollaborative learning project. What's more, if approached as a sequence, they help one understand the relationship between the design and facilitation of such activities while anticipating the needs of telecollaborators around the world.

Question #1: What Is the Purpose of the Dance?

Every dance, whether a formal wedding dance or an impromptu New Year's Eve celebration, has a purpose. The same applies to the telecollaborative dance. This should not come as news to teachers conditioned to state the learning objectives for each study unit. Indeed, this is the same starting point teachers have for most classroom activities: How will it meet students' needs and fulfill the curricula inherited from a department, school district, or national examinations board? Though the objectives are liable to change, teachers should at least state the starting goals for a global telecollaborative project, making sure it fulfills curricular aims rather than becoming an "extracurricular" activity that places undue stress on everyone involved.

For this reason, and others, teachers should explore the possibilities, conducting online research to see what kinds of projects exist. Before one tries to write a sonnet or paint a watercolor picture, after all, it helps to become familiar with the genre. The same applies to global, telecollaborative learning activities. Not all of them are alike. In fact, there are many variations on this theme. Familiarity with telecollaborative learning activities will help classroom teachers in two ways: First, they will know what they are looking at when they encounter an online project; second, familiarity will strengthen their own repertoire, affording a number of choices as they begin to design an original project to suit their students and curricula.

Until late in the 1990s this was difficult to do, but classroom experiments and research studies have led to a taxonomy of activity structures for telecollaborative learning activities. Harris's (1998) investigation and categorization has yielded three primary genres:

- Interpersonal Exchanges
- Information Collection and Analysis
- Problem-solving Projects

In addition to describing these archetypes, Harris also provides several variations on each in her book, *Virtual Architecture* (Harris 1998). This research helps classroom practitioners envision different approaches to telecollaborative learning and how it might fit within their curricula. By familiarizing themselves with these approaches or "lurking" as silent apprentices in an existing project, teachers can take "dance lessons" that will help them feel more comfortable once they get out on the floor. There are also a number of telecollaborative "dance instructors" that offer online assistance. Here, for example, are a few sites where one may glean project archives and learn about the ways in which educators have designed telecollaborative activities:

1. Blue Web 'N (www.kn.pacbell.com/wired/bluewebn)
2. International Education & Resource Network (I*EARN) (http://www.iearn.org)
3. The Global Schoolhouse (http://www.globalschoolhouse.org/)
4. NickNacks (http://home.talkcity.com/academydr/nicknacks/NNindex.html)
5. Schoolworld Internet Education (www.schoolworld.asn.au)
6. Virtual Architecture's Web Home (http://ccwf.cc.utexas.edu/~jbharris/Virtual-Architecture/index.html)

Question #2: What Is the Dance Venue?

While the purpose of some dances may be subtle and difficult to decipher, their physical space is usually well defined. Where does one "meet" to dance with partners in global, telecollaborative dances, though? Online projects do not occupy a physical space, so where are they happening? Aren't they all floating around in the same environment, one that we call *cyberspace*? Actually, no. There are different places to meet within cyberspace, from synchronous chat rooms and multiuser domains (MUDs) to asynchronous newsgroups, electronic mailing lists, and discussion forums. Because of this, the creators of telecollaborative dances must give careful thought to their "venue," taking into consideration a number of variables before deciding which is best for their virtual dance. The question of venue must be addressed almost immediately after the question of "purpose," since it will influence the atmosphere and interactions. Think of it this way: The dance at a wedding reception held in a church basement will be quite different from the one held at a country club or in a family's backyard. What does this have to do with a telecollaborative dance?

For one thing, due to limited access to the Internet, not everyone around the world can get to the same venue. Many teachers in developing nations lack a stable connection and advanced technology. Therefore, the only way many of them could join a telecollaborative dance would be through the lowest common denominator: electronic mail and mailing lists. This is an important consideration for anyone attempting a truly global telecollaborative dance. Educators shouldn't allow infatuation with new technology and all the "special effects" of the dance floor to distract them from their purpose or partners. If the purpose of the dance is "interaction" with a diverse group, then simple technology proves most inclusive, particularly since e-mail goes to the dancers while Web-based forums and newsgroups demand that the dancers come to them—if they can.

What this reveals is that every venue for a telecollaborative activity will simultaneously afford and constrain interactions. In other words, the online venue enables certain possibilities and imposes certain limitations. Choosing the right venue requires attention to both the project's purpose and partners. To put this in concrete terms, imagine that Mrs. Capello, a high school Spanish teacher, wishes to create a telecollaborative dance in which bilingual students in San Antonio, Texas, can interact with students in Spain and South America. Perhaps she conceives of this as an "interpersonal" project, which she hopes will help her students learn more about language and culture. What would be the appropriate venue for this undertaking? Figure 7.2 shows seven different options recommended by the computer coordinator at her school. Consider the pros and cons of each venue.

So, what's the right choice for Mrs. Capello? Well, that depends largely upon the purpose of her telecollaborative dance and the partners who join her. However, as one can see from this list, she faces an obvious dilemma. On the one hand, schools in Spain may have the technology necessary for synchronous interactions like MUDs, Internet Relay Chats, or video conferences, but the difference in time zones will make scheduling difficult, if not impossible, within the school day. Meanwhile, many of the schools she might like to work with in South America may lack some of the technology necessary for a high-tech dance. In some cases, limited Web access could make it difficult for those schools to join a Web-based discussion forum or newsgroup. Mrs. Capello needs to determine the best compromise. If she wants a diverse group that does not exclude "technology-poor"

The Pros and Cons of Common Telecollaborative Venues

Venue	Pro	Con
E-mail	The "lowest common denominator" among schools and most accessible means of communication	Difficult to follow the conversational threads and establish a "public" meeting place for more than two participating schools
Mailing lists	Accessible means for the creation of a "public" meeting place	Confusion over "public" and "private" discourse; difficulty following discussion threads and sustaining reciprocal conversations
Newsgroups	Enables conversation with limited technology and creates online archive	Internet Service Provider must subscribe to the newsgroup; difficult to sort through cryptic or redundant "subject lines" as messages accumulate
Web-based Discussion Forums	Creates an online archive of discussion threads	Requires Web access and proactive participants who are willing to visit the forum regularly (as opposed to having messages come to them)
Multiuser Domain (MUD)	Allows "real time" communication and an informal atmosphere	Often chaotic and disorienting for inexperienced users; time zone differences create scheduling problems
Internet Relay Chat (synchronous)	Allows "real time" communication with an informal atmosphere	Usually requires Web access; time zone differences create scheduling problems; often chaotic and disorienting for inexperienced users
Video Conferencing (synchronous)	Allows "real time" communication and opportunity to see counterparts	Bandwidth limitations, access problems, and time zone differences often frustrate telecollaborative efforts

Figure 7.2

schools and students, perhaps her best choice for now is electronic mail and a mailing list. However, this could change as more schools acquire the necessary hardware, and developing nations improve their technological infrastructures. That thought brings up the question of dance partners.

Question #3: Who Will Be the Dance Partners?

As just seen, in order to select a telecollaborative dance venue, one must give careful thought to the needs of potential partners. However, what qualities should one look for in a dance partner? What would be the "dream date," and how might one find such telecollaborative dance partners? The initial temptation is to seek counterparts in exotic locations who might provide unusual perspectives. While that carries potential for a diverse discussion, it could also wreak havoc due to limited technology and inexperience. In the case of a novice who is new to this dance, it might be wiser to seek partners who can help "share the labors" of this difficult initiation. This doesn't mean refusing to dance with other novices as much as it argues for inexperienced dancers to work with more experienced partners until they become comfortable enough to tutor apprentices. It also suggests that there's far more to the matchmaking process than simply locating educators with Internet connectivity in an exotic location.

Perhaps it would help, at this point, to consider the perspective of educators in developing countries who seek telecollaborative dance partners. At a World Links for Development workshop held in September 1998 at the World Bank Institute in Kampala, Uganda, a group of thirty educators described the ideal telecollaborative dance partner as someone who is:

- Patient and understanding
- Flexible and "agile"
- Dependable (committed to the project and the people involved)
- Communicative (with regularity)
- Culturally sensitive
- Linguistically talented
- Considerate and proactive
- Good-natured and lively
- Open-minded
- Technically competent

Creating a Dance Card: The Call for Collaboration

Before one announces a telecollaborative project and invites others to "contact the coordinator for more information," it's a good idea to set realistic limits and expectations. Remember, this is a global telecollaborative project. That means thinking of a global audience and taking responsibility for coordinating the dance of virtual colleagues. Experienced dancers know the value of a KISS (Keep it simple, stupid!). So it's often wise to begin with just one dance partner, or possibly two, acquiring the confidence and skills necessary to enjoy the inaugural dance. There will be time for more complicated dances in the future. To help fill out one's dance card, though, it might help to visit the telecollaborative dance instructors once more, many of whom keep a list of people looking for partners, or to use the services provided by the following matchmakers:

1. Community Learning Network's Education Listservs (http://www.cln.org/lists/)
2. Epals (http://www.epals.com/)
3. Intercultural Email Classroom Connections (http://www.iecc.org)
4. Kidlink (http://www.kidlink.org/english/index.html)
5. World Links for Development (WorLD) (http://www.worldbank.org/worldlinks)
6. Youthnet (http://youth.net/#K-12)

Question #4: What's the Music and Rhythm?

While designing a telecollaborative dance, it's important to recall the difficulty and disorientation of the improv dance described in the "Music of the World" exercise. That brief simulation teaches important lessons about cultural differences, particularly with respect to their "music and rhythm." Indeed, it underscores the greatest challenges of the telecollaborative dance. For once one overcomes the technological concerns—acquiring Internet access and the hardware and software necessary to go online—one must choreograph learning activities that will accommodate diverse people and cultures. It would be naïve to assume, for example, that everyone would be able to attend a telecollaborative dance at the same time of year. Yet classroom teachers are often asked to accommodate the academic calendars of colleagues on another continent or hemisphere. When *should* they schedule a telecollaborative dance in order to suit a global academic calendar? Once again, this depends on the partners involved, but for the sake of argument let's imagine that Mr. Apakabar, a history teacher in Singapore, wishes to arrange a telecollaborative project that focuses on "Life After Colonialism."

Mr. Apakabar has a clear sense of purpose (to discuss both the pros and cons of postcolonial life); plans a simple venue of an electronic mailing list (to enable technology-poor schools in developing nations to join); and hopes to locate dance partners from countries that gained independence within the past century. So, shortly before his school's December holidays begin, he posts a note to educational mailing lists, inviting interested teachers to contact him with information about their academic calendars and vacation periods. He is thrilled to hear from five different teachers but is dumbstruck by what he discovers when he looks at their respective schedules:

South Africa	School year: January–September Terms: 3 (January–March, April–June, July–September) Vacations: October–December
Brazil	School year: February–November Vacations: July, December, January
Chile	School year: March–December Vacations: July–August, December–January
Peru	School year: April–November Vacations: end July/begin August, January–March
Senegal	School year: October–June Terms: 3 (October–December, January–March, April–June) Vacations: July–September

Mr. Apakabar has an obvious problem. His experience as a classroom teacher has not prepared him for this. He has learned to accommodate *his* school's academic schedule, which presented enough obstacles on its own. How on earth will he manage to juggle half a dozen schedules, though? Because the schools interested in his project idea begin the school year at different times and pause for different holiday schedules, the only time that accommodates everyone would be April and May. Unfortunately, Mr. Apakabar's own schedule cannot accommodate this because he teaches history in the International Baccalaureate program, which administers final examinations in May. What to do? He decides this will have to be a four- to five-week discussion beginning in early April and concluding at the start of May. However, he is still not sure what type of "music" they should play. Should this be a fast dance or a slow one? What rhythm would be best—daily or weekly dance sessions with partners?

Mr. Apakabar realizes he underestimated the complexity of choreographing a global telecollaborative dance. Fortunately, he gave himself enough lead time to prepare for the dance. In fact, though he teaches in Singapore, his school follows a northern hemisphere academic calendar. So he maps out his "Project Timeline" (Figure 7.3), intuitively realizing that he needs to "flesh out" the logistics and collaborate with his dance partners to make sure everyone is comfortable with the music and rhythm of this particular dance. After he establishes his purpose, venue, partners, music, and rhythm, however, he has to address the most important question of all: What exactly will the dancers do when they meet? Must they know the steps in advance, or can they simply improvise?

PROJECT TIMELINE—A PARADIGM

January					February				March			
1	8	15	22	29	5	12	19	26	5	12	19	26

Brainstorm

Research—Partners and Projects

Project Logistics—Venue, Music and Rhythm, Steps

Call for Collaboration

Student Prep

Figure 7.3

Question #5: What Are the Dance Steps?

How should one design a telecollaborative project? When they rendezvous at the designated venue, what should the dance partners do?

Questions of Design

The structure of the activity, and the learning activities it inspires, will certainly be influenced by the purpose, venue, partners, music, and rhythm of the project. As indicated earlier, there are many variations on the telecollaborative theme. Harris's text, *Virtual Architecture* (1998), provides a fuller discussion of these activity structures, along with examples, but it's worthwhile to take a brief look at the three primary genres and consider the types within them. Teachers should consider which types of telecollaborative activities will suit their particular purpose and work within their technological constraints while accommodating a diverse population, various academic calendars, and the rhythm of an online community of learners.

Interpersonal exchanges, the first type of telecollaborative project, includes all of the following:

- Keypals—the online equivalent of the traditional "pen pals" exercise
- Global Classrooms—two or more classes meet online for topical discussions
- Electronic Appearances—an online meeting with experts or special guests
- Telementoring—student interaction with subject area specialists serving as mentors
- Q and A activities—student-generated questions submitted to subject area experts
- Impersonations—role-playing activities in which students adopt a character and correspond from that character's point of view (Harris 1998)

While interpersonal exchanges may appear the easiest way to begin, teachers need to monitor these "exchanges," encouraging healthy discourse and reciprocal relationships, lest students lose interest due to unrequited efforts or the problems of discourse literacy previously cited.

The second type of telecollaborative learning activity, information collection and analysis, offers the following variations on the dance theme:

- Information Exchanges—thematic, curriculum-based studies of student-collected data
- Database Creation—the collection and organization of information in digital archives
- Electronic Publishing—the exchange of student writing for collaborative publications

- Telefieldtrips—virtual field trips conducted through various online media
- Pooled Data Analysis—the collection of data at multiple sites followed by telecollaborative analysis (Harris 1998)

While there's far less concern with reciprocity in information collection and analysis, this approach can quickly become a glorified scavenger hunt. The teacher needs to emphasize analysis, lest the activity should become little more than the collection and exchange of data. Information is not knowledge until students have acted upon it, interrogating the information until they can make meaning of it through social interactions.

Problem solving, the third, and final, type of telecollaborative learning activity, is the most complex and ambitious. To succeed, participants need to synthesize interpersonal skills with their ability to collect and analyze information. Although problem solving is a worthy and commendable goal, projects of this type may prove too demanding for novices. However, with good planning and a collaborative spirit, good things may come of the following approaches to the telecollaborative dance:

- Information Search—a scavenger hunt providing clues and online resources to help students answer difficult questions
- Peer Feedback—online workshops for students to critique their peers' work and ideas
- Parallel Problem Solving—students in multiple locations work on the same problem, using online interactions to discuss findings and problem-solving methods
- Sequential Creations—collaborative efforts to produce a text and overcome the problems of artistic creation
- Telepresent Problem Solving—a virtual meeting of students from different geographical locations to engage in problem-solving activities
- Simulations—collaborative efforts to solve authentic, real-world problems by moving beyond understanding to social activism (Harris 1998)

Choosing an appropriate activity structure that is well-suited to the students' ability and the teacher's purpose makes good sense. However, while familiarizing oneself with archetypes it's important to continue to experiment and innovate, lest one fall prone to "paradigm paralysis." Also, a good design alone will not suffice. For a global, telecollaborative dance to succeed there must be far more than a good design. There must be a commitment to global literacy, a desire to "read" others, interpreting their ideas and responding to them in a manner that indicates careful thought and genuine respect. This takes one beyond the issue of design to questions of facilitation.

Facilitating the Global Dance

Once a design has been chosen, what exactly "goes on" at this dance party? How does the "chaperone" interact with the dancers and other chaperones? Unfortunately, trying to describe what goes on inside a telecollaborative learning activity from outside the medium that gives it life is like trying to describe a new dance without moving. Attempts to describe what takes place on the online dance floor through offline printed text demand a movement from a dynamic environment to a static one. For this reason it seems appropriate to offer three different strategies, beginning with a simulation, proceeding to an illustration, and concluding with a narrative response to the elusive question: "What goes on at the telecollaborative dance?"

GLOBAL LITERACY CHALLENGE #2

Simulating the Dance

How might one demonstrate the dynamic interactions and challenges of an electronic mailing list without using computers? The Listserver Game, a simple classroom simulation, will do just that.

What to Do

1. Have the following supplies on hand:

    - Four lengths of colored rope (to simulate subscription to a listserver)

    - One ball of string (lengths of which will signify private e-mail)

    - Colored hard candies (which symbolize e-mail messages)

    - Two large cups or two small buckets (to catch e-mail messages)

    - Name tags (to identify subscribers)

    - Six volunteers (to serve as telecollaborative dancers)

2. Station two of the volunteers in the center of the room, placing them back to back. They represent the "listserver" and should receive appropriate name tags. In reality, of course, there is only one listserver for an electronic mailing list, but this simulation requires two sets of hands to handle the flow of messages. Give each of the listserver volunteers a large cup or small bucket, which they'll use to catch the messages. Tie two lengths of colored rope to each of the listserver volunteers' belt loops, one length on each side of each of them. (Note: The listserver volunteers will need to have their hands free to send and receive e-mail messages, so be sure the rope is tied to their clothing, not their arms or hands).

3. Arrange the other four volunteers in a square around the listserver pair (see Figure 7.4). Each of these volunteers will represent a subscriber to the mailing list from schools in different countries around the world. To give the simulation more substance, tell students that these schools will collaborate on the "Lakes of the World" project, which has attracted participants from the "four corners" of the globe. This project will combine elements of interpersonal, information collection/analysis, and

Figure 7.4

problem-solving projects. Participants will study the folklore, myths and legends, economics, and environmental concerns of local lakes, then discuss global parallels online. Place a name tag on each of the volunteers so the rest of the class will be able to identify the subscribers from Uganda (Lake Victoria); Peru (Lake Titicaca); Indonesia (Lake Tobah); and Scotland (Loch Ness).

4. With the principal players at their stations, simulate an online community's interactions via electronic mailing list.

Subscribe: How does one subscribe to an electronic mailing list? By sending a "subscribe" message to the listserver. Give each of the subscribers a piece of candy, and instruct them (one at a time) to gently toss the candy to the listserver. The listserver volunteers should catch the candy in their cups. After they've caught it, they toss the candy back, indicating that the sender has successfully subscribed to the mailing list. Hand each subscriber one length of colored rope to tie to their clothing, indicating their connection to the community network.

What if one of the "subscribe" messages should miss its target? What would an errant throw or dropped piece of candy represent? A "bounced" message! When this happens, simply give the subscriber another piece of candy and ask them to try again. Proceed until all four participants have subscribed, tying the colored rope to themselves to indicate a network with four lengths of rope going to the four corners of the globe.

Send a Message: To approximate the experience of telecollaborators, one volunteer tosses a piece of candy (message) to the listserver. The listserver must distribute four copies of that message, one to each of the subscribers, including the person who sent it. To simulate this, the listserver will toss a piece of candy of the same color to each of the four subscribers.

This is a good time to discuss the importance of a message's "subject line." Discuss why a vague subject line ("Hello!") might not be a good idea in a global discussion. If students can't see a problem with a vague subject line, the next step demonstrates the problem for them.

Send a reply: Have each of the other three volunteers send a reply in response to the initial message, prompting the distribution of those three messages (pieces of candy) to all four subscribers. This quickly demonstrates the exponential growth of e-mail messages in a telecollaborative project. That initial message caused the listserver to send out four copies; the three responses will generate twelve copies. What if one group should suddenly decide that each student in a class of 25 should send a greeting? That question should prompt further discussion of why the "subject line" is so important. If the subject line of the first message said "Hello!," odds are the subject line of the three replies will offer the equally vague "Re:Hello!" While this may not pose a problem initially, it will soon become difficult for this online community to keep track of discussions. Thus, it is important to use descriptive subject lines such as "Greetings from Lake Titicaca!"

Bounced messages: Throughout this process, pieces of candy will miss their mark, bouncing off the listserver and falling to the floor. Students are likely to find this amusing, and teachers should certainly make light of it, but they should also use that moment to teach an important lesson: Technology can and will fail. Why is this significant? Ask the students to think about the consequences of "bounced" messages. Why did the message bounce? Perhaps it wasn't sent to the appropriate address? Perhaps there was a typographical error in the address itself? If so, this means a message did not pass through the list and that no one received it. Thus, if students simply wait for a reply they may grow frustrated. It's essential, therefore, that they pay close attention to details and make certain that their messages have passed through the list. The best way to check this is to look for a copy of the message from the listserver.

Public Versus Private Messages: This simulation underscores a number of important points, but none is more important than the distinction between "public" and "private" messages. At any point in time, the subscribers could send private e-mail to each other by tossing a piece of candy directly to them. Let's say, for example, that the students in Uganda wish to send a private message to students in Peru, saying that they have never had the opportunity to exchange letters with people in South America before. The volunteer representing Uganda tosses a piece of candy to the volunteer representing Peru. Run a piece of string from "Uganda" to "Peru," symbolizing this private connection. The same could be done to connect all four schools in a crisscrossed fashion. While this seems a wonderful thing, enabling both public and private discourse, the teacher must point out the dangers of conflating the two.

To illustrate this: Ask students to imagine that a participant in Indonesia had visited Scotland a few years earlier, taking a tour around the Loch Ness region. Eager to share memories of that journey, this student decides to describe his tour of the "Whisky Trail," recounting a few bawdy tales. However, instead of simply sending this private message to a "keypal" partner in Scotland, the student makes the mistake of submitting it to the public forum of the mailing list. Now what? Every subscriber to the mailing list will be privy to this information. As shown in the chapter 5 exercise, "Putting E-mail in the Right E-nvelope," this places obvious strains upon a global, telecollaborative community. Many subscribers will be confused, some titillated, and at least one person reminded to send only public messages to the listserver address.

Illustrating the Dance

While a simulation such as The Listserver Game can prove useful, many students appreciate a graphic representation of the dynamics involved in a telecollaborative dance. How might one illustrate participants' roles and interactions in a telecollaborative project? Let's return for a moment to *Utopian Visions*, the project mentioned briefly in the previous chapter's discussion of visual literacy. Figure 7.5 describes the interactions between the Utopian Visions' project coordinator, faculty site coordinators, student participants, and silent "lurkers" who communicate through an electronic mailing list that is archived on the World Wide Web.

Although it fails to convey the dynamic quality of online interactions, this illustration does offer an accurate representation of the "distributed cognition" that is involved in such endeavors (Hutchins, 1996). Distributed cognition challenges more traditional, organizational structures, since it describes a distribution of ideas and ownership rather than a hierarchy. Notice that the project coordinator and site coordinators are not placed in the center of the diagram. While they play significant roles, they are not central to every facet of the project. They are part of a complex system that includes student participants and "lurkers" who may begin on the periphery as apprentices but gradually assume more ownership and influence as they are drawn into the online discourse (Lave and Wenger, 1991). Finally, notice that the technology of a listserver and "time capsule" (database) provide the connective tissue that binds this community, enabling students

What goes on "inside" a telecollaborative dance?

Figure 7.5

to correspond with distant peers, site coordinators, or the project coordinator by way of mailing lists while simultaneously conducting research through the online database.

Case Study: Putting the Dance Into Words

Finally, let's take a narrative approach to the elusive question. The following description of "what goes on inside" a telecollaborative project was written for participants in *Utopian Visions '99*. It was written by the project coordinator to give students and teachers some idea of what to expect as the project evolved. By no means a definitive statement, it is an attempt to "translate" a dynamic, hypertextual experience into a linear narrative.

> Each year, at the start of this project, I am asked to describe its goals and the activities that will take place during it. How does one describe what "goes on inside" a

telecollaborative project? It's a difficult challenge, but here is an attempt to explain, as briefly as possible, the theoretical goals and rationale for online activities that will take place during Utopian Visions '99.

* In Theory—A Rationale for Telecollaboration

We want to inspire students to think critically. That means helping them learn how to ask thoughtful questions and explore possible answers instead of accepting cliches or unexamined assumptions. This is not an easy task, however, nor is it one that technology will accomplish by itself. In fact, there are ways in which technology can make this a more difficult assignment if we are not clear about our purpose. In theory, then, the Utopian Visions project was designed to stimulate authentic inquiry and discussion among students around the world. We are not satisfied with the recital of information that students encounter in textbooks or Web sites. Instead, we want them to interrogate the information they encounter, questioning its validity and accuracy. Only by such careful scrutiny will they arrive at a deeper understanding of the utopian visions that have shaped their municipality and human history. Clearly, access to information is not enough to accomplish such important goals. Today's students are saturated with information, but they often lack the skills necessary to interrogate that information and its sources, as well as the ability to synthesize, analyze and speculate—all of which are essential to answering an essential question: "What does this information mean?"

* In Practice—The Making of Utopian Visions

This project actually began in 1993, when two schoolteachers conducted an experiment linking classrooms on opposite sides of the globe. I was a humanities teacher in Kuala Lumpur (Malaysia), and my colleague, Lowell Monke, was a computer science instructor in Des Moines (USA). We initiated "Project Utopia" so that our students could exchange ideas about the perfect society through telecommunications. Although new and interesting, the project remained too much a "fiction" in our students' minds. They failed to see how their own visions might one day affect the societies in which they lived. We wanted something more realistic, something that would inspire utopian ideals while asking them to consider existing conditions. This inspired the "South African Elections '94 Internet Project" the following year, an extraordinary educational experience that asked students to consider the impact of that historic occasion—the realization of a utopian vision that changed South Africa—upon their own country and region.

That experience was transformative for many of us, students and faculty alike. Lowell Monke and I wanted to re-create some of that when we began designing Utopian Visions shortly thereafter. We were not aware, however, of research that had identified three primary types of telecollaborative projects (Harris, 1998):

* Interpersonal Exchange (Keypals, Electronic Mentors, etc.)

* Information Collection & Analysis (Scavenger hunts, electronic publishing, etc.)

* Problem-based Learning (e.g. Environmental studies, etc.)

However, when we did learn of this research we realized that Utopian Visions combined elements from all three types of projects, creating a robust, new paradigm.

*Utopian Visions '99—An Interpersonal, Analytical, Problem-Solving Project

The project begins with students describing their personal vision of utopian/dystopian elements within their municipality, speculating upon the origins of these elements as well as proposals for preserving utopian qualities while reforming dystopian ones. These personal visions prompt interpersonal exchanges through electronic mail "dialogues" with peers who subscribe to the project mailing list around the world.

Most often, the dialogues reveal that students need to move beyond initial ideas, conducting research that will lead to more informed questions. Their research produces category reports on twelve designated topics, offering an argument on whether or not their municipality was moving toward utopia or dystopia in the century leading to 1899. It's essential that these reports offer more than "information collections." They should present an argument that stimulates "dialogues" with distant peers studying the same category around the world. These dialogues are central to the project, but they are not simply "keypal" exchanges about social lives and entertainment. Instead, they should enable students to ask questions that the reports have prompted, presenting opportunities for clarification, deeper reflection and further research. This relies on student-generated questions, which, if authentic and serious, could prompt the kind of "problem-based learning" that we would like to see in telecollaborative projects. The problem at the heart of this project, after all, is one that unites all of humanity: "What can we learn from the past and present that will guide us toward a better future?"

This is, of course, an open-ended question. No single answer will satisfy, but if we inspire students to strive for what I've just sketched imagine what they might gain from the experience? We will have introduced them to an online "community-of-inquiry" where they learn how to debate some of the most critical issues that their generation will confront. Indeed, we will have asked them to explore their collective past, examine the present, and predict the future. How often does schoolwork ask them to "study" the future? How often do they have an opportunity to engage in authentic inquiry that could change their lives and help them envision a better society? If this seems too much to ask of a school project, then imagine what impact this endeavor will have upon an adolescent who offers a personal vision, engages in online dialogues, asks thoughtful questions, conducts research that leads to insightful category reports, then follows those reports with more online dialogues and questions, culminating with predictions for the future of their municipality. Is there not the chance for personal transformation within this process? And where there's personal transformation might there not be opportunities for positive, social transformations?

I realize this is an idealistic perspective, but what did you expect from a telecollaborative project called "Utopian Visions"? ;-)

Of course, it is difficult to accomplish what I've just described. The first step, though, is to empower students to think for themselves. The best way to achieve that, we feel, is to give them opportunities to ask serious questions and engage in a community-of-inquiry. That community begins in their local classrooms and families, but extends to the

```
online community that gathers for this project. For it to
succeed we need the help of dedicated teachers who inspire
students to think deeply and question openly. This is, from
start to finish, a truly collaborative project. It is also a
deeply humbling experience for those who take it seriously,
embracing the power of personal visions and human imagina-
tion. We are grateful to everyone who has ever participated
in this project, and look forward to the 1999 edition, which
will surely give life to a new generation of Utopian Visions.

Sincerely,

R. W. Burniske

Project Coordinator, Utopian Visions '99
```

Taking the First Steps: A Process Approach to Project Designs

Let's take a look at what happens when teachers use the five questions necessary to choreograph a global telecollaborative dance as guidelines. It's worth pausing to recall what one is trying to accomplish with these complicated undertakings, from the basics of computer literacy to the sophisticated demands of global literacy. Toward that end, educators at a World Links for Development (WorLD) workshop in Uganda were asked to describe the characteristics of a good project design. Although newly initiated to such endeavors, they reached consensus on five essential features for global, telecollaborative learning activities, arguing that they should be:

- realistic and manageable within the given time frame
- universal in theme (to attract a diverse group of telecollaborators)
- designed for geographical diversity and distance learning
- full of potential for educational activities online
- truly collaborative within local classrooms and telecollaborative online

These are certainly worthwhile goals. However, educators may not achieve them without a process approach to telecollaborative projects that parallels a writer's composition. This requires multiple drafts and peer critiques before the dissemination of the idea via electronic mailing lists or online databases. What follows is the evolution of one telecollaborative project, created during an intensive, five-day workshop that introduced participants to the concept of telecollaboration, project designs, and the process described in this chapter. The creators began with a simple topic proposal that led to a rough draft, peer reviews, and several revisions before culminating with a final project design.

Case Study: Women and Tradition

Before one can dance the telecollaborative dance, one must take a tentative step, sketching the general aims and purpose of this activity. Toward that end, three educators posted the following proposal in a Web-based discussion forum to invite their colleagues' review.

Project Proposal

> Project Proposal—This keypal project will look at women in a
> traditional setting. This project aims at studying the role
> of women in society and how that role is influenced by tradi-
> tion.

Proposal Critique

Shortly thereafter, participants in the workshop read each other's proposals, offering brief critiques to help the writers of the proposal sharpen their vision by asking more questions.

> Proposal Critique—What are the specific roles that you want
> to focus on? Family? caregiver? career prospects? What spe-
> cifically do you want the students to explore? The changing
> roles of women around the world? A comparison of women's
> roles in Uganda v. other parts of the world? The future roles
> for women?

Questions like these prove central to the process of project design, for they help the creators anticipate queries from potential "dance partners." This type of response is not as threatening as a judgmental review ("I don't like this project idea"), nor as meaningless as a vague compliment ("I like your project idea"). Often, the best response one can give is a thoughtful question that encourages a sharper vision, which comes about through re-vision.

Project Description: Rough Draft

```
Project title: Women and Tradition

The project category is interpersonal exchange and the type
is keypals.

Purpose: The aims of this project are: To understand the role
of women in a traditional community. To appreciate women's
contribution to positive development. To understand the myths
and facts about the role and position of women in society.
Students will compare and contrast the role of women in their
respective societies.

Dance Venue: The correspondence will be done through E-mail
using listservers.

Partners: We wish to collaborate with students of either sex
aged between 11 and 16 years from all continents.

Music/Rhythm: We would like to communicate with our partners
at least once a fortnight, starting in October and continuing
to February.

Dance Steps:

1. Students will define terms like tradition, society and
roles.

2. They will explain how traditional values/beliefs contrib-
ute to society.

3. Write short essays of between 250 to 400 words on how
tradition affects women.
```

```
4. Cite examples of how women have tried to change tradition
for their emancipation.

5. Students to propose any other activities they would like
to work on.

Coordinators: Kiganda A., Nakanwagi C., Mutiibwa F.
```

Rough Draft Critique

At this point, the project coordinators need a response from another set of colleagues, who will supply a fresh perspective on the project idea as well as careful scrutiny of the rough draft. While questions remain an integral part of the process, the response must also include suggestions and recommendations to help the authors clarify their aims and consider their audience as they put the finishing touches on their project description.

```
It's a great idea! However, the aims have to be given a
global touch. Regarding your schedule, there is a need to be
more definite about the year(s) when the project is running.
Collaborators should know the application deadline. It also
does not cater to vacation and examination time. The reports
about your project should be sent to the participants at
definite times and covering the different sub-categories for
your project. Also, we recommend a shorter time period for
the project. Collaborators may not wish to commit so much
time to a pilot project. Finally, this does not tell us who
you are. There are no contact addresses.
```

Project Description: Final Draft

Finally, after another round of revision—and perhaps another critique—the project coordinators are ready to broadcast their telecollaborative dance. However, since project participants do not all dance to the same beat—or live by the same metaphors—they will need to change their terminology to address a global audience.

Telecollaborative Project Title: Women and Tradition

Application Deadline: October 1st

The project category is interpersonal exchange and the type is keypals.

Educational Aims: The aims of this project are: To understand the role of women in a traditional community. To appreciate women's contribution to positive development. To understand the myths and facts about the role and position of women in society. Students will compare and contrast the role of women in their respective societies.

Communication Media: Correspondence will be through electronic mailing list.

Partners: We wish to collaborate with students of either sex aged between 11 and 16 years from all continents.

Schedule: We would like to communicate with our partners at least once a fortnight, starting in October and continuing through November.

Activities:

- October 1 - 8: (a) Students will be required to introduce themselves by submitting their names, age, sex and schools and country of residence, in a maximum of 50 words. (b) They will define the terms: tradition, role and society in a maximum of 50 words.

- October 10 - 17: students will research and exchange information on the effects of traditions on women in their societies. The essay should be 250 to 400 words.

- October 19 - 26: Students will write a presentation on the myths and facts as per the position and role of women in society. (350 words).

- October 27 - November 2: students will research and exchange information on the role of women in society. (350 words).

- November 5 -12: students will analyse and appreciate by briefly writing about traditional values they feel can be adopted in their own societies.

Coordinators: We are secondary school teachers in Uganda. You can reach us at the following email addresses for more information.

Kiganda A., kiganda@fakemail.co.ug

Nakanwagi C., nakanwagi@fakemail.co.ug

Mutiibwa F. mutubwa@fakemail.co.ug

Dancing Globally, Evaluating Locally

It's easy to forget that global literacy does not come easily, but it's important to keep that fact in mind at all times. Educators are likely to trip, stumble, and occasionally fall while trying to learn this new dance. But, as Alexander Pope once observed,

> Not to go back is somewhat to advance
> And men must walk, at least, before they dance. (1980, 339).

With time, the global literacy that students and teachers acquire will provide greater ease and comfort, perhaps even grace, as they take to the telecollaborative dance floor.

Clearly, thinking and acting globally compels students and teachers to draw upon the previous literacies we've discussed. While one pursues global literacy, however, one cannot forget his or her responsibilities to local concerns. After all, teachers must still satisfy the requirements of a local curriculum and attend to the needs of their own students. All this talk of global literacy and the potential for new learning activities may leave readers wondering how teachers will assess student learning and evaluate their performance while all of this occurs. How might students reflect on both the process and product of their work? How might teachers give student effort and performance the attention and weight they deserve? These questions should give one pause, as they do in the next chapter, while inspiring discussions of *evaluative literacy*.

CHAPTER

8

Evaluative Literacy:
Peer Reviews, Electronic Portfolios, and Online Learning Records

Reading maketh a full man, conference a ready man, and writing an exact man.

(Bacon 1939, 150)

In every academic discipline, students need to acquire better understanding of their own learning style and process, as well as become better critics of their own work. Often, they suffer the delusion that it's acceptable for either the style or content of their work to be weak so long as the strength of its counterpart compensates for that weakness. This may be true occasionally, but, regardless of the academic discipline, students must become critical of both the style and substance of their work. Critical judgment is essential, for it helps them discover the flaws in their work, which is the first step toward the kind of *evaluative literacy* necessary for self-improvement (see Figure 8.1).

Evaluative Literacy

Evaluative literacy is the ability to distinguish excellence from mediocrity as it applies to both the process and product of one's labor.

Figure 8.1

Without knowledge of alternative approaches to a task, and without an understanding of the strengths and weaknesses of those approaches, students remain ignorant of the process that led to a finished project, report, or essay. This, in turn, may lead to misunderstandings about evaluation because the euphoria that attends the completion of a project may have more to do with overcoming a flawed process than producing quality work. What's more, students often believe they can cut corners on the process and still arrive at a quality product. Sometimes they can, but what if they cannot? How can teachers demonstrate a good process approach to writing essays, reports, and more with new technology? How might they use networked computers to help students change their approach—refining their process—so that they can produce better quality work? How can educators teach students to turn a critical eye toward their own work, judging both its strengths and weaknesses? Ultimately, how can teachers in networked classrooms use technology to help students develop more evaluative literacy?

This chapter's literacy challenges and case studies respond to those questions, presenting a sequence of "building blocks" that become increasingly complex. First, the "Hypertext Writing Workshop" focuses upon one draft of a written project. Next, "Electronic Portfolios" enables students to collect the respective pieces involved in a particular project, revealing both their process and final product. Finally, the "Online Learning Record," a hypertext collection of a semester's work, encourages students to select their best work, reflect on both the process and product, and offer a summative report and self-evaluation. Thus, the narrative moves from evaluation of a part to the whole, giving careful consideration to the process of learning, the quality of student work, and the evaluative skills necessary to understand the relationship between the two.

Let's begin with an exercise written for students, which guides them through an electronic variation of a tried-and-true method.

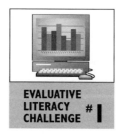

EVALUATIVE LITERACY CHALLENGE # 1

The Hypertext Writing Workshop

What to Do

1. Share the following letter with students.

Dear Writing Workshop Participants,

To build a "community of writers" we need to help each other "see" our writing through another's eyes. However, this means we must learn to trust one another, as both readers and writers. When asked to critique someone's essay or report, you are helping them "re-see" their work. That is what "re-vision" means; literally, we "see again," but this time, hopefully, we see from a different perspective, one that improves our judgment. Your observations and comments will make a strong impression, so please be responsible and compassionate with them. This doesn't mean saying only nice things, but it does mean trying to "show and tell" what you're seeing so that the writer receives it as constructive criticism. If you work diligently at this, helping the writer improve, you'll develop the skills necessary to critique your own writing and strengthen your evaluative literacy.

In the past, peer review sessions were usually conducted on paper, asking classmates to exchange papers, scribble notes in the margins, and circle typos and grammatical errors. How might we transfer this process to sessions in a computer lab? Where are the margins in which we write notes to the author? How do we highlight errors? How do we allow for more than one reviewer to comment on the style and content?

Actually, it's not that hard if you know a few HTML tags or work with a "WYSIWYG" editor (What You See Is What You Get). Either way, a little ingenuity will allow you to call attention to troublesome words and phrases, highlight awkward sentences, and comment on confusing passages. This exercise will help you "see" what's going on inside an essay. It begins with close reading of a text. In fact, it asks you to give the text three close readings. This may seem odd, but with practice you'll learn that re-reading is essential to the process of "re-vision." You will have approximately 30 minutes for the entire exercise, so you'll have to budget your time well. And remember the golden rule: "Do unto others' compositions as you would have them do unto yours."

2. Instruct students that all editing will be done on a copy of the author's electronic draft, which means using HTML tags for notations. The authors should save a backup of their original draft as well as a "Review" copy. Each review session will last approximately 30 minutes. Reviewers should work carefully through the essay, following the instructions below.

3. Participants will "rotate" by shifting two computer terminals to their right. They should work on the essay at that terminal for the first 30 minutes. Before beginning, remind reviewers to make sure the author saved his/her draft as "roughreview.html." This means they'll be working on a separate copy of the text, not the original. Upon completion of the reviews, the authors can link to their reviews from the original, using it to guide revisions.

4. Tell students to use the following conventions:

   a. Wherever the instructions say to *highlight* something, they'll need to use the HTML "tags" or the menu bar of their WYSIWYG editor to accomplish the following:

Reviewer 1: Highlight by using boldface: Highlight = \<B\> **BOLDFACE TYPE** \</B\>

Reviewer 2: Highlight by using italics: Highlight - \<I\> *ITALIC TYPE* \</I\>

b. To indicate agreement/disagreement with their co-reader, they should follow these rules:

If, as Reviewer 2, they *disagree* with Reviewer 1, they are to offer a comment at the end of the paragraph. If, as Reviewer 2, they *agree* with Reviewer 1, they are to use *ITALIC TYPE* on top of the **BOLDFACE** to reinforce the concern.

For example, let's say they encounter a sentence like this.

"The truth cannot be told by me."

Reviewer 1 finds this awkward, so he or she highlights it and offers a parenthetical comment:

"The truth cannot be told by me." (Awkward)

Reviewer 2 agrees, so he or she highlights the sentence as well and adds to the parenthetical comment:

"The truth cannot be told by me." (Awkward—*Passive Voice!*)

This will tell the author that both reviewers see a problem here and that the second reviewer offers a diagnosis. Remind students that neither reviewer is responsible for fixing the problem. Rather, they merely call attention to the problem, helping the author see the text through a fresh set of eyes.

What if Reviewer 2 disagrees with Reviewer 1? Then the highlighted item would appear in boldface, but not in italics. This indicates that the reviewers do not agree on the matter. Fair enough: The author will serve as final arbiter.

5. When instructed, everyone should shift to the next terminal on their right, serving as the second reviewer for the essay before them.

6. Tell students they should try to accomplish three major objectives in their three readings.

FIRST READING—TAKE INVENTORY: Ask students to take inventory in the first reading. This applies mostly to Reviewer 1, but Reviewer 2 should verify Reviewer 1's work.

a. *Underline the essay's claim* and the reasons supporting it.

b. *Underline the "grounds"* upon which the claim and reason are founded.

c. *Underline the first sentence* of each paragraph.

d. *Number each paragraph* (chronologically) by placing a number at the start of it.

e. *Highlight typos* and other "distractions."

(Reminder—Do *not* fix any of the mistakes; simply help the author see them.)

SECOND READING—EVALUATE THE BASICS: In the second reading, ask both Reviewer 1 and Reviewer 2 to evaluate the basics by accomplishing the following:

a. Assess the "Thesis paragraph"—Is it clear? Well supported? Does it indicate the direction the essay will take? Does the diction reveal an awareness of audience? Does it hint at "conditions for rebuttal" or "qualifiers?" Type a brief comment at the end of the opening paragraph.

b. Transitions—At the start of each paragraph, judge the transition from the previous paragraph as "strong," "fair," or "weak." What do the underlined topic sentences at the start of each paragraph reveal about the structure of the essay? Where is it flawed?

c. Highlight confusing phrases, and write a brief comment in parentheses (Ex: "I'm not sure what you're saying here. Are you?")

d. Use the "strikethrough" command to draw a line through redundant words/phrases.

e. In the space below each paragraph, offer a brief commentary on the paragraph's weaknesses; let the author know if the prose is vague or confusing; suggest additional material if the support seems "thin." Be specific!

Remember: Reviewer 1, type your comments in **BOLDFACE**; Reviewer 2, in *ITALICS*.

THIRD READING—THE BIG PICTURE: STYLE AND STRUCTURE: For the third reading, ask students to concentrate on the big picture—the style and structure of an argument. This applies equally to both Reviewer 1 and Reviewer 2.

a. After each paragraph, assess the author's use of supporting evidence. Is it persuasive? Is it documented properly?

b. Highlight errors with in-text citations, and offer a parenthetical comment on bibliographic documentation.

c. Critique each paragraph, referring to it by number. Tell what each paragraph says/does. Is it coherent? Does it "show and tell" effectively?

d. Prepare a final commentary. At the end of the essay, each reviewer should provide their full name, type a one-paragraph commentary that addresses the following questions, and "Save" the document. Again, Reviewer 1 should type the commentary in **BOLDFACE**, and Reviewer 2 should use *ITALICS*. Here are a few questions to guide responses:

Argument: Assess the strength of the author's claim and reasons. Is the author aware of his/her own assumptions? Does a lack of evidence undermine the author's ethos at any point? If so, where? Which point of the rhetorical triangle (logos, ethos, or pathos) should the author emphasize more (or less) in the next draft?

Structure: Overall, how do the reviewers like the structure of this essay? Would they move a paragraph to give it more prominence in the essay as a whole? Would they delete one altogether? Does the essay "flow" naturally from one paragraph to the next? Are the transitions graceful or forced?

Style: Where is the prose interfering with the argument instead of making it clear? Is the tone and voice of the essay appropriate for the audience that the author addresses? Is the documentation complete and reliable?

Suggestions: What, if anything, is missing from this essay? What needs the most attention in the next phase of revision?

Rather than isolate a peer review sample, examining it out of context, let's see how this works within a process approach that integrates hypertext and portfolio assessment. By doing so, one can glimpse a number of the advantages to conducting peer reviews as hypertext writing workshops.

Case Study: Electronic Portfolios

As students learn to evaluate their peers' efforts and see their own work through another's eyes, they must also learn to transfer evaluative literacy skills to their own work. Toward that end, they need a strategy that encourages reflection upon their research and writing processes, as well as a way to collect the disparate pieces of their work. Borrowing from the idea of portfolio assessment with printed materials, teachers can help students through this process by arranging electronic portfolios for a given project. Although this exercise grows out of language arts and humanities instruction, it's applicable to projects in most academic disciplines. It begins with the creation of a simple hypertext template that emphasizes research, reflection, and a process approach to writing. By constructing electronic portfolios, students create a record of their research and writing process, develop HTML skills, and strengthen their evaluative literacy.

What's the appeal of an electronic portfolio? Does this variation accomplish anything that print portfolios couldn't? Certainly, this activity shares a good deal with its print cousin. For one thing, it provides context for student work. How often does a school curriculum encourage students to think in holistic terms, situating disparate learning activities and fragmented disciplines in a larger context? As a result, they often think of learning activities as "busywork" a teacher creates to keep them occupied, rather than as part of a coherent learning process. As much as anything, portfolio assessment tries to overcome this. The electronic portfolio, by extension, will help students think of their work not as an isolated essay or report for a particular teacher or class, but as part of a larger conversation—one that connects them with a community of scholars. The electronic portfolio process distinguishes itself from print variations because the medium allows students to link directly from their composition to online resources. Meanwhile, internal links between the respective portfolio sections encourage a self-conscious and reflective approach to composition.

To illustrate the importance of this type of approach, let's consider a common academic assignment: the research essay. Typically, the process goes something like this: The student chooses a research topic and submits a proposal that the teacher must approve. Then, the student conducts research, taking notes from secondary sources that will help support a particular argument (often a preconceived argument the research will merely reinforce rather than question). Finally, the student outlines an essay, writes a draft or two, and produces a final draft replete with citations and bibliography. Now stop to consider this process. How much time did the student spend reflecting upon it? How much of the process has the teacher seen? How much of it will be reflected by the final draft? How much of the process does the student retain? Does the student see the relationship between that process and the final product? Or has the obsession with that destination blinded the student to the journey?

The answers to these questions will depend largely on the particular students and teacher, but, generally speaking, the final draft of a conventional research paper reveals only a fragment of the process involved in its creation. With a portfolio, however, the final draft is placed within the context of the entire project. The electronic portfolio offers the unique opportunities of hypertext, which allows one to move through the internal links of the portfolio sections as well as depart from it to consider the secondary sources that informed the writer's thinking.

How might one design an electronic portfolio? Figure 8.2 presents the template created for students in *The Rhetoric of Utopia* course introduced in chapter 5.

In this instance, the teacher established six discrete portfolio sections, though these could certainly be modified depending on the academic discipline and project. From the "index" page of this portfolio, which is shown in Figure 8.2, the reader can follow one of the following internal links:

- Biographical Sketch
- Topic Proposal
- References
- Process Journal
- Rough Draft(s)
- Final Draft

To illustrate each of these sections and discuss their significance within the electronic portfolio, let's look at selected samples rather than follow a particular student's progress through a research assignment. This will allow a wider sampling, offering a variety of approaches to the required tasks.

What follows is a brief explanation of the electronic portfolio's respective sections. Although the selected "screenshots" truncate some pages, they illustrate the way in which the respective parts relate to the whole.

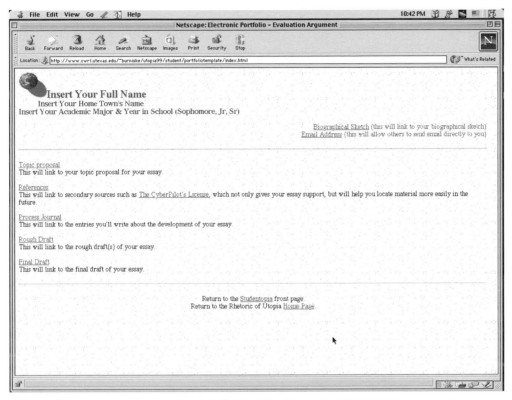

Figure 8.2 Reprinted with permission of R. W. Burniske. Copyright 1999. All rights reserved.

What's more, they demonstrate how an electronic portfolio, conceived as an online hypertext, may contribute to a student's evaluative literacy.

a. *Biographical sketch.* Every essay or report has a story behind it. The author is the protagonist, drawn to his or her subject because of personal interests or curiosities. This section offers the writer a chance to tell the background to this story. Why did he or she choose this topic? Or, perhaps more accurately, why did this topic choose him or her? It's often best to save this exercise for last, providing one last chance for the student to reflect on the intellectual journey. As Figure 8.3 indicates, pausing to consider the "story" behind an individual's topic selection yields privileged insight. Not only does it help the student and teacher understand the thought process involved in making this decision, but it also reveals the level of personal commitment.

Readers who prefer to examine an individual portfolio or see more samples should visit the online collections archived in *The Rhetoric of Utopia* course Web site for the Fall 1998 and Spring 1999 semesters:
Fall 1998 – (http://www.cwrl.utexas.edu/~burniske/utopia98/student/index.html)
Spring1999 – (http://www.cwrl.utexas.edu/~burniske/utopia99/student/index.html)

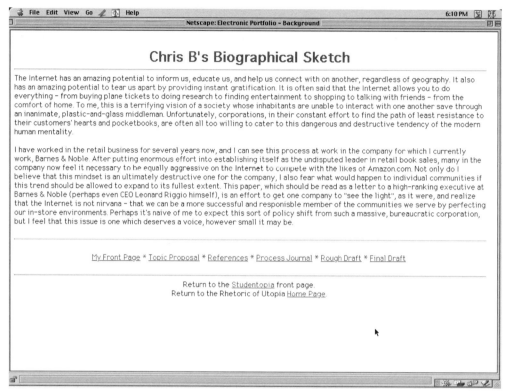

Chris B's Biographical Sketch

The Internet has an amazing potential to inform us, educate us, and help us connect with on another, regardless of geography. It also has an amazing potential to tear us apart by providing instant gratification. It is often said that the Internet allows you to do everything – from buying plane tickets to doing research to finding entertainment to shopping to talking with friends – from the comfort of home. To me, this is a terrifying vision of a society whose inhabitants are unable to interact with one another save through an inanimate, plastic-and-glass middleman. Unfortunately, corporations, in their constant effort to find the path of least resistance to their customers' hearts and pocketbooks, are often all too willing to cater to this dangerous and destructive tendency of the modern human mentality.

I have worked in the retail business for several years now, and I can see this process at work in the company for which I currently work, Barnes & Noble. After putting enormous effort into establishing itself as the undisputed leader in retail book sales, many in the company now feel it necessary to be equally aggressive on the Internet to compete with the likes of Amazon.com. Not only do I believe that this mindset is an ultimately destructive one for the company, I also fear what would happen to individual communities if this trend should be allowed to expand to its fullest extent. This paper, which should be read as a letter to a high-ranking executive at Barnes & Noble (perhaps even CEO Leonard Riggio himself), is an effort to get one company to "see the light", as it were, and realize that the Internet is not nirvana – that we can be a more successful and responisble member of the communities we serve by perfecting our in-store environments. Perhaps it's naive of me to expect this sort of policy shift from such a massive, bureaucratic corporation, but I feel that this issue is one which deserves a voice, however small it may be.

My Front Page * Topic Proposal * References * Process Journal * Rough Draft * Final Draft

Return to the Studentopia front page.
Return to the Rhetoric of Utopia Home Page.

Figure 8.3 Reprinted with permission of R. W. Burniske. Copyright 1999. All rights reserved.

b. *Topic proposal.* All stories have a beginning, middle, and end. The topic proposal is the beginning. Students may decide to change their topic, but unless they write a topic proposal they could delay the decision unnecessarily, procrastinating while they search for the "perfect topic." What they learn from this exercise, more often than not, is that the starting point isn't as important as the subsequent journey. The proposal, nonetheless, helps them overcome inertia at the start of a research project, compelling them to locate sources that will engage them in discussion of their chosen topic. This piece of the portfolio may help them see where things ran amok, helping them recall the process of topic selection and evaluate its impact upon their performance. In the example depicted in Figure 8.4, students began with a "Why List" (see chapter 4), before writing a topic proposal indicating their proposed audience and three references that would spur further research.

c. *References.* This is perhaps the most unique feature of an electronic portfolio. Not only does this section allow students to link directly from their in-text citations to full bibliographical references, but in the case of

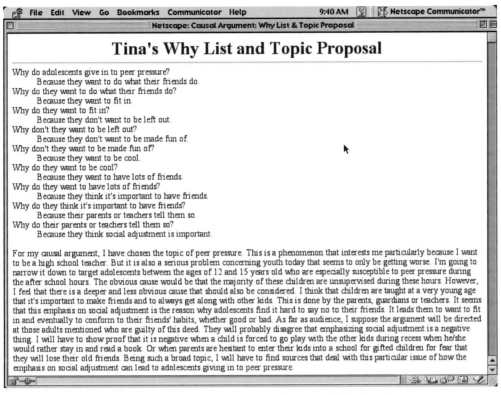

| File | Edit | View | Go | Bookmarks | Communicator | Help | 9:40 AM | Netscape Communicator™ |

Netscape: Causal Argument: Why List & Topic Proposal

Tina's Why List and Topic Proposal

Why do adolescents give in to peer pressure?
    Because they want to do what their friends do.
Why do they want to do what their friends do?
    Because they want to fit in.
Why do they want to fit in?
    Because they don't want to be left out.
Why don't they want to be left out?
    Because they don't want to be made fun of.
Why don't they want to be made fun of?
    Because they want to be cool.
Why do they want to be cool?
    Because they want to have lots of friends.
Why do they want to have lots of friends?
    Because they think it's important to have friends.
Why do they think it's important to have friends?
    Because their parents or teachers tell them so.
Why do their parents or teachers tell them so?
    Because they think social adjustment is important.

For my causal argument, I have chosen the topic of peer pressure. This is a phenomenon that interests me particularly because I want to be a high school teacher. But it is also a serious problem concerning youth today that seems to only be getting worse. I'm going to narrow it down to target adolescents between the ages of 12 and 15 years old who are especially susceptible to peer pressure during the after school hours. The obvious cause would be that the majority of these children are unsupervised during these hours. However, I feel that there is a deeper and less obvious cause that should also be considered. I think that children are taught at a very young age that it's important to make friends and to always get along with other kids. This is done by the parents, guardians or teachers. It seems that this emphasis on social adjustment is the reason why adolescents find it hard to say no to their friends. It leads them to want to fit in and eventually to conform to their friends' habits, whether good or bad. As far as audience, I suppose the argument will be directed at those adults mentioned who are guilty of this deed. They will probably disagree that emphasizing social adjustment is a negative thing. I will have to show proof that it is negative when a child is forced to go play with the other kids during recess when he/she would rather stay in and read a book. Or when parents are hesitant to enter their kids into a school for gifted children for fear that they will lose their old friends. Being such a broad topic, I will have to find sources that deal with this particular issue of how the emphasis on social adjustment can lead to adolescents giving in to peer pressure.

Figure 8.4 Reprinted with permission of R.W. Burniske. Copyright 1999. All rights reserved.

online documents they can provide direct hyperlinks from their final draft to secondary sources. By reinforcing the lessons learned about intellectual property in chapter 2 (see "Borrowing Without Stealing"), the reference section compels attention to detail (see Figure 8.5). Unless they're carefully documented, the links from this section to the online references will not work, which obviously damages the author's credibility. Best of all, the reference section places the essay within the context of the larger discussion conducted by the community of scholars the writer has joined. By linking from their own essay to the online resources, the writer allows the reader to see how secondary source material influenced his or her thinking. What's more, the quality of those sources is revealed, calling attention to the fact that the choice of secondary materials affects one's ethos.

    d. *Process journal.* This section of the electronic portfolio allows students to demonstrate the process behind their final product. Teachers may require one or two journal entries per week, but to keep students honest (avoiding the "creative writing" that results from composing entries the night before they're due), it's wise to request that entries be turned in at

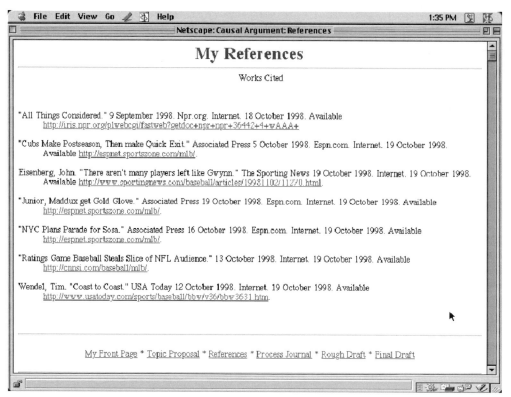

Figure 8.5 Reprinted with permission of R.W. Burniske. Copyright 1999. All rights reserved.

the end of each week. This will encourage periodic reflection, giving students a better understanding of their own process and what they might do to improve it in the future. In effect, the process journal is the "story behind the story," a behind-the-scenes glimpse of the project's evolution. Raising student awareness in this manner proves remarkably useful, empowering them with a critical literacy that begins with an honest assessment of what went well, what didn't, and what they need to do differently in the future. In just a few brief sentences, the student can speak to the difficulties of settling on a topic; share important research discoveries; describe struggles with initial drafts and revision; reveal the agony and ecstasy of peer review; and speculate on a future course of action. Indeed, all of this appears in the process journal depicted in Figure 8.6, which consists of two brief entries per week over a three-week period.

e. *Rough drafts and peer reviews.* This section draws on exercises such as the "Hypertext Writing Workshop," offering a detailed portrait of the composition process, including peer reviews. Once students learn how

My Process Journal

April 8
I am considering writing about trees. My parents and I have been planting and researching native trees from Texas. I believe that students would benefit from learning more about their enviroment. Mr. B. had a good idea with targeting Earth Day

April 13
I have changed my mind. I want to write about Mexico and studying abroad. I am going to Mexico this summer. I have experience traveling as a high school student four years ago. I believe more students should receive the opportunity to experience other countries.

April 15
Rick Williams has a lot of good information to offer on Rational and Intuitive Intelligences. It ties to what will be accomplished when students study abroad.

April 20
I feel very frustrated. My paper is just not making sense. I am dwelling too much on Williams theory. It is important to what I am talking about, I just need to figure out how to incorperate it.

April 22
I had a great review from Jennifer B. Clay was a bit ctitical, but my paper was confusing. I lost his review when we lost our folder. I have found more studies that prove studying abroad inproves education

April 27
I am just tying up odds and ends. I would really like to send this to my former spanish teacher. I think he would be receptive to this idea. I would be willing to go to my old high school to talk to student about this.

My Front Page * Topic Proposal * References * Process Journal * Rough Draft * Final Draft

Figure 8.6 Reprinted with permission of R. W. Burniske. Copyright 1999. All rights reserved.

to create copies of an HTML document (which takes one keystroke at the computer), they can link to multiple rough drafts and peer reviews. With their own drafts and peer reviews on display in this section, the depth of the students' commitment to the writing process and to peer review is quickly revealed. As the sample in Figure 8.7 indicates, peer review sessions that provide time for two reviewers to mark the text using a hypertext editor often produce remarkably thorough commentaries. As a result, hardly a word escapes scrutiny, making the rough drafts an essential part of the portfolio, as well as a key to the students' development of evaluative literacy skills.

f. *Final draft.* This, of course, is the ending, but it should not be considered an isolated piece. The internal links at the foot of the document allow the reader to trace the evolution of this finished "product" back through its rough drafts and peer reviews, its process journal and topic proposal, right to the origins described in the biographical sketch. With all this background information, the reader gains insight into the trials and tribulations

Critique #1: Helping Elementary School Readers

There has been an ongoing study in Seattle (**Washington -- specify the state**), at Mirror Lake Elementary school. *(Weak introductory sentence -- give it some "oomph" to grab the reader's attention)*. Here, ~~Ele~~ mentary students in 3rd and 4th grade have exhibited difficulty in reading. (****First two sentences could easily be one. See suggestion below**) These students were removed from class to undergo an intensive eight week reading *rehabilitation (Is this the correct word choice? do you mean "remediation" instead?)* The program is a key example of how elementary students' reading skills can be *recovered (Is "recovered" the right term? Don't you mean "developed" or "improved"?)* (**What was the result of the Mirror Lake program? Do you want to offer it as a good model before moving to more general stats? If so, tell us WHY it is a "key example".**) Over 40% of 4th graders do not read at their standard reading level *(Source of info?)*. These statistics (**perhaps "this situation" would be better? - people are more than just statistics**) can be improved by the implementation of a reading subject *(do you mean "subject" or "class"?)* outside of language arts. (***Why outside of Language Arts? Does that hold more benefit than increasing the time spent in Language Arts?***) This separate subject will allow all elementary students to help themselves **be more capable** in their future ~~school and life~~. The ability to read will not only help comprehension but make them more apt to stay in school because they will be interested in the classes. (**Why will they be more interested in classes? I agree with the argument here, but explain it to the reader. You're assuming readers will accept this cause-and-effect relationship.**)

** **Reviewer #1 - Suggestion: In an ongoing study at Mirror Lake Elementary, in Seattle, students in the third and fourth grades have displayed numerous problems with reading skills.**

All subjects in school require ***reading such as;*** math, science, art, foreign language, etc. this makes reading a focus in which all students can excel. (***Awkward sentence structure. This should be at least two sentences***).

** *Reviewer #2 - Do all subjects really lend themselves to reading? Math is primarily a subject of equations and it might be difficult to force reading into it. A good idea, certainly, but perhaps not all subjects need added reading work.*

Therefore, the extra time spent reading in elementary school ~~will allow us to have~~ **allows** faster paced ***curricullum*** ~~s~~ in middle and high school, allowing the student to learn and get a better grasp on concepts. *(What evidence do you have to support this claim? Be sure to show the reader how you arrived at the causal relationship implied by "therefore".)*

** **Reviewer #1 - What kind of potential benefits can be seen from this? How might the improvement of reading levels in primary education improve student intiative and actually save schools money while bolstering communities?**

<u>COMMENTS</u>
Reviewer #1 - A solid plan for background information and real-life sources would strengthen your argument.
Reviewer #2 -- How do you plan to close your paper? What is the best way of giving the reader some sense of closure?

Figure 8.7 Reprinted with permission of R.W. Burniske. Copyright 1999. All rights reserved.

involved in this intellectual odyssey. Embedded within the text of the final draft are hyperlinks to the references, which will take the reader directly to secondary sources. For example, the underlined in-text citations in Figure 8.8 may provide a hyperlink to the complete bibliography located in the References section of the electronic portfolio, or take the reader directly to the online secondary sources.

Portfolio assessment requires a reorientation, shifting students and teachers away from simplistic grading schemes and standardized tests toward holistic evaluation. Also, it asks students to become self-conscious, paying attention to not only what they learn, but also how they learn it. There are a number of benefits to this, including a change in classroom dynamics. Once students become aware of their learning style, acquire a deeper understanding of their writing process, and realize that they play a role in their own evaluation, they're more likely to view the teacher as an ally in the learning process rather than as an adversary in the "grading game."

Final Draft: Bilingual Education

(1) "Excellence and Equity for all of our Students" reads the motto at the bottom of the **Texas Education Agency** homepage. Although the Texas Education Agency runs several programs that strive toward that goal, the area of bilingual education is suffering. The few programs the Texas Education Agency does have for children with limited-English proficiencies are inadequate. Unknown to many, in 1968 the U.S. Congress passed the **Bilingual Education Act** mandating that schools provide these types of bilingual education programs. The act however, gives much discretion to individual state agencies in deciding how and what programs should be instituted. The result has been a lackluster attempt at implementing bilingual education programs. Texas for instance, has used its federal funds to support only 49 bilingual education programs **(Latino Link)**. Rather than looking at the 1968 mandate as a set of "discretionary funds" or as merely a "grant", the Texas Education Agency should take the act for what it is, and institute a number of these programs with a long-term intent. I propose however, that a good portion of this new focus be dedicated to the creation of an entirely new type of bilingual education programs. Programs aimed at those Already English Proficient (AEP) should be instituted simultaneously with bilingual education programs. Texas, as a border state, has a constantly growing immigrant population. Consequently, a student's need for bi-lingual education grows as well. The existing language requirements in Texas schools, and recent legislation passed on the issue, do not ensure that a second language will be adequately acquired. If students do not acquire a second language, particularly one relevant to their region, they will fall behind culturally and socially.

(2) The term "melting pot" has become synonymous with American culture. This term is often used to refer to a society in which cultures, races or ethnicities have become homogenized. The Texas public education system, however, is not reflective of this, even as the demographics of the state transform significantly each year. Thousands of people cross the United States' borders for business and recreation each day and a significant portion of them decide to take up permanent residence. The 1997 Census reports for example, that the number of foreign-born citizens numbered approximately 25,779,000- about 9.6% of the population, up from 7.9% in 1990 and 4.8% in 1970 **(Census 1997).** The Federation for American Immigration Reform Organization has found that the percentage of foreigners entering the U.S. is steadily increasing, even in rural areas **(FAIR)**. A common notion is that immigration is something that affects only border states, but Mississippi has the fastest growing immigrant population, up by 476% since 1990. Other non-border states have also witnessed rapid increases in their immigrant population, including Colorado(136%), North Carolina (129%), Oregon (115%), Nebraska (107%), and Utah (102%) **(FAIR)**. Although staggering, these statistics fail to describe the face of Texas in the year 2030. The **Texas State Data Center** estimates that by 2030, Hispanics will comprise the majority group with a population of almost 15 million.

(3) In light of this statistical information, it is unclear why primary and secondary schools have not instituted more rigid language requirements. Science perhaps, provides an even more convincing argument for mandating AEP bilingual education. Children are naturally adept at learning new languages. Many children with limited-English proficiencies who are able to start and continue bilingual education past primary school remain fluent. The common scientific explanation given is that because children use a different area of the brain, and use all of that area to process languages, they are able to learn them more rapidly than adults. Adults on the other hand have to create a new area in the brain to process new languages **(Addis Tribune)**. If students already proficient in English begin learning a second language from grades one thorough five, scientific research supports their retaining it.

Figure 8.8 Reprinted with permission of R. W. Burniske. Copyright 1999. All rights reserved.

However, this transformation remains incomplete unless students also have some input into the evaluation of a semester's work. How, then, do teachers take the final step in this journey, moving from peer reviews of a single draft and electronic portfolios representing an individual project to consideration of academic coursework as a whole? How might they help students develop a greater awareness of the way in which a community of inquiry has influenced their intellectual development and affected their literacy skills? This invites the final evaluative literacy case study: the Online Learning Record.

Case Study: Online Learning Records

Adapted from the California Learning Record (http://www.electriciti.com/lrorg/), a portfolio model inspired by the Primary Language Record developed in Great Britain during the mid-1980s, the Online Learning Record

(OLR) feels like a natural progression from peer reviews and electronic portfolios. Just as the electronic portfolio allowed students to pull the disparate pieces of a single project together, the OLR provides an opportunity to represent a semester's work, from postings on class mailing lists or discussion forums to transcripts of synchronous chats or asynchronous telecollaborations, as well as peer reviews, essay drafts, and more. In essence, the OLR allows students to showcase both the quality and quantity of their work while participating in the evaluation of their overall performance. Here is how one of its principal creators, M. A. Syverson, describes its purpose:

> The Online Learning Record integrates research, assessment, and teaching and learning practices for computer-enhanced literacy development. The Learning Record provides a format for documenting student progress and achievement, based on interviews, observations over time, samples of students' naturally-occurring work, and well-supported interpretations of learning across five dimensions. (Syverson 1998)

To accomplish these goals, the Online Learning Record asks students to provide the following information, which could be entered into a hypertext template that the teacher creates or an original, student design:

- Background information and data collection
- Summary interpretation of five dimensions of learning
- Self-evaluation

Selection of materials is left to the students' discretion, but by addressing these three fundamental concerns, they acquire privileged insight into their own process and the work that it produces. The teacher may choose to employ the OLR as a supplement to conventional assessment, or use it as the only assessment tool, in which case students would submit an OLR at both midterm and end of term. A template like the one featured in Figure 8.9, meanwhile, will help students understand the relationship between the respective sections and encourage them to focus on the content of the OLR rather than on its appearance and hyperlinks.

What follows is a brief discussion of the respective sections and how they contribute to a student's evaluative literacy. Admittedly spare, this introduction cannot do justice to the Online Learning Record but should, at the very least, provide a thumbnail sketch that encourages teachers to learn more about this alternative assessment method.

Figure 8.9 Reprinted with permission of R. W. Burniske. Copyright 1999. All rights reserved.

a. *Part A—Background information and data collection.* As with the electronic portfolio, background information provides a glimpse of the student's personal and intellectual journey. However, it shifts the focus from the relatively short time span of a course project to the life span of the student. Teachers may choose to modify this section of the OLR to suit a particular discipline, but the fundamental prerequisite is a description of the student's development, as described by the student and someone who knows that student well. For example, in a humanities course the teacher may ask that both the student and acquaintance describe this individual's development as a reader, writer, and thinker. This accomplishes several things, including self-evaluation, corroboration from another, and privileged insights into an individual's history as a student. More important, it situates the present work within the context of personal history, helping both the student and teacher gain critical perspective.

The second part of this section, Data Collection, presents two important elements: observations and evidence of work. Similar to process journal entries, the observations offer short, informal responses to readings, class discussions, and online activities. They are not the activities, but reflections upon them. As such they constitute a "meta-level" narrative, encouraging students to step back from their work to periodically reflect on their reactions and assess the impact of particular learning activities. The Evidence of Work section, meanwhile, provides students with an opportunity to select representative samples of their best work. The selection process itself forces students to evaluate their work, deciding which pieces deserve a place in this online showcase. There are three principal categories from which to choose:

- Samples of written work—writing exercises that culminate with a final draft (topic proposal, rough drafts, etc.), electronic portfolios, etc.
- Samples of comments by others—e-mail messages from the class mailing list, discussion forum postings, peer reviews, etc.
- Samples of other activities—e-mail exchanges through the class mailing list, postings in the class discussion forum, excerpts from synchronous discussions, etc.

Obviously, these categories could be amended to suit different disciplines, while their present form leaves them open to a range of interpretations. What's essential, however, is giving students an opportunity to select their best work, demonstrating the quality of their effort and performance through a variety of materials that might otherwise be forgotten due to their ephemeral nature.

b. *Part B—Summary interpretation.* The temptation for students who are new to the Online Learning Record is to leap from data collection to self-evaluation. However, they should resist that temptation, for it neglects an essential step in the process: summary interpretation. As its name suggests, this segment of the OLR will ask students to interpret their performance. To do so, they must isolate individual strands of work and interpret them along specific learning dimensions. For students in a rhetoric and composition course, Syverson recommends the following breakdown:

Four major strands of work: Rhetoric, research, technology, and collaboration.
Five dimensions of learning: 1) confidence and independence; 2) knowledge and understanding; 3) skills and strategies; 4) use of prior and emerging experience; and 5) reflectiveness. (1998)

Students may choose to write this summary as a lengthy paragraph or break it into disparate pieces, dedicating a paragraph to each of the major strands (and their learning within them). This, too, is left to the discretion of the students and teacher. Regardless of the form the summary takes, it's important to impress on students the significance of this segment of the OLR. At both midterm and end of term, this summative interpretation draws upon the observations and evidence of work highlighted in Part A, considering them with respect to the four major strands of work and the five dimensions of learning. This is not "busywork," but a prerequisite to a thoughtful self-evaluation in the final section of the Online Learning Record. Having selected exemplary work and reflected on their learning experiences, students are ready to apply evaluative literacy skills to the final topic: themselves.

c. *Part C—Evaluation.* Upon completion of the previous sections—and not before—students evaluate their performance. At the midterm, this requires looking forward and backward, simultaneously assessing the work they've accomplished while stating resolutions for the remainder of the semester. The OLR encourages students to offer suggestions for improving the course, from new learning activities to a change of pace or classroom dynamics. This provides students with a sense of ownership while demonstrating the teacher's interest in their input. It's important that the teacher take these ideas seriously, either by addressing proposals in a brief narrative response or by acting on them, altering the classroom activities and environment. Otherwise, students will lose interest in the exercise, viewing it as a meaningless ritual. Much the same applies to the final requirement of the midterm evaluation: an estimation of their work in terms of a letter grade.

At the end of term, this section of the final OLR spends more time looking backward than forward, though students are welcome to offer the teacher suggestions for future classes. Based on the previous sections, as well as supplementary information, students evaluate their work in terms of a letter grade. This feels strange to many students. Some will balk, others will underestimate their performance, and some will reveal an inflated sense of accomplishment. However, each response invites dialogue with the teacher, who can use the opportunity to help the student evaluate his or her work more objectively, demonstrating respect for the student's efforts and evaluative judgment while articulating the principles that inform the teacher's assessment. While this may seem awkward initially, it transforms the "grading game" into a rhetorical exercise. The teacher must not allow students to offer an unqualified assertion: "I deserve an A." Rather, students must make an argument based on thoughtful criteria and careful consideration of the ethos, logos, and pathos of their semester's work. For examples of completed Online Learning Records, visit the collection at *The Rhetoric of Utopia* Web site: (http://www.cwrl.utexas.edu/~burniske/ utopia98/olr/finalolr/index.html)

For a more thorough account of its history, theory, and uses, visit the OLR Web site: (http://www.cwrl.utexas.edu/~syverson/olr/ contents.html)

Pedagogical Literacy

While much of this chapter's discussion focused on the development of student literacy skills, the respective exercises and case studies— Hypertext Writing Workshop, Electronic Port- folios, and Online Learning Records—will undoubtedly affect teachers as well. By engaging in alternative assessment the teacher challenges conven- tions, which provokes questions about the strengths and weaknesses of various assessment methods. Portfolios deliver far more insights on stu- dent processes than teachers acquire through a conventional final draft of an essay, report, or project. In most cases, this breaks down barriers be- tween the student and teacher, encouraging a more collaborative environ- ment. However, changes in assessment methods often prompt changes in pedagogical approaches. Thus, one needs to consider the teacher's role more carefully. This explains the focus of the final chapter, *pedagogical literacy*.

Pedagogical Literacy:
Plugging Into Electronic Pedagogy

*. . . we need to guide ourselves—remember cyber means steer—
in all our assembled forms and multiple selves right between the
towers of promise and danger, of desire and technology.*

(Stone 1996, 183)

It seems appropriate to conclude this discussion by considering pedagogy
as a form of literacy. How so? In ancient Greece, the *paidagogos* was a
slave who escorted children to school. Thus, pedagogy was comprised of
all the tricks employed to accomplish that task. One can only imagine the
trials suffered while trying to get rebellious youngsters to obey. Indeed,
pedagogy required skill in "reading" the child's disposition, writing a plan
of action (syllabus) that would fulfill the objectives (curriculum), and articulating that plan in a persuasive manner (rhetoric).

Despite technological advances, modern educators have much in common with the ancient *paidagogos*. Today's educator must learn to "read"
learning styles and write syllabi that fulfill mandatory curricula culminating with standardized examinations. The introduction of computers and
networked technology hardly simplifies matters. In fact, it often compli-
cates them. While integrating new technology, therefore, educators must
continually ask which forms of literacy they value most and how technology might help students acquire it. To accomplish this, the classroom practitioner needs to become fluent in various technologies, learning how to

"read" their strengths and weaknesses. Then, depending upon the age group, learning styles, and curriculum of the students, educators must determine when to use these tools and when to set them aside. This constitutes *pedagogical literacy*, a fluency with the strategy and tactics we can employ along with networked technology for educational purpose (see Figure 9.1).

Pedagogical Literacy

Pedagogical literacy is a fluency with the methods that one can employ for teaching and learning as well as the critical judgment necessary to determine which activities and media are most appropriate for a particular group, time, and purpose.

Figure 9.1

The pedagogically literate teacher draws upon a wide range of skills while developing an instructional repertoire. Only through a demanding process called *praxis*, which Paolo Freire described as a combination of "reflection and action," can we arrive at a point where our rhetoric and action, our means and our ends, form a coherent system (1997, 107). This requires periodic detachment and critical thinking about the choices we make, from our rhetoric and actions to the literacies we've inspired. Though it makes us uncomfortable, we as educators must hold a mirror up to nature to see what has happened to ourselves and our schools along the way.

After all, not every use of computer technology enhances the learning environment. Not all pedagogical strategies succeed all of the time with all of our students. Nonetheless, how can educators determine whether something will work if we never give it a try? How will we acquire computer literacy, or a sophisticated degree of pedagogical literacy, if we never try to develop our "vocabulary" and understanding? We must move at our own individual pace, starting from a comfort zone that allows us to transfer skills acquired with one medium to that of another. As always, our colleagues prove instructive, particularly those who define the extremes of the pedagogical spectrum. With that in mind, this final chapter presents two illustrative cases: first, the traditionalist who refuses to try new gadgets or practices; then, an experimentalist who flourishes when tinkering with the status quo.

Mr. Wynegar's Pastime: Tradition and the Individual Teacher

Technology alone will not save teachers from weak pedagogy or literacy skills. We've learned this from experiences with one technology or another, often learning to simplify because we let the technology dictate too much of the activity in our classroom. After all, pressing "Play" on a VCR hardly qualifies as thoughtful pedagogy, though pressing "Stop" at a critical moment to heighten suspense and inspire speculative discussion might!

Teachers would do well, therefore, to remember traditional approaches even as they experiment with new ones. Every educational institution has its share of dedicated teachers who have succeeded without depending on electronic technology to teach literacy skills. For centuries, students have learned about reading, writing, and speaking from these people, traditionalists like Mr. Wynegar.

Mr. Wynegar taught for nearly forty years.

He was rather fixed in his ways, for they served his students well.

He was also fond of his idiosyncracies, including a profound hatred of the word "very."

So great was his disdain for this adverb that when he returned student compositions their stationery sported rectangular holes, the result of tiny scissors clipping the offensive adverb from every sentence where it appeared.

Some would argue this was not a *very* professional response.

It was not the kind of behavior one might learn in a course on, say, "The Methodology of Writing Assessment."

Still, it was effective.

Why? Perhaps because it was so "unprofessional." Perhaps because it had so much personality to it. Perhaps, just perhaps, because it was so human.

Most students felt fortunate to have Mr. Wynegar as their English teacher. He taught them a lot about word choice, sentence structure, the mechanics of writing, and the personality of language and people. He also had a good point to make about the word "very," and his method for making that point, unconventional and quirky though it was, made a lasting impression. Students would never forget holding their essays up to the light and finding them riddled with more holes than a colander. They would frequently shove a returned essay into a notebook without letting others see it, but their furtive glances confirmed what they knew instinctively: They had much to learn about writing. And while they might never reach Mr. Wynegar's extreme in their writing style, they had to respect the conviction those scissored perforations represented.

More important, though, they admired the strength of personality, the courage, that those perforations revealed. Mr. Wynegar was not afraid of being unconventional; he didn't care what those holes said about his personality, nor what his colleagues might say about his teaching methods. Unlike many educators, he knew that teaching began as the expression of personality and ended as an escape from it. Unfortunately, the evolution of teaching in this century makes one wonder how much room is left for personality in the classroom. While teachers pay lip service to the "craft" of teaching, the emphasis on outcome-based learning, standardized tests, "plug-and-play" software packages, and Internet connectivity threatens human exchanges in their classrooms. Critics of these trends argue that

> the work of teachers has been increasingly subject to the rationalizing logics of management. The results have been the deskilling of teaching with its accompanying loss of control over the activity of classroom life, an overstandardization of curricula and teaching, an introduction of management ideologies and techniques that may be utterly inappropriate in an education that aims at promoting democracy in more than name only. (Apple 1990, x)

One explanation of such developments, which signal a shift from art to science and the attendant concern for "objectivity," is the educator's desire for professionalism, a magical commodity that some believe will secure the respect that has often eluded educators. While the pursuit of professionalism pleases administrators, school board members, and a society obsessed with appearances, it does not guarantee effectiveness in a classroom. In the zealous rush to "professionalize" educators (borrowing the conventional definitions of that term from other fields, in particular the corporate world), the gain in "objectivity" is offset by a loss of personality in the classroom and humanity in our schools. Objectivity is often a

Pyrrhic victory, however, for while it invests educators with professionalism it separates them from those with whom they must establish a more personal, individual relationship: their students.

Teaching, particularly in the K–12 classroom, cannot be divorced from a teacher's personality. Regardless of how many education courses one may take in classroom management, child psychology, or teaching methods, the teacher's professionalism will be useless if it overwhelms the personality that must convey it. Teachers would do well to remember the counsel of a flawed educator who failed to practice what he preached: "To thine own self be true." A music teacher with a sense of humor should not attempt seriousness at all times. Students see through this. They know when teachers are not being true to themselves. They lose respect for the teacher who is phony and become indifferent to those who seem diluted in character, shadows of a previous, more lively self. This is not to say that a sudden break from character is ineffective, as when a soft-spoken teacher quiets an unruly group with an unprecedented raising of the voice, just that "faking it" or repressing one's true character are recipes for disaster in the classroom.

The best teaching, like the best writing, occurs when one allows for spontaneity. Writing that follows a strict guideline, never deviating from a syllabus or lesson plan, may be efficient, economical, and persuasive, but it often feels contrived and uninspiring. The same applies to teaching. Teachers encumbered by an outline, pressuring themselves to "cover everything" before the bell rings, are likely to lose sight of the students before them. Teachers who commit themselves to the material more than the human beings in the classroom are making a mistake. This transforms them from human beings into automatons, refusing to let anything distract them from their syllabus. Course objectives, little notes in a black book, will satisfy their professionalism, but at what price? We need to think of professionalism in new terms, encouraging teachers to experiment with pedagogical strategies, deviate from rigid curricula, and challenge their students intellectually without stifling personality—either their own or their students.' Contrary to current trends, perhaps the most "professional" thing teachers can do is resist the impulse to standardize and objectify their pedagogy and classroom demeanor. Standardization and objectification are counterproductive in an environment where each student deserves to be treated with the dignity and respect their humanity demands.

The analogy between teaching and writing helps illustrate the importance of not only having personality, but also knowing how to use it for didactic purpose. In his celebrated essay, "Tradition and the Individual Talent," T. S. Eliot claimed that, "It is not in his personal emotions, the emotions provoked by particular events in his life, that the poet is in any way remarkable or interesting" (1978, 506). By substituting "teacher" for "poet," one may gain a sense of the analogy's force. Do not be deceived by Eliot's words, however. He argued that poetry is an escape from emotion and personality, though not the dissolution of it. The writing of poetry, like the teaching of children, demands clear expression of emotions and ideas, though not necessarily unique emotions or ideas, which Eliot claimed would only "discover the perverse." It's important to understand the prerequisites to such an escape, by either poet or teacher:

> Poetry is not a turning loose of emotion, but an escape from emotion; it is not the expression of personality, but an escape from personality. But, of course, only those who have personality and emotion know what it means to want to escape from these things. (Eliot, 1978, 507)

What this means, really, is that teachers must use all their human qualities—from vocal inflection to facial expression, cognitive ability to emotional response—to educate. In so doing, they express a personality that gives shape to ideas, much as the artist's craft gives shape to thought and emotion. This leads to one of life's paradoxical truisms: By offering the personal anecdote and allowing for one's own vision to give shape to a curriculum, one discovers the universal through the personal. This is what Eliot meant by the individual's "escape from these things." If teachers do not take risks, sharing something of themselves and their interests, their quirks and contradictions, the very things that make human beings human, what chance is there that young students will gain a sense of humanity from schools? Students who reflect on great teachers often recall what was original and unique about them. In a word, what gave them, and their classes, such "personality." Critics of this argument may call it egocentric, but they miss the point. With apologies to Mr. Eliot, one could argue that "teaching is not a turning loose of emotion, but an escape from emotion; it is not the expression of personality, but an escape from personality." And yes, "only those who have personality and emotion know what it means to want to escape from these things," to push beyond their own limited definitions of the self and the rhetoric used to construct that "self," to engage the universal.

Mr. Wynegar knew what it meant to escape from personality and emotion, but, unfortunately, he never took that final step. By the time he retired, leaving the school where he'd taught for nearly 40 years, he had become a caricature of his former self, a man more renowned for his idiosyncratic teaching strategies than a dynamic personality. He had, in effect, become an extension of his pedagogical routines, rather than making his pedagogy the extension of a dynamic self. Do we really want this to happen to our teachers? Do we really want to make schools and curricula "idiot-proof" by reducing education to strategies and tactics that are to be replicated by "guides on the side" who avoid the expression of individual personality? Shouldn't we encourage teachers to keep growing, challenging themselves and their students to search within themselves, their personal interests, emotions, and beliefs, to discover the universal? Failure to do so will produce a generation of people who are strangers to themselves, detached from emotions and human society.

Society owes a great deal to people like Mr. Wynegar, educators who passed the "sacred fire," not only to young students who would eventually become writers, but also those who went on to become teachers of reading and writing. We learned a great deal from teachers like Mr. Wynegar. However, current trends in education, particularly the embrace of technology that displaces the teacher, promoting the "guide on the side" while dismissing the "sage on stage," may signal yet another triumph of technique over humanity, science over art, and professionalism over personality. For all those idiosyncratic quirks and all the remarkable strategies he employed—from standing behind a podium to snipping adverbs from student essays—were initially an expression of Mr. Wynegar's personality. Unfortunately, they eventually became an end in themselves; the tools Mr. Wynegar had shaped for performing his craft eventually shaped him in ways he hadn't foreseen.

What educators need is encouragement to continue growing and learning, reinventing themselves and their practice. Early in his career, Mr. Wynegar knew this without articulating it. That individual possessed what one educator described as "knowing-in-action," a wisdom that is hard to classify, yet indispensable.

> When we go about the spontaneous, intuitive performance of the actions of everyday life, we show ourselves to be knowledgeable in a special way. Often we cannot say what we know. When we try to describe it, we find

ourselves at a loss, or we produce descriptions that are obviously inappropriate. Our knowing is ordinarily tacit, implicit in our patterns of action and in our feel for the stuff with which we are dealing. It seems right to say that our knowledge is *in* our action. (Schön 1995, 29)

Mr. Wynegar had a "feel" for what he was doing, as well as "the stuff with which [he was] dealing." At least, he did before he became a slave to his own conventions and his idiosyncratic methods stunted his personality. At the start of his career he had an intuitive feel for the classroom and the courage to teach universal lessons through personal expressions. And, though he'd bridle at the use of an offensive adverb, he was a *very* good teacher because of those expressions.

Ms. Sabadilla and The Electronic Chalkboard

And now, a word on behalf of innovators, those who wish to experiment with new technology and pedagogical strategies. Despite the ways in which they differ from Mr. Wynegar, many of these people, particularly those who work in the humanities, share a belief he espoused for decades.

"The art of writing is rewriting."

Teachers of language arts chant this mantra during composition workshops. Ironically, though, these same instructors have often resisted the use of computer labs for facilitating workshops. Initially, many in the humanities pledged allegiance to the Luddites, describing the word processor as an instrument of evil in the hands of a young writer. Extremists called for the prohibition of computers in language arts instruction because they feared students would develop a harmful dependency, using technology to check spelling, grammar, and other fundamentals, instead of refining their skills.

While one might understand such concerns, even empathize with them, they remain as reactionary as the protests of humanists in the sixteenth century who feared the adoption of printed texts would destroy the memory of students. In the twentieth century, teachers of mathematics expressed a similar anxiety when they claimed the use of calculators would prevent students from developing fundamental skills and the mnemonic devices that had supported the study of their discipline for centuries. In recent years, teachers have seen how uncoached word processing can harm the writing of secondary students. Weaker students sometimes do confuse the appearance of a manuscript with its content, believing justified margins, a spellchecker, and sleek fonts hold the secrets to a first-rate essay. However, it shouldn't take more than one set of papers to disabuse them of this fallacy. And then, if one really wants to use the word processor to advantage, the real fun begins.

Despite its drawbacks, the word processor is the best tool for editing prose ever invented. It's that simple. Ms. Sabadilla worked as a journalist in college. She enjoyed writing articles, but she loathed editing on "hard copy." She had learned to type articles and essays in triple space, allowing room for editing marks. By the time an article was done it looked like a road map; though instead of interstate highways running at all angles, grease pencil corrections sprawled across the page. It wasn't until she graduated from college and began teaching that word processors became common, revolutionizing the editing process forever.

Now, as a high school journalism teacher, Ms. Sabadilla uses the computer as an integral part of her teaching, particularly the teaching of composition skills. Some of her colleagues still take perverse pleasure (or is it pride?) in declaring that they know almost nothing about the computer and have no desire to learn about it. She wonders what they would say, though, if one of their students expressed similar feelings about whatever topic they were teaching at that moment. Open-minded folks interested in improving their instruction of writing and editing skills, however, may find her experience enlightening.

For years Ms. Sabadilla slaved over essays that repeatedly contained the same mistakes. She scribbled "awkward" in margins, crossed out unnecessary words, and often retyped sentences or paragraphs that were in special need of editing. This required loads of time and usually did little to improve the next set of papers. The only exercise that seemed helpful to the class as a whole was writing sentences out on the chalkboard and asking students to revise them. In some cases, though, the chalkboard was not big enough to accommodate a full paragraph, or else her penmanship was not good enough to make the exercise efficient.

Then Ms. Sabadilla discovered the digitized projection screen, or liquid crystal display (LCD) panel. This device, when placed atop an overhead projector, was the magic wand she'd been seeking for writing and editing workshops. The digitized projection screen allows one to insert a disk with writing samples into a word processor, open a file, and immediately project it onto a screen or wall for the entire class to see. Ms. Sabadilla likes to select half a dozen paragraphs from student essays, type those onto a disk, and collate all the paragraphs onto one sheet, which she prints out and copies for her students. The paragraphs, perhaps the introductions or conclusions of essays (without names attached), are then distributed to the class. Students are directed to edit the paragraphs as carefully as possible, removing unnecessary words or cliches, improving awkward word choices, and generally tightening and clarifying the paragraph as a whole. After they've had time to do this on paper, they are ready for a collaborative session at the projection screen.

This is when the technology feels like magic. For at this point the teacher has an opportunity to do more than "tell" students what should or shouldn't be done; he or she has the chance to "show" them how to go about editing and revising. The effort is a collaborative one that involves the entire class, not just a single student who may or may not understand cryptic notes in the margin of a paper. What is especially good about using the computer for this exercise is that one can save different versions of the same paragraph, including the original, for comparison after everyone is satisfied with the editing. The advantages of this technology over the traditional chalkboard should be obvious, for the latter becomes an enormous road map of insertions, cross-outs, and chalk smears, obliterating the original paragraph entirely by the time a single paragraph is edited.

Most important, the innovation of an "electronic chalkboard" introduces new possibilities for teaching and learning. Writing teachers can usually edit several times as much work on the computer as they could on the traditional chalkboard in the same class period. With a computer and digitized projection screen, teachers spend more time editing and discussing the virtues of a good sentence and far less time with the mechanics of assembling a sentence for student inspection. They also discover—and invent—a wide range of learning activities that the conventional chalkboard never enabled. In Ms. Sabadilla's class, for example, students now use the LCD panel, along with a computer connected to the Internet, to offer hypertext presentations, review online articles, and analyze the rhetorical impact of Web sites.

Electronic Pedagogy: The Web Site

Mr. Wynegar deserves respect for his high standards and steadfast commitment to principles, pedagogy, and pupils. However, Ms. Sabadilla's innovations are equally commendable and merit respect for the courage and convictions they require. Of course, not all innovations are good, for some are simply "improved means to unimproved ends." However, one example of a positive innovation when it comes to teaching literacy skills is the shift from a slate chalkboard to a digitized screen. Mr. Wynegar never tried using one of these, though he did employ an overhead projector from time to time. Perhaps the LCD panel came along too late in his career, at a time when his skills and practices had been honed to such an extent that to alter his pedagogy would have required a profound alteration of himself.

It is worth noting that Mr. Wynegar retired several years ago, prior to the push for integrating networked technology into school curricula. He never had to learn about meaningful, instructional uses of computer technology. Perhaps this was just as well for Mr. Wynegar, but it's not an option for many of today's educators. The extraordinary effort to connect classrooms to the Internet has placed a tremendous burden upon teachers. Unfortunately, expenditures on infrastructure have not generated similar expenditures on the people charged with the mission of introducing electronic pedagogy to their curricula. Because of their limited professional development opportunities, educators need a place to learn about electronically supported, pedagogical tools. That conviction, and the desire for continued discussions about classroom *praxis*, has inspired the creation of the Electronic Pedagogy Web site (http://www.cwrl.utexas.edu/~burniske/eped).

This Web site (see Figure 9.2) offers educators an opportunity to examine "Pedagogy in Action" through links to interactive sections where one will find "Cyberwriters at Work" as well as "Online Conferences and Courses" and a discussion forum dedicated to "Composing Ourselves Online." Meanwhile, for those seeking archives of "Pedagogy in Reflection," there are hypertext links in "The Library of Electronic Pedagogy" to print and online resources as well as a listing of online "Institutes & Archives" and a growing collection of online resources dedicated to "Distance Learning." Hopefully, efforts such as these will provide the kind of support often missing from instructional technology initiatives. Certainly, educators

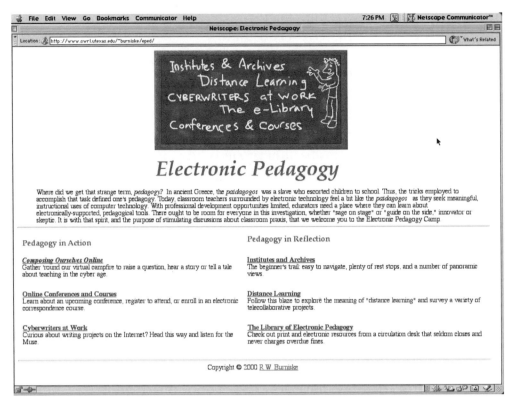

Figure 9.2 Reprinted with permission of R. W. Burniske. Copyright 1999. All rights reserved.

need an antidote for the malaise caused by a paucity of professional development opportunities and the excesses of corporate rhetoric praising technology as the panacea for what ails modern education. Technology alone will not solve teachers' problems. On the contrary, if we don't attend to the pedagogical literacy of our teachers, helping them strengthen their skills and repertoire, technology could simply exacerbate the situation.

Ultimately, a book like this is simply one statement within a much larger conversation. What's necessary at this point, and what this book has aimed to inspire, is a more critical discussion of technology in education. Indeed, without an open inquiry and continued debate over critical issues, educators not only slow their pedagogical progress, but may also forfeit the opportunity to use the current interest in technology to reinvigorate our schools and curricula. There's no shortage of challenges, of course, since the introduction of networked computers raises new problems even as it solves old ones.

Rather than wring our hands, however, we should look upon the outrageous expenditures for wiring schools as a challenge. It's no longer a question of whether we should introduce computer technology into our classrooms. [. . .] that "choice" has already been made for us. The question now is how we should make use of this technology for educational purposes. How can we use it to help young students acquire a literacy that's more hospitable to dialectical discourse? (Burniske 1998, 157)

It seems only fitting to draw this book's discussion to a close by extending it through a telecollaborative effort. By now there must be a number of arguments that readers wish to contest, questions they'd like to ask, or comments they'd like to make. Fortunately, modern technology allows us to stretch the parameters of conventional texts, accommodating readers who wish to participate in the conversations it has provoked. One way to do that is to continue composing ourselves online by joining the discussion forum or contributing to the digital archives at the *Electronic Pedagogy* Web site.

There's no obligation, of course, but consider this an open invitation for you to join an authentic discussion of electronic pedagogy. You can listen to what others have to say, post a question, or simply browse through the Web site's collection of annotated links. Teachers throughout the world need opportunities to collaborate with colleagues—sharing questions, concerns, and experiences that deepen the discussion of innovative practices in the classroom. The *Electronic Pedagogy* Web site offers such an opportunity, enabling educators to continue a conversation that will help them develop pedagogical literacy. It also encourages a collective pause, enabling a community of educators to ensure that our acquisition of computer literacy serves something more than itself.

It should go without saying, but let's say it anyway: Telecomputing is *not* about computers. It's about educating our students, serving our communities, and improving our societies. If it's not about those things first and foremost, it has no place in our curricula. Indeed, this book sprung from the hope that a discussion of literacy in the cyberage would inspire reflection upon the critical literacies fundamental to a well-rounded education: media literacy, civil literacy, discourse literacy, personal literacy, community literacy, visual literacy, global literacy, evaluative literacy, and pedagogical literacy. It is now up to students and teachers to define a more meaningful and satisfying form of *computer literacy*. Here's hoping this book contributes to that cause—one teacher, and several students, at a time. To do so, it must inspire further dialogue and pedagogical innovation, which are necessary to discover—and invent—improved means for helping twenty-first-century students become truly literate individuals.

Appendix:
Index of Web Sites

Web Site Name	URL	Cited in Chapter
All Search Engines	http://www.allsearchengines.com	2
Blue Web 'N	www.kn.pacbell.com/wired/bluewebn	7
California Learning Record	http://www.electriciti.com/lrorg/	8
Center for Democracy and Technology	http://www.cdt.org	2
Classroom Connect: Acceptable use policies	http://www.wentworth.com/classroom/aup.htm	2, Bibliography
Community Learning Network's Education Listservs	http://www.cln.org/lists/	7
Computer Professionals for Social Responsibility	http://www.cpsr.org/	2
Computer Writing and Research Lab (CWRL)	http://www.cwrl.utexas.edu	2
Critical Tools	http://www.cwrl.utexas.edu/~criticaltools	5
CyberPilot's License, The	http://www.cwrl.utexas.edu/~burniske/cpl	2
Cyber-Rights Homepage	ftp://www.cpsr.org/cpsr/nii/cyber-rights/index.html	2
Deja News archive	http://www.deja.com/	2
Electronic Pedagogy	http://www.cwrl.utexas.edu/~burniske/eped	9
Epals	http://www.epals.com/	7
European Computer Driving License	http://www.ecdl.com/	2
Evaluating Web Resources	http://www2.widener.edu/Wolfgram-Memorial-Library/webeval.htm	6
Flight School Forum	http://www.cwrl.utexas.edu/~burniske/cpl/teachers/index.html	2
Global Schoolhouse, The	http://www.globalschoolhouse.org/	7
Glossary of Internet Terms	http://www.matisse.net/files/glossary.html	2
Guide for Educators	http://discoveryschool.com/schrockguide/eval.html	6
Hobbes' Internet Timeline	http://pollux.com/compuweb/timeline.htm	2
Intercultural Email Classroom Connections	http://www.iecc.org	7

Web Site Name	URL	Cited in Chapter
International Education & Resource Network (I*EARN)	http://www.iearn.org	7
Internet Public Library: Citing Electronic Resources	http://www.ipl.org/ref/QUE/FARQ/netciteFARQ.html	2
Kidlink	http://www.kidlink.org/english/index.html	7
Learn the Net	http://www.learnthenet.com/english/index.html	2
NetLearn	http://www.rgu.ac.uk/~sim/research/netlearn/callist.htm	2
NickNacks	http://home.talkcity.com/academydr/nicknacks/NNindex.html	7
Ohio University: Censorship	http://www.tcom.ohiou.edu/OU_Language/project/censorship.html	2
Onion, The	http://www.theonion.com	6
Online Learning Record	http://www.cwrl.utexas.edu/~syverson/olr/contents.html	8
Papert, Seymour: Obsolete skill set: The 3 Rs	http://www.wired.com/wired/archive/1.02/1.2_papert.html	Bibliography
PBS: Using and Understanding the Internet	http://www.pbs.org/uti/	2
Piloting Skills and Netiquette	http://www.cwrl.utexas.edu/~burniske/cpl/skills.html	2
Pilot's Place, The	http://www.cwrl.utexas.edu/~burniske/cpl/students/index.html	2
Plato: The Republic	http://www.utm.edu/research/iep/text/plato/rep/rep.htm	3
Reference Desk, The	http://www.cwrl.utexas.edu/~burniske/cpl/reference.html	2
Rhetoric of Utopia-Fall 1998-index	http://www.cwrl.utexas.edu/~burniske/utopia98/student/index.html	8
Rhetoric of Utopia-Online learning records	http://www.cwrl.utexas.edu/~burniske/utopia98/olr/finalolr/index.html	8
Rhetoric of Utopia-Spring 1995-student samples	http://www.cwrl.utexas.edu/~burniske/utopia99/student/index.html	8
Rhetoric of Utopia-Spring 1998-student samples	http://www.cwrl.utexas.edu/~burniske/utopia98/student/index.html	8
Rhetoric of Utopia-Spring 1999-index	http://www.cwrl.utexas.edu/~burniske/utopia99/student/index.html	5, 8
Rice University: Acceptable Use	gopher://riceinfo.rice.edu:1170/11/More/Acceptable	2
Rogers, Al: Global literacy in a Gutenberg culture	http://lrs.ed.uiuc.edu/Guidelines/Global-Literacy-Rogers.html	Bibliography
Schoolworld Internet Education	www.schoolworld.asn.au	7
Selfe, Cynthia L.: Technology and literacy: A story about the perils of not paying attention	http://www.ncte.org/forums/selfe/	Bibliography
Syverson, M. A.: Beyond portfolios: The online learning record	http://www.cwrl.utexas.edu/~syverson/olr/	8
Utopian Visions	http://www.en.utexas.edu/uv	2, 6
Virtual Architecture's Web Home	http://ccwf.cc.utexas.edu/~jbharris/Virtual-Architecture/index.html	7
World Links for Development (WorLD)	http://www.worldbank.org/worldlinks	7
Youthnet	http://youth.net/#K-12	7

Bibliography

Anderson, D., Bret B., and Paredes-Holt, W. 1998. *Connections: A guide to on-line writing*. Boston: Allyn and Bacon.

Apple, M. W. 1990. Series editor's introduction. In *The new literacy: Redefining reading and writing in the schools*. New York: Routledge.

Ba, M. 1986. *Scarlet song*. Translated by D. S. Blair. Harlow, England: Longman.

Bacon, F. 1939. Of studies. In *Essays*. New York: E. P. Dutton.

Barton, D. 1994. *Literacy: An introduction to the ecology of written language*. Oxford, England: Blackwell.

Berger, J. 1972. *Ways of seeing*. London: Penguin.

Bolter, J. D. 1991. *Writing space: The computer, hypertext, and the history of writing*. Hillsdale, NJ: Lawrence Erlbaum.

Brewer, B., Davis, H., and Jeutonne, P. 1997. *Electronic discourse: Linguistic individuals in virtual space*. Albany: State University of New York Press.

Bump, J. 1990. Radical changes in class discussions using networked computers. *Computers and the Humanities* 24: 49–65.

Burniske, R. W. 1998. The shadow play: How the integration of technology annihilates debate in our schools. *Phi Delta Kappan* 80(2): 155–157.

Burniske, R. W. 1999. Computer illiteracy: Vice or virtue? *AFT On Campus* 18(5): 18.

Burniske, R. W., and Monke, L. Forthcoming. *Breaking down the digital walls: Learning to teach in a post-modem world*. Albany: State University of New York Press.

Classroom Connect. December 1994–January 1995. Acceptable use policies: Defining what's allowed online and what's not. *Classroom Connect Newsletter*. Available online: http://www.wentworth.com/classroom/aup.htm

Costanzo, W. 1994. Reading, writing and thinking in an age of electronic literacy. In *Literacy and computers: The complications of teaching and learning with technology*, edited by C. L. Selfe. and S. Hilligoss. New York: Modern Language Association.

Edgar, C., and Wood, S. N., eds. 1996. *The nearness of you: Students and teachers writing on-line.* New York: Teachers and Writers Collaborative.

Eisner, E. 1985. *The educational imagination.* New York: MacMillan.

Eliot, T. S. 1978. Tradition and the individual talent. In *The Scribner quarto of modern literature*, edited by A. W. Litz. New York: Charles Scribner's Sons.

Freire, P. 1997. *Pedagogy of the oppressed.* Translated by M. Bergman Ramos. New York: Continuum.

Gergen, K. 1991. *The saturated self: Dilemmas of identity in contemporary life.* New York: Basic Books.

Getzels, J. W. 1982. The problem of the problem. In *Question framing and response consistency,* edited by R. M. Hogarth. San Francisco: Jossey-Bass.

Gibaldi, J. 1999. *MLA handbook for writers of research papers.* 5th ed. New York: Modern Language Association.

Gilster, P. 1997. *Digital literacy.* New York: John Wiley.

Graff, G. 1990. Other voices, other rooms: Organizing and teaching the humanities conflict. *New Literary History* 21: 817–839.

Graff, H. J. 1995. *The labyrinths of literacy: Reflections on literacy past and present.* Pittsburgh, PA: University of Pittsburgh Press.

Haas, C. 1996. *Writing technology: Studies on the materiality of literacy.* Mahwah, NJ: Lawrence Erlbaum.

Harris, J. 1998. *Virtual architecture: Designing and directing curriculum-based telecomputing.* Eugene, OR: IFTE Publications.

Hirsch, E. D. 1987. *Cultural literacy: What every American needs to know.* Boston: Houghton Mifflin.

Hutchins, E. 1996. *Cognition in the wild.* Cambridge, MA: MIT Press.

Kelly, K. 1996. The electronic hive: Embrace it. In *Computerization and controversy: Value conflicts and social choices,* 2nd ed., edited by R. Kling. San Diego, CA: Academic Press.

Kling, R., ed. 1996. *Computerization and controversy: Value conflicts and social choices.* 2nd ed. San Diego, CA: Academic Press.

Landauer, T. K. 1996. *The trouble with computers.* Cambridge, MA: MIT Press.

Lanham, R. 1994. *The electronic word: Democracy, technology and the arts.* Chicago: University of Chicago Press.

Lave, J., and Wenger, E. 1991. Situated learning: Legitimate, peripheral participation in *Learning in doing: Cognitive and computational perspectives,* edited by J. F. B. Roy Pea. Cambridge: Cambridge University Press.

Liddell, H. G., and Scott, R. 1973. *A Greek-English lexicon.* Oxford, England: Oxford University Press.

Lipman, M. 1991. *Thinking in education.* New York: Cambridge University Press.

Lunsford, A. A., Moglen, H., and Slevin, J., eds. 1990. *The right to literacy.* New York: Modern Language Association.

Lunsford, A. A., and Ruszkiewicz, J. J. 1999. *Everything's an argument.* Boston: Bedford/St.Martin's.

McLuhan, M. 1964. *Understanding media: The extensions of man.* New York: Signet.

Messaris, P. 1994. *Visual "literacy": Image, mind, and reality.* Boulder, CO: Westview Press.

Miller, S. E. 1996. *Civilizing cyberspace: Policy, power and the information superhighway.* New York: Addison-Wesley Publishing Co.

Myers, M. 1996. *Changing our minds: Negotiating English and literacy.* Urbana, IL: National Council of Teachers of English.

Ong, W. 1982. *Orality and literacy: The technologizing of the word.* London: Methuen.

Papert, S. June 1993. Obsolete skill set: The 3 Rs. Available online: http://www.wired.com/wired/archive/1.02/1.2_papert.html

The New Shorter Oxford English Dictionary, Vol. 3. 1993. "Pedagogue." Oxford, England: Clarendon Press.

Plato. 1996. The Republic. In *The Internet encyclopedia of philosophy.* Available online: http://www.utm.edu/research/iep/text/plato/rep/rep.htm

Pope, A. 1979. An essay on criticism. In *The Norton anthology of English literature,* edited by M. H. Abrams. New York: W. W. Norton.

Pope, A. 1980. Imitations of Horace, Epistle I. In *Familiar quotations,* edited by E. M. Beck. Boston: Little, Brown.

Postman, N. 1993. *Technopoly: The surrender of culture to technology.* New York: Vintage.

Queneau, R. 1981. *Exercises in style.* Translated by B. Wright. New York: New Directions.

Ramage, J. D., and Bean, J. C. 1998. *Writing arguments: A rhetoric with readings.* 4th ed. Boston: Allyn and Bacon.

Rheingold, H. 1993. *The virtual community: Homesteading on the electronic frontier.* New York: Addison-Wesley.

Rogers, A. 1998. Global literacy in a Gutenberg culture. Available online: http://lrs.ed.uiuc.edu/Guidelines/Global-Literacy-Rogers.html

Schön, D. 1995. Knowing in action: The new scholarship requires a new epistemology. *Change* (November/December): 27–34.

Selfe, C. L. 1998. *Technology and literacy: A story about the perils of not paying attention.* Available online: http://www.ncte.org/forums/selfe/

Selfe, C. L., and Hilligoss, S., eds. 1994. *Literacy and computers: The complications of teaching and learning with technology.* New York: Modern Language Association.

Shakespeare, W. 1964. *The sonnets.* New York: Signet.

Snyder, I., ed. 1998. *Page to screen: Taking literacy into the electronic era.* New York: Routledge.

Stone, A. R. 1996. *The war of desire and technology at the close of the mechanical age.* Cambridge, MA: MIT Press.

Suzanne de Castell, A. L., and Maclennon, D. 1989. On defining literacy. In *Literacy, society and schooling: A reader,* edited by A. L. Suzanne de Castell and K. Egan. Cambridge, England: Cambridge University Press.

Syverson, M. A. 1998. *Beyond portfolios: The online learning record.* Available online: http://www.cwrl.utexas.edu/~syverson/olr/

Talbott, S. L. 1995. *The future does not compute: Transcending the machines in our midst.* Sebastopol, CA: O'Reilly & Associates.

Tuman, M. C. 1987. *A preface to literacy: An inquiry into pedagogy, practice and progress.* Tuscaloosa: The University of Alabama Press.

Tuman, M., ed. 1992a. *Literacy online: The promise (and peril) of reading and writing with computers.* Pittsburgh, PA: University of Pittsburgh Press.

Tuman, M. 1992b. *Word perfect: Literacy in the computer age.* London: Falmer Press.

Turkle, S. 1997. *Life on the screen: Identity in the age of the Internet.* New York: Simon & Schuster.

Twain, M. 1964. *Pudd'nhead Wilson.* New York: Signet.

Tyner, K. R. 1998. *Literacy in a digital world: Teaching and learning in the age of information.* Mahwah, NJ: Lawrence Erlbaum.

Warschauer, M. 1999. *Electronic literacies: Language, culture, and power in online education.* Mahwah, NJ: Lawrence Erlbaum.

Welty, E. 1981. A sweet devouring. In *The Riverside reader,* edited by J. Trimmer and M. Hairston. Boston: Houghton Mifflin.

Willinsky, J. 1990. *The new literacy: Redefining reading and writing in the schools.* New York: Routledge.

Windschitl, M. 1999. The challenges of sustaining a constructivist classroom culture. *Phi Delta Kappan* 80(10): 751–755.

Wordsworth, W. 1979. My heart leaps up. In *The Norton anthology of English literature,* edited by M. H. Abrams. New York: W. W. Norton.

Index

There are
one-story intellects,
two-story intellects, and
three-story intellects with skylights.

All fact collectors, who have no aim beyond their facts, are

one-story minds.

Two-story minds
compare, reason, generalize,
using the labors of the fact collectors
as well as their own.

Three-story minds
idealize, imagine, predict—their best illumination
comes from above,

through the **skylight**.

—Oliver Wendell Holmes

SkyLight

PROFESSIONAL DEVELOPMENT

We Prepare Your Teachers Today
for the Classrooms of Tomorrow

Learn from Our Books and from Our Authors!

Ignite Learning in Your School or District.

SkyLight's team of classroom-experienced consultants can help you foster systemic change for increased student achievement.

Professional development is a process not an event. SkyLight's experienced practitioners drive the creation of our on-site professional development programs, graduate courses, research-based publications, interactive video courses, teacher-friendly training materials, and online resources—call SkyLight Professional Development today.

SkyLight specializes in three professional development areas.

Specialty # **1**

Best Practices

We **model** the best practices that result in improved student performance and guided applications.

Specialty # **2**

Making the Innovations Last

We help set up **support** systems that make innovations part of everyday practice in the long-term systemic improvement of your school or district.

Specialty # **3**

How to Assess the Results

We prepare your school leaders to encourage and **assess** teacher growth, **measure** student achievement, and **evaluate** program success.

Contact the SkyLight team and begin a process toward long-term results.

2626 S. Clearbrook Dr., Arlington Heights, IL 60005
800-348-4474 • 847-290-6600 • FAX 847-290-6609
info@skylightedu.com • www.skylightedu.com